LOVING IN THE WAR YEARS

LOVING IN THE WAR YEARS

AND OTHER WRITINGS, 1978-1999

CHERRÍE MORAGA

Haymarket Books
Chicago, Illinois

Published in 2023 by
Haymarket Books
P.O. Box 180165
Chicago, IL 60618
773-583-7884
www.haymarketbooks.org
info@haymarketbooks.org

ISBN: 978-1-64259-906-0

Distributed to the trade in the US through Consortium Book Sales and Distribution (www.cbsd.com) and internationally through Ingram Publisher Services International (www.ingramcontent.com).

This book was published with the generous support of Lannan Foundation, Wallace Action Fund, and Marguerite Casey Foundation.

Special discounts are available for bulk purchases by organizations and institutions. Please email info@haymarketbooks.org for more information.

Cover artwork, *Skirt* © 2014 by Celia Herrera Rodríguez.
Cover design by Rachel Cohen.

Printed in the United States.

Library of Congress Cataloging-in-Publication data is available.

10 9 8 7 6 5 4 3 2 1

"Where resides the rebel heart?"

In honor of activist/artist, Harry Belafonte
3/1/1927 – 4/25/2023

and in remembrance of my father, Joseph Phillip
6/14/1923 – 2/17/2023

For the warrior women . . .

Contents

An Estranged and Unrecognizable City   1

Words on Wording   8

LOVING IN THE WAR YEARS, 1978–1983

Amar en los años de guerra   14

What Kind of Love Have You Made Me, Mother?

The Pilgrimage   23

Later She Met Joyce   24

La Dulce Culpa   28

The Slow Dance   31

The Voices of the Fallers   33

Loving on the Run

An Open Invitation to a Meal   41

You Upset the Whole System of This Place   42

Lovin' on the Run   44

Loving in the War Years   48

Fear, A Love Poem   50

Passage   54

View of Three Bridges

Raw Experience   57

For the Color of My Mother   59

La Güera   62

It's the Poverty   73

What Does It Take?   76

Anatomy Lesson   78

It Got Her Over   79

Winter of Oppression, 1982   83

The Road to Recovery

Minds & Hearts   89

No Born-Again Children   90
You Call It "Amputation"   93
Glamorous   94
Heading East   96

Lo que nunca pasó por sus labios
A Long Line of Vendidas   98
RiverPoem   145
Feed the Mexican Back into Her   146
And Then There's Us . . .   149
Querida compañera   150

THE LAST GENERATION, 1985-1992
Prophecy of a People   156
The Last Generation   160

The Ecology of Women
En Route para Los Angeles   166
Girls Together   169
The Ecology of Woman   171
Just Vision   176
Poema como Valentín (or a San Francisco Love Poem)   178
Reunion   180
Dreaming of Other Planets   182
New Mexican Confession   183

War Cry
War Cry   188
Ni para El Salvador   189
We Have Read a Lot and Know We Are Not Safe   190
La Despedida   192
Proposition   196
Art in América con Acento   197

La fuerza femenina

Credo 207

Blood Sisters 209

If 210

En busca de la fuerza femenina 211

La Ofrenda 217

The Breakdown of the Bicultural Mind

Red 227

Peloncito 229

If a Stranger Could Be Called Family 231

I Was Not Supposed to Remember 234

Half-breed 238

It's Not New York 239

Indian Summer 241

The Grass, Not Greener 243

The Breakdown of the Bicultural Mind 245

Queer Aztlán

Meditation 264

I Don't Know the Protocol 265

Our Lady of the Cannery Workers 267

Queer Aztlán—The Re-formation of Chicano Tribe, 1992 271

En Memoriam 296

Where Beauty Resides 300

Codex Xeritzín—El Momento Histórico 305

COYOLXAUHQUI REMEMBERED, 1995-1999

Moon in Memoriam 315

Coyolxauhqui Re-membered 316

Canto Florido 320

Looking for the Insatiable Woman 323

Entre nos 333

Thistle 334

Out of Our Revolutionary Minds—Toward a Pedagogy of Revolt   335

La danzante   350

The Dying Road to a Nation—A Prayer para un Pueblo   355

Afterword   364

Agradecimientos   365

Notes   366

References/Selected Works   382

Index   387

An Estranged and Unrecognizable City

INTRODUCTION, 2023

THE DREAM

I arrive in a strange city. There is a male guide, a friend. I push a stroller, protective of its contents. We roll along the sidewalk in the effort to avoid crossing the impossible bumper-to-bumper traffic. Suddenly an elder woman appears—literally out of nowhere. She collapses onto the cement in front of us. I run to her while a young woman whisks past me and carries off with the stroller. I catch a quick glimpse of her face, her resemblance to the baby is unmistakable. And, I am left cradling my own mother in my arms.

Elvira's face is as ancient and beautifully chiseled as the last look I had of her upon her death, seventeen years ago.

Mamá, I say, are you hurt? How did you get here?

Her only answer is the calming gaze of her eyes. And, although I am holding my mother, she has linked her arms around mine, so that it is more she who carries me.

I am aware that I am beginning to wake up, so I hold my eyes closed to hold fast to the dream, to sustain the tactile physicality of Elvira's presence in my life. It lasts for an extended moment—somewhere between the material and dream world.

And in that place I am reminded that I am loved.

Even in an estranged and unrecognizable city, we are reunited with our relations. This is what is required of us now—to find other ways of knowing, of transmitting messages to one another across generations living and gone. From all parts of the world, peoples are sent into migration, so that even the ground beneath their feet may no longer speak to them. What was wrong before has gotten worse. More so than we could have imagined.

How does one speak of spirit, not as escape, but as a radical reckoning with the horrific conditions of a dying world?
This is what we ask of one another in low whispers.
This is how we continue to love.

LOVING

The right to love was the original impetus for *Loving in the War Years* and would impact all of my writings that would follow. In 1977, this meant for me the right to be a lesbian. At the time, I didn't know it would come to mean so much more.

This collection of selected writings reflects the trajectory of some twenty years of selected works that affected the production of another twenty thereafter. The selections were drawn from three published texts—*Loving in the War Years/Lo que nunca pasó por sus labios* (1983); *The Last Generation* (1993); and the second edition of *Loving* (2000) that included an additional chapter from the late 1990s (herein retitled "Coyolxauhqui Remembered"). The reissue of these texts is an effort to speak of a not-so-distant past in order to aid in the formation of more livable and less compromising liberatory strategies for people of color and queer communities in the future. We desperately need a cross-generational freedom movement.

For me, the beauty of this re-vision process of writings, some more than four decades old, is that it has allowed me to consider the younger writer who first composed these works as "she," not me.

I admit, I miss that young writer, especially in the earliest works—her unabashed bravura in breaking taboos: writing of the desirous body, the Chicana mixed-blood/mixed-up queer female body—the color and class of it in all its shameless struggling viscerality. And all in the effort to get herself and perhaps some of us free.

I admire the young poet-lover—frequently recognize her in my own students' writings. They (and she) challenge me to speak to what remains unsaid, hidden in the shadows of unacknowledged censorships: to proclaim aloud that theory can never wholly comprehend desire. This is the work of poets.

The first writings in *Loving* emerged from that poetic impulse. Reviewing the pages that come after, I find myself saddened to discover how the poems become fewer as the política presses on and harder.

And so it continues, today, even harder.

THE WAR YEARS

The real war is not just the senseless fodder of the Ukraine-Russia conflict, nor the cruel dregs of the mercenary twenty-year US occupation in Afghanistan. Nor is it even the forever wounding of Palestine. The real war is one that truly warrants the title "World War." Marx was right in his prediction that capitalism would eventually destroy itself, but did he think it would destroy the planet in the process?

For some of us there is occasional reprieve from these thoughts—but reprieve is, by nature, fleeting. We may decide to look away from the slow meltdown of our planet and its once impermeable monuments—the Iceland glacier, the coral reefs, the old-growth redwoods of Califas. We keep telling ourselves the latest virus will be the last one, in a global economy where disease can travel more fluidly and frequently than human beings. But everywhere we turn there is another masked cashier, a drought turned flood, a burning sequoia, a disappeared island, a shuttered diner, a classroom of checkerboard squares of sleepy-eyed, disinterested students, and a well-meaning teacher trying to make contact. There is always another fresh hill of grave dirt and another creature-carrier to blame for it.

We are not immune. In the public collective consciousness, there can be no reprieve. There is only pain, only loss, only the forced removal of hundreds of thousands from their homelands due to environmental upheaval and stupid wars of avarice off and online.

Coyolxauhqui Remembered

The reissue of these works was prompted by a desire to rescue, in some small way, the personal and political past of la Chicana from oblivion, to preserve a radical activist women of color feminism that reflected the complexity of our experience, as described in *This Bridge Called My Back: Writings by Radical Women of Color.* I bemoan the fact that Chicanas, and Raza in general, still have such a limited public face nationally and internationally. I am hungry to see our work—our images and writings, our worldviews—realized across borders of language and culturas because I believe there are communities of peoples just like us, who may speak a different language, but know what it is to feel displaced—that they, like us, are not truly full members in what was once their homeland. We are the measure of multiple colonizations in América, external and internal, and we cannot forget what has been lost.

But generations *are* forgetting. So much has changed. We imagine we have become freer than we had ever hoped. But, if viewed through the vantage point of the liberation movements of the 1960s and '70s—all the civil rights and antiestablishment movements that have shaped the world in which my generation came to consciousness—we may have only encountered a more sinister system of imprisonment today. The cultural dominance of AngloAmerica has required us to imitate the colonizer to survive. We speak in his first-world tongue to such a degree that we begin to believe the masquerade of the performance and we grow speechless in the lie of it. Trying to express ourselves to the generations that follow in the tracks of our own amnesia, we fail them.

If, for example, the immigrant children of los pueblos originarios from the South grow up to find no resonance, no value, in twenty-first century Chicanx política, what does this mean about our collective participation in the future of radical activism in the US? For whom, and with whom, do we continue to evolve a movimiento?

The Mexica(n) figures invoked in this collection—Coyolxauhqui, Malinche, La Llorona, and Coatlicue—reflect part of the Chicana feminist writer's project of recuperation. They are "presente," in the way we Raza call upon our ancestors aloud by name. They appear and reappear on these pages, corresponding to my own stages of evolving consciencia and to the litany of hungry women in whom their fuerzas resonate. Mesoamerican in origin, these diosas are the pantheon of story, of mythology, of our first Américan literatures. I find my way free through them, unlocking the prison of their male-centric colonizations and my own.

There is much to lament in what is not known. I bear witness to a dying breed of Xicana,[*] neither compromised nor complicated by academic and new-aged appropriation, but grounded in actual conocimiento garnered through suffering. Something Gloria Anzaldúa understood porque sufrió mucho. Perhaps this is why we believe (in) her. She learned through suffering. I do not romanticize nor quantify. I only recognize the hard road it is to live a life of unrelenting consciencia, with spirit as one's singular guide. This was Gloria.

---

* When Xicana is spelled with an "X" it is to emphasize the indigenous identification with our self-naming as mestizo peoples. In náhuatl, the "x" is pronounced closer to a "ch" sound as in me/xi/cana.

FROM THE LAST GENERATION

At seventy, I am learning to inhabit that place of the last generation—to be free to tell the story differently; to write without convention; to script in an original tongue; to reimagine how we continue to love in writing, unbound by the warring languages of the corporate academy, the parroting in the evening news, the one-upmanship of pundits and scholars, the often violent verbiage of social media and its ubiquitous platforms.

I look forward to the next twenty years, although one is not guaranteed the longevity. Still, this is the last generation for *my* generation and in that, we have a calling—a personal and public responsibility to continue to say what has not been said, or was once said but now forgotten. We, who were young during one of the most liberatory moments in US history—let us name them so we do not forget:

The civil rights movement, the United Farm Workers, Black Power, El Movimiento Chicano, the Young Lords, AIM (the American Indian Movement), the Asian American Political Alliance, the Anti (Vietnam) War Movement, SNCC, the Third World Liberation Front, the Panthers, the Brown Berets, the I-Hotel Filipino protests, Women's Liberation, the Gay and Lesbian Movement, Anti-Apartheid (South Africa), Central American solidarity (FSLN, FMLN), HIV/AIDS Activism, the Third World Women's Alliance, Free Palestine, Immigrant Rights, Trans Liberation, Reproductive Rights (Abortion/Anti-Sterilization Abuse), Transnational Women of Color Feminism, and onward.

Today, in the United States, as Xicanx peoples, old and young / queer and straight, we have been systematically separated and censored from one another by the mythologies of free enterprise, the rights of property, and a rabid consequential competitive individualism. In many traditional societies, cross-generational exchanges provided consejo y conocimiento and our daily labors threaded a fabric of continuity within the community. From the vantage point of forty years of political and arts engagement, I can only say that there is so much to know from the past in the radical reconstruction of a future. As I have aged, I have learned to look further and further back to find respuesta—to insist that to re-member is to re-create and that decolonization requires the re-indigenization of heart and mind.

Perhaps we can uncover what that means by simply deciding to make our way home again. I don't know.

FOR THE NEXT GENERATION

What do you know, the young ones ask.
Teach me of what I have not seen.
Our time together is short on this planet.

The onus on the next generations is impossible to contemplate. Everything and nothing is required of you. My generation can't presume to ask you to make the world well. I only offer these early works because they were brave once upon a time, for their time, and you all will need to be brave. But, only you can determine what that requires.

In the inquiry resides the hope.

January 2023
Sacramento, CA

The ancestral homelands of the
Maidu, Miwok, Me-Wuk, and Nisenan

Words on Wording

In this collection of writings, I have tried to retain the evolving late twentieth-century usage of politicized terms as they were then applied to sites of identity, e.g., ethnicity, race, sex, sexuality, and gender. For example, in the early 1980s, the generic masculine Chicano was used to refer to us as a people and/or specifically to Chicano males. Chicana was used only when referring specifically to females. The usage of Chicana/Chicano and Chican@ to reflect more inclusive gender designation became popular in the 1990s, eventually arriving at today's (twenty-first-century) nonbinary Chicanx/Latinx or Chicane/Latine (preferred by some Spanish-speakers) and its concurrent gender neutral pronouns.

For my part, in more recent writings, I often use "Xicana/x," placing an "x" on both ends of the word to speak to an Indigenous and feminist* political praxis, in which we recognize ourselves as mestizo/indigenous peoples of an América sin fronteras, with women (including transwomen) as central.

"Latino" (and its evolving gendered variations) is at times used herein when speaking more generally of US Latin American, Caribbean, Mexican, and Central American peoples as a whole.

In this collection and moving forward, I often prefer the use of "Raza," meaning "the people," to refer to US Latinos generally and to Chicanos specifically. It's an old word with less than complimentary

---

* Retaining the female "a" while including the nonbinary "x."

origins in early Spain. But, in my lifetime, it has been a word that created community, with no gender bias, which is why I like it, along with its cultural and ethnic inclusivity; but, admittedly, the word contains a complicated racial history.*

The Mexican philosopher José Vasconcelos adopted the term in his 1925 post-revolution treatise *La raza cósmica*. The work argued that mestizos of Latin America represented a future "fifth race" that promised, through continual miscegenation, to eliminate race and racism. The dangerously eugenic message of the work required the gradual disappearance of the indigenous and all races deemed inferior in favor of mixed-raced peoples, improved by virtue of their blending with the European.

But, forty and fifty years later, Chicanos understood all this quite differently. If we *are* mestizos, they reasoned, then we are also *Indigenous* Americans, and with that the hyphenated "Mexican-American" became "Chicano" and took their rightful place among people of color liberation struggles, proclaiming en masse "Viva La Raza!" The word still feels radical to me, as I experienced it fifty years ago. And that is how I use it here in these pages.†

---

* Associated Press, "Why the Term 'La Raza' Has Complicated Roots in the US," *CPR News*, July 13, 2017, https://www.cpr.org/2017/07/13/why-the-term-la-raza-has-complicated-roots-in-the-us/.

† It's also important to note that the actual language used on barrio streets and in our homes may differ considerably from all of the above.

LOVING IN THE WAR YEARS /

LO QUE NUNCA PASÓ POR SUS LABIOS

1978–1983

Cover of the 1983 edition of *Loving in the War Years*, published by South End Press

Para mis compañeras
for the duration.

———

Para mi familia de "scratch"
and all the rest of the tribe.

Amar en los años de guerra

Introduction, 1983

Sueño

My lover and I are in a prison camp together.
We are in love in wartime.
A young soldier working as a guard has befriended us.
We ask him honestly: the truth—"are we going to die?"
He answers, "yes, it's almost certain."
I contemplate escaping.
Ask him to help us. He blanches.
"That is impossible," he says.
I regret asking, fearing recrimination.

I see the forest through the fence on my right. I spot a place between the trees. I think, I could burrow through there, toward freedom? Two of us would surely be spotted. One of us has a slim chance. I consider leaving my lover, imprisoned. But know that we must, at all costs, remain with each other. Even unto death. That it is our being together that makes the pain, even our dying, human.

Loving in the war years.

1

Tonight, the summer heat takes on the liquid flavor it had when I first moved into this room, a six-floor walk-up in Brooklyn, Nueva York. I am tired by the thought of all this moving and working—how slow and hard change is to come. How although this book has taken me from Los Angeles, north to Berkeley, across the Bay to San Francisco, across the country to Boston and Brooklyn, south to Mexico and back again to Califas, sigo siendo la hija de mi mamá. My mother's daughter.

My mother's daughter who at ten years old knew she was queer. Queer to believe that God thought so much of me, he intended to see me burn in hell; that unlike other children, I was not to get by with a clean slate. I was born into this world with complications, marked as "other," chosen to prove my salvation. Todavía sigo siendo bien católica—with all its obligatory guilt and velas burning, but also with the inherent Mexican faith that there is meaning to nuestro sufrimiento en este mundo.

The first time I went to la basílica in Mexico City, where el retrato de La Virgen de Guadalupe hovers over a gilded altar, I was shocked to see that below it ran a moving escalator. The escalator was not one that brought people up to the image that we might reverently put our fingers to our lips and press them against the painting of the angelito at the foot of her garment. Instead, it moved people along horizontally, from side to side and through, as quickly as possible. A moving sidewalk built to keep the traffic going. In spite of the irreverence imposed by such technology, the most devout y humilde de las mujeres, Indígenas mayores, clung to the ends of the handrailing, crossing themselves, gesturing besos al retrato, their hips banging up against the moving railing over and over again as it threatened to remove them. They stayed. In spite of the machine, they had come to spend their time con La Virgen.

I left the church in tears, knowing how for so many years I had closed my heart to the passionate pull of such faith that promised no end to the pain. I grew white; fought to free myself from my culture's claim on me. It seemed I had to step outside my familia to see what we as a people were doing suffering. This is my politic; this is my writing. For as much as both have eventually brought me back to my familia, the "consciousness" my education provided initially separated me from them and forced me to leave home. This is what has made me the outsider so many Chicanas, very near to me in circumstance, fear.

I am a child, lying on my bed midday. The sun streaming through the long window, thin sheer curtains. Next door I can hear them all—my aunties, my mom—arguing. Mi abuelita giving the cold shoulder, not giving in. Each daughter vying for a place with her. The cruel gossip. Las mentiras. My mother trying to hold onto the truth, her version of the story, su integridad.

I put my head back on the pillow and count the years this has been going on—todas las mujeres en una procesión cada día llegando a la puerta de mi abuela. Needing her, never doing enough for her. The competition for her favor. My grandmother's control of them. I count my mother's steps; hear her click high-heeled angry down the gravel driveway, through the fence, up the back steps, and back into our house. Estará llorando. Otra vez. I tell my sister reading a novel next to me—

"How many years, JoAnn? It can't be this way for us too when we grow up."

. . . . .

Mi abuelita se muere muy lentamente, sus ojos cerrados y la boca callada. El hospital le da comida por las venas. Ya no habla. No canta como cantaba. She does not squeeze my mother's hand tight in her fight against la sombra de su propia muerte. She does not squeeze the life out of her. Ya no. Está durmiendo mi abuela, esperando a La Muerte.

And what goes with her? My familia's claim to an internal dialogue where el gringo does not penetrate? Born in 1888, su memoria de noventa y seis años extends to a time where nuestra cultura was not the daily subject of debate.

I write this book because we are losing ourselves to the gabacho.

SUEÑO: 5 DE ENERO 1983

My grandmother appears outside la iglesia. Standing in front as she used to después de la misa. I am so surprised that she is well enough to go out again—be dressed, be in the world. I am elated to see her, to know I get to have the feel of her again in my life. She is, however, in great pain. She shows me her leg, which has been operated on. The wound is like a huge crater in her calf—crusted, open, a gaping hole. I feel her pain so critically.

SUEÑO: 7 DE ENERO 1983

En el sueño, intento de sacar una foto de mi abuela y de mi mamá. Mientras una mujer me espera en la cama. The pull and tug present themselves in my dreams. Deseo para las mujeres, anhelo para la familia. I want to take the photo of my grandmother because I know she is dying. I want one last picture. The woman keeps calling me to her bed. She wants me. I keep postponing her.

The dream then transitions to my brother. He has returned to la familia, not begging forgiveness, but acknowledging his transgressions against us. Somos unidos.

2

Can you go home? Do your parents know? Have they read your work? These are the questions I am most often asked by young Raza.* It's as if they are hungry to know if it's possible to have both—your own

---

* Chicano expression for "the people"—"our community"; often extended to mean Latinos in general.

life and the life of our familias. Sadly (or perhaps, gratefully), this is a book my family will never see. And yet, how I wish I could show them how much I have taken them to heart, even my father's silence. What he didn't say working inside me as intensely as my mother wept it.

My first poems were love poems. El amor, el deseo para la mujer also brought me to Chicana feminism. Writing is the measure of my life. I cannot write what I am not willing to live up to in the world. Is it for this reason I so often fear my own writing, fear that it will jump up and push me off some precipice of self-doubt?

Women daily change my work. How can it be that I have always hungered for, and feared, falling in love as much as I do writing from my heart? Each changes you forever. For me, sex has always been part of the question of freedom, the freedom to want passionately—to live it out through the body of the poem, with the body of the beloved. So that when I feel the stirrings of creativity, it is a fresh inhale of new life, life I want to breathe back into my work. And I long to be a lover like youth.

I watch my changes in the women I love.

JOURNAL ENTRY: 2 DE JULIO 1982

It takes the greatest of effort even to put pen to paper—so much weighing on me. It's as if I am bankrupt of feeling, but that's not really so. My comes into my room, sees me face flat on the bed, gathers me into her arms. I say I am depressed and she reminds me of how I tell her so often how depression is not a feeling. Depression covers a feeling that doesn't have a chance to come out. Keeping it down. Keeping the writing back.

So often throughout my work on this book I felt I could not write because I have a movement on my shoulder, a lover on my shoulder, a family over my shoulder. On some level you have to be willing to lose it all to write—to risk telling the truth that no one may want to hear, even you. En el acto de escribir radica el riesgo, siempre amenazándote. Paradoxically, my writing has drawn me closer to my familia, for it has freed me to love them from places in myself that had been mired in unexpressed pain. Writing has ultimately brought me back to them.

They don't need this book. They have me.

The issue of being a "movement writer" is altogether different. Because of the sudden published visibility of my writings, I feel my back will break from the pressure I feel to speak for others. A friend told me once how it was no wonder that I had titled my first book *This Bridge Called My Back*.* "You have chronic back trouble," she says.

Riding on the train with another friend, I ramble on about the difficulty of finishing this book, feeling like I am being asked by all sides to be a representative of the race, the sex, the sexuality—or at all costs to avoid that. I hear the contempt in their voices. "You don't speak for me! For the community!" My friend smiles at me kindly, almost amused. We are on the commuter train among a sea of gray suits. We speak in secret code.

"Ah, Chavalita," she says to me. "Tú necesitas viajar para que veas lo que en verdad es la comunidad. There's really no such thing as community among políticos. Community is simply the way people live a life together. And they're doing it all over the world. The only way to write para la comunidad is to write so completely from your heart what is your own personal truth. This is what touches people."

Some days I feel my writing wants to break itself open. Speak in a language that maybe no readership can follow. What does it mean that the Chicana writer, if she truly owns her voice, may depict a world so specific, so privately ours, so "foreign" to the Anglo reader, there will be no publisher for it. The people who can understand it, don't/won't/can't read it. How can I be a writer in this? I have been translating my

---

* *Writings by Radical Women of Color*, coedited with Gloria Anzaldúa.

experience out of fear of an aloneness too great to bear. I have learned analysis as a mode to communicate what I feel the experience itself already speaks for. The combining of poetry and essays in this book is the compromise I make in the effort to be understood. Conversely, in Spanish "compromiso" refers to "obligation," "commitment." And yes, I write as I do in contract with both sides of myself.

I am the daughter of a Chicana and an Anglo. I think most days I am an embarrassment to both groups. I sometimes hate the white in me so viciously that I long to forget the obligation my light skin has imposed upon my life. To speak two tongues, one of privilege, one of oppression. I must. But I will not double-talk and I refuse to let anybody's movement determine for me what is safe and fair to say.

3

The completion of this book finds me in the heart of change. So, there is no definitive statement to make here in this introduction that will prepare the reader for the ever-evolving story of a life—a story of change. But for whom have I tried so resolutely to communicate? Whom have I worried over in this writing? Who is my audience?

Todavía soy la hija de mi mamá. I keep thinking, *this is for the daughters.* It's the daughters who remain loyal to the mother, although this loyalty is not always reciprocated. To be free means on some level to release that painful devotion when it begins to punish us. Stop the chain of events—la procesión de mujeres, sufriendo. Dolores my grandmother, Dolores her daughter, Dolores her daughter's daughter. Free the daughter to love her own daughter.

I write this on the deathbed of my abuela. We have made one last procession to her: my mother, my sister, her daughter, and I. My grandmother's eyes are open today. I hold the bone of her skull in the palm of my hand. It is a light bird-weight.

I whisper into her better ear. "¿Abuelita? ¿Me reconoce? Soy Cherríe. Acabo de llegar de Nueva York."

She opens her eyes. "¡Ay, Chorizo! ¡Mi'jita!" She pulls my head down into the deep bowl of her thin neck, she kisses me. "Mi chorizito! ¡Tengo hambre! ¡Quiero Chorizo!" And I give her the fleshy part of my arm for her to pretend a bite from it.

"¿Dónde está tu mamá?"

"Aquí estoy, mamá." My mother grabs her hand.

"Elvira. ¿y la JoAnn, está aquí también?"

"Sí, grandma, aquí 'stoy y la Erín."

"Hi, little grandma," Erin says, softly kissing her cheek.

"¡Ay, mi chulita!" She wraps her thin veined hands around Erin's cheeks, then gnashes her teeth together, shaking her head, pretending like she wants to eat her up, too. Suddenly, it seems my abuelita has never been so full of life.

I hold the moment. La línea de las mujeres, la raíz de nuestra familia. A sadness begins to seep in.

Porque nunca podía hablar con mi abuelita,

no completamente,

en el idioma de su corazón.

1983
Brooklyn, New York

WHAT KIND OF LOVE
HAVE YOU MADE ME, MOTHER?

The Pilgrimage

She saw women
for the first time
when they had streamed in long broken
single file
out from her mother's tongue—

      "En México, las mujeres crawl
      on their hands and knees
      to the basílica door.
      This proves their faith."

The brown knotted knees were hers
in her dreaming, she wondered

where in the journey
would the dusty knees begin
to crack

would the red blood of women
stain the grey bone
of road.

Later She Met Joyce

1

Later, she met Joyce
and after they had been friends for a whole
school year, formed their own
girls' gang with code words & rhymes
that played itself coolly
on *this* side of trouble
they got separated by the summer.

> Joyce, without a phone
> and so far away
> into the bordering
> town.

But just once, they rendezvoused
on the front porch of a pair
of old white folks, friends of her family.
> "Come see me," Joyce whispered
> over the telephone line.
> "I'm only a few blocks away."

And without expecting to, Cecilia climbed
right up those steps and straight into Joyce's
arms and she would never forget the shape
of the girl's chest, a good one
and a half years older and
how her own small chest & cheek
sunk into it.

It spread through her body the cool
breath and release of a tightness
she didn't know she had held
back, waiting
for summer's end.
Waiting to look
into Joyce's round-like-an-olive
face and see it full
of tears, too.

It was the first time for both of them.
And Cecilia thought,
So, this is love.

2
Later, she met Joyce
who didn't come back
to cath-lic school
it being too hard she guessed
(there *was* no telephone)
in a big winter coat
after mass one sunday
looking more like a mama
than her childhood friend,
rounder than Cecilia had ever seen her
hair teased high off her head.

      "Hi," Cecilia said.
      "Eh, ésa, 'ow you doing? Wha chu say, man?"

Joyce moved back and forth, her suedes
toeing the ground, talking that talk

that Cecilia's mama called
a difernt claz a people
that had something to do with your tongue
going thick on you, wearing
shiny clothes and never getting
to college.
Seems in other people's eyes
Joyce was a fat half-breed
that flunked close-to-twice
in other people's eyes
in other people's eyes.

In Joyce's eyes that morning
Cecilia looked for a sign—

> *C'mon, Joyce   be kidding   please*
> *you remember me   you remember*
> *me   you remember*
> *please*

and thought she detected
some trace there between the two thick lines
of turquoise, of the brown eyes that cried
over missing her.

Missing Joyce turned
pachuca on her, walking away
talking about the "guyz"
she would like to have
ride her low
through the valley floor.

3
Later that year,
Cecilia was picked
by the smart
white
girls
for president.

La Dulce Culpa

What kind of lover have you made me, mother
who let me into bed with you
at six
at sixteen
oh, even at sixty-six you do still
lifting up the blanket with one arm
lining out the space for my body with the other

       as if our bodies still beat
       inside the same skin
       as if you never noticed
       when they cut me
       out
       from you.

What kind of lover have you made me, mother
who took belts to wipe this memory from me

       the memory of your passion
       dark & starving, spilling
       out of rooms, driving
       into my skin, cracking
       & cussing in spanish

       the thick dark *f* sounds
       hard *c*'s splitting
       the air like blows

       you would *get a rise outta me*

you knew it in our blood
the vision   of my rebellion

What kind of lover have you made me, mother
who put your passion on a plate for me
nearly digestible. Still trying to swallow
the fact that we lived most of our lives
with the death of a man
whose touch ran
across the surface of your skin
never landing nightly
where you begged it
to fall

>   to hold
>   your desire in the palm
>   of his hand
>
>   for you to rest there
>   for you to continue.

What kind of lover have you made me, mother
so in love
with what is left
unrequited.

          . . . . .

What is left.

Mamá
I use you

like the belt
pressed inside your grip
seething for contact

I take
what I know
from you and want
to whip this world
into shape.

The damage
has defined me
as the space you provide
for me in your bed.
          . . . . .

I was not to raise a hand against you—
but today
I promise you
I *will* fight back.

Strip the belt from your hands
and take you

into
my arms.

The Slow Dance

Thinking of Mari and Elena—those two dancing together. The images return to me. Hold me. Stir me. Prompt me to want *something*.

Mari moving Elena around the floor, so in control of the knowledge: how to handle a woman, while I fumble around them both. When Mari and I kissed, just once, I forgot and let too much want show, closing my eyes, all the eyes around me seeing me close my eyes. I am a girl wanting so much to kiss a woman. She sees this too, cutting the kiss short.

But not with Elena, Elena's arm around Mari's neck. Mari's body all leaning into the center of her pelvis. This is *the way she enters a room*, leaning into the body of a woman. The two of them, like grown-ups, like the women I silently longed for. Still, I remember after years of wanting and getting and loving, still I remember the desire to be that *in sync* with another woman's body.

And I move women around the floor, too—women I think enamored with me. My mother's words rising up from inside me, "A *real* man, when he dances with you, you'll know he's a *real* man by how he holds you in the back." I think, *yes,* someone who can guide you around a dance floor. And so, I do, moving these women kindly, surely, even superior. *I can handle these women. They want this.* And I do too.

Thinking of my father, how so timidly he used to take my mother onto the small square of carpet we reserved for dancing, pulling back the chairs. She really leading the step, he learning to cooperate so it *looked* like a male lead. I noticed his hand, how it lingered awkwardly about my mother's small back, his thin fingers never really getting a hold on her.

I remember this as I take a woman in my arms, my hand moving up under her shoulder blade, speaking to her from there. It is from *this* spot that the dance is directed. From *this* place, I tenderly, with each fingertip, move her.

I am my mother's lover. The partner she's been waiting for. I can handle whatever you got hidden. I can provide for you.

But when I put this provider up against the likes of Mari, *I* am the one following/falling into her. Like Elena, taken up in the arms of this woman. *I want this.*

Catching the music shift again; the beat softens, slows down. I search for Mari through the bodies, the faces. *I am ready for you now.* I want age. Knowledge. *Your body that still, after years, withholds and surrenders—keeps me there, waiting, wishing.* I push through the bodies, looking for her. Willing. Willing to feel *this time* what disrupts in me. Girl. Woman. Child. Boy. Willing to embody what I will in the space of her arms. Looking for Mari, I'm willing, wanting.

And I find you dancing with Elena. My body both hers and yours in the flash of a glance.

I can handle this.

I am used to being an observer.
I am used to not getting what I want.
I am used to imagining what it must be like.

The Voices of the Fallers

*Because Jay Freeman was imprisoned at the age of nineteen
for more than twenty years for murdering the son of her lesbian lover, throwing him off a cliff. And, because, at the age of
nineteen, my high school friend Charlotte, also a lesbian, fell
from a cliff and died.*

For M.

You were born queer with the dream
of flying
from an attic with a trap
door   opening
to a girl who could
handle a white horse
with wings   riding her
away   opening
to a girl who could
save a woman
on a white horse
riding her
away.

I was born queer with the dream
of falling
the small sack of my body
dropping
off
a ledge
suddenly.

Listen.
Can you hear my mouth crack
open   the sound
of my lips bending
back against the force
of the fall?

Listen.
Put your ear deep
down
through the   opening
of my throat and
listen.

.....

The nun said
"Young lady
you have a chip
on your shoulder
that's going to get you
in plenty of trouble
someday."

The queer
flicks off
the chip
with the nonchalance
with the grace
with the cool
brush of lint

from a 200-dollar
three-piece

the chip tumbling
off
her shoulder
first tumbling
off
the cliff   the legs
following
over
her head

the chip
spinning onto the classroom floor
(silently imagined)
her body's
dead
silent
collision
with the sand.

> *I'm falling.*
> *can't you see*
> *I'm*
> *falling?*

. . . . .

DARE ME
DARE ME

DARE ME
to push this kid off
the cliff   DARE
ME
Some queer
mother I am
who would kill her kid
to save her own neck
from cracking
on the way
down.

You bet your ass I am
if push comes to shove the kid goes
queer

I'm falling.
can't you see
I'm
falling?

. . . . .

It was not an accident.
I knew then sitting in the row next to her she would not
        survive she
could not survive this way this unprotected defiance her
        shoulders
pushing up against me grabbing me by the collar
        up against the locker "motherfucker you mess
        with my girlfriend?"

her pale face twitching
cover it up
cover it up
I wished she would
cover it up
for both our sakes she would not
survive this way pushing
people
around.

. . . . .

When I fell
from the cliff   she tells me
it was the purest move
I ever made   she tells me
she thought of me
as a kind of consolation
surviving
just
as she made
the move
to fall
just
as her shoulders split
the air.

Do you know what it feels like finally
to be up against nothing?
Oh, it's like flying, my friend,
 I'm flying

I'm falling.
can't you see
I'm
falling?

. . . . .

She confesses to me—
I held the boy's body between my hands
for a moment it was like
making love
the bones of my fingers resting
between the bones of his ribcage
I held him there
I guess we both felt   safe
for a split   second
but then he grew
stiff and then he resisted
so I pushed
up against him
I pushed until the wall
of his body vanished
into the air so thick
it was due to eat both of us up
sooner or later.

I'm falling.
can't you see
I'm
falling?
Momma, I tell you
I'm falling

right
now

. . . . .

In this child
killer I could have
buried the dead
memory of Charlotte
falling   once
and for all
I could have
ended there   holding
the silence
but it is
this end
I fear.

      Waking to the danger
of falling
again

    falling

in love
the dream.

LOVING ON THE RUN

An Open Invitation to a Meal

I am
you tell me
a piece of cake.

I wonder about your eating habits
which make me dessert
instead of staple
a delicacy, like some chocolate mousse
teasing your taste buds, melting in your mouth
stopping there.

There's nothing fancy about me.
I am brown and grainy and can stick to the ribs
a food source that won't run out on you
through the toughest winter.

Come, sit down.

Give up that sweet tooth and we'll put it in a jar
to remind us of the polite society that can afford such things.

Right now, it's beginning to snow.

Come, sit down.
The day is getting shorter and it's beginning to snow.

Yes, here.
Sit down.

Here.

You Upset the Whole System of This Place

Remembering her.

I've been inside all day.

You enter sleek, wet from winter rain, hot heaving chest, hot breath. The still heated air of this house melts around your shoulders as you pass through it, dripping down along your thighs to bare calloused feet. You upset the whole system of this place.

Approaching, your footsteps are solid and silent.

I wrapped in bedclothes, billows of quilts and pillows. I rock to the rhythmic sound of my own breathing inside my head, stuffed mucus. My small chest, a battleground, it is fragile and bony, a cough that scrapes it dry each time, an ache like a rash beneath my ribs.

All that keeps you from me is this Guatemalan drape which lines my bed like a mosquito net, only one simple striped panel. You wave it aside with a backhand motion, you move into the bed with me, not afraid of catching cold. The thick warm dough of your hands pours into the hollow parts of me.

"I've been trying not to cry for you all day," I say. You stroke my mouth closed. "I need you now, I have this terrible cold."

Without reply, you go into the green kitchen and pull out the remains of a gallon of cider. I imagine you crushing the nutmeg into the liquid while it warms over the low flame, squeezing in lemon, imitating me.

You return, mug in hand, you are dry now, your hair straggly. I drink the hot cider and you stay and roll with me until dinnertime. You ease me a half an hour into the night.

"Are you coming back?" I lean into your cheek, breathing in with my mouth.

"Yes," you answer, "when you're better."

I follow your footsteps exiting through the hardwood hallway, down a step, across the carpet, out the door and down the many red wet steps into the neon night that swallows you up.

Lovin' on the Run

For women who travel in packs of one

1
I found you on a street corner
hangin' out with a buncha boys
lean brown boys
you too lean
into them
talkin your girl-head off
with your glasses
like some wizard
sayin—
"I know what that feels like."

I found you there
you guys hangin out like family
talkin about women
you sayin—
how they make your hips roll
without thinkin
those pale olive
hips of yours
deep and oiled
like a woman

they don't catch on
bout you bein' one
for all your talk about women/likin them
they don't catch the difference

for all your talk bout
your common enemy
you operatin on street sense
so keen
it spots danger
before he makes it around the corner
before he hardly notices you
as a woman
they marvel at this

they don't catch on
them seein your words
like the body of a dark brother
you sayin—
"I know what that feels like"
bein' shitted on
and they believin you
about your allied place on the block
about the war going on
they believe you
because you know
you got
no reason
to lie to them

2
I found you
among blarin boom boxes
walkin thru the hood
there you were
kicked back on some porch
actin like family

like you belonged
callin to me
hangin over the railing
wavin
coaxin me to your steps
gettin' me to sit there
you strokin my head
slow and soft,
sayin—
"you are soooo sweet"
drawin' out the "so"
like a long drink
like a deep moan
comin out from inside you
like a deep sigh of lovin

lovin
like your brothers
lovin hard-won lovin
gotten in snatches in collisions
in very desperate situations lovin
which sometimes squatted
rested
took a vacation
would not get up off its ass
to meet a woman
face on
lovin on the run

3
collecting me
into your thin arms

you are woman to me
and brother to them
in the same breath
you marvel at this

seeing yourself
for the first time
in the body of a sister
like family
like you belong
you moving right up into
this me
this streetfighter
like you
who you take under your bruised wing
your shoulder blade bent
on bearing alone

seeing yourself
for the *first* time
in the body of her boyhood
her passion to survive
female and unyielding

taking all this under your wing
letting it wrestle there
into your skin
changing you

Loving in the War Years

Loving you is like living in the war years.
I *do* think of Bogart & Bergman
not clear who's who
but still singin' a long smoky
mood into the piano bar
drinks straight up
the last bottle in the house
while bombs split
outside, a broken
world.

A world war going on
but you and I still insisting
in each our own heads
still thinking how
if I could only make some contact
with that woman across the keyboard
we size each other up
          yes ...

Loving you has this kind of desperation
to it, like do or die, I
having eyed you from the first
time you made the decision to move
from your stool
to live dangerously.

All on the hunch
that in our exchange of photos

of old girlfriends, names
of cities and memories
back in the states
the fronts we've manned
out here on the continent
all this on the hunch
that *this* time there'll be
no need for resistance.

Loving in the war years
calls for a certain kind of risking
without a home to call our own
I've got to take you as you come
to me, each time like a stranger
all over again. Not knowing
what deaths you saw today
I've got to take you
as you come, battle bruised
refusing our enemy—fear.

We're all we've got. You and I

maintaining
this wartime morality
where being queer
and female
is as warrior
as we can get.

Fear, A Love Poem

1
If fear is two girls awakening in the same room
after a lifetime of sleeping together
she saying, *I dreamed it was the end of the world*
sister, it was the end   you knowing this in your sleep
her terror seeping through skin into your dreams, holding
    her
sensing something
moving too fast

                  as with a lover,
                  dressing and dreaming
                  in the same room.

If fear is awakening in the same room
feeling something moving too fast
the body next to you awake—the back ignoring
your dream which breaks *her* sleep, too   you
waiting for the embrace to be returned   you
waiting to be met in the nightmare
by a sister, by a lover—

If fear is wishing there were some disease to call it
saying, I AM GOING CRAZY always for lack
of better words   always because we have no words
to say we need
attention, early on.

If fear is this, these things
then I am neither alone, nor crazy

but a child, for fear of doom, driven
to look into the darkest part
of the eye—

      the part of the eye that is not
      eye at all
      but hole.

At thirteen, I had the courage
to stare that hole down   face up
to it, alone in the mirror.
I can't claim the same simple courage
now, moving away from the mirror
into the faces of other
women   to *your* face which dares to answer
mine. That it is

      in
      this
      hole
      round, common and black
      where we recognize each other.

      That
      in looking to the hole
      the iris, with all its shades
      of contrast and persuasion,
      blurs peripheral
      and I am left, standing
      with your face
      in my hands
      like a mirror. This clear
      recognition I fear

to see our hunger bold-faced like this
sometimes turning the sockets in your head
stone cold, *sometimes*
enveloping your eyes with a liquid
so pure and full
of longing I feel
it could clean out the most miserable parts
of myself   melt down
a lifetime of turned backs.

2
I know now, with you
no one's turning her back.
I may roll over and over
in my mind, toss back and forth
from shoulder to shoulder the weight
of the child in me, battered wanting walking
through the streets armored and ready to kill
a body wrestling now with the touch of your surrender
but I won't turn my back.

You reach for me in bed.
It is 4 am
your arm stretching
across a valley of killings I fear
no one can survive.
                    all this in one night, again?

You reach for me in bed.
Look at me, you say,
turning my chin into your hand
what do you see?

It is
my face wanting
and refusing everything.

And at that moment
for a moment, I want

to take that slender hand
and place it between my breasts
my hand holding it there.
I want

to feel your touch *outside*
my body, on the *surface*
of my skin.

I want
to know, *for sure,*
where you leave off
and I begin . . .

Passage

on the edge of the war near the bonfire
we taste knowledge
—Stephen Berg, *Nothing in the Word: Versions of Aztec Poetry*

There is a very old wound in me
between my legs
where I have bled, not to birth
pueblos or revolutionary
concepts or simple
sucking children

       but a memory
       of some ancient betrayal.

So that when you touch me
and I long to freeze, not feel
what hungry longing
I used to know
nor taste in you a want
I fear will burn
my fingers to their roots
it's out of my control.

Your mouth opens, I long for dryness.
The desert untouched.
Sands swept without sweat.
Aztlán.[1]

Pero, es un sueño—the safety
of the desert.
My country was not like that.
        Neither was yours.

We have always bled
with our veins
and legs open
to forces
beyond our control.

VIEW OF THREE BRIDGES

Raw Experience

1
There is this motor inside me
propelling me
forward
I watch myself for clues.

The hands in front of me
conducting me through this house
a spoon too soon wiped clean
the hands sweeping it away
barely experiencing the sensation
of fullness usefulness
I watch myself for clues.

Catch my face, a moving portrait
in a storefront window
am taken aback by the drop
in cheek line   my face sinking
into itself
I watch myself for clues.

Say "extricate"
for the first time in my life
feel the sound
bulldoze from my mouth
       I earned that word somewhere
       the syllables secretly meeting within me
       planning to blast me open.

There is this motor inside me
propelling me
forward.

I watch myself for clues,
trying to catch up
inhabit my body again.

2
On the highest point of a hill
sitting, there is the view
of three bridges
      each one with a special feature—
      a color
      an island
      a lone red rock
each with a particular destination
coming and going.

I watch them for clues
their secrets
about making connections
about getting
someplace.

For the Color of My Mother

I am a white girl gone brown to the blood color of my mother
speaking to her through the unnamed part of the mouth
the wide-arched muzzle of brown women.

at two
my upper lip split open
clear to the tip of my nose
it spilled forth a cry that would not yield
that traveled down six floors of hospital
where doctors wound me into white bandages
only the screaming mouth exposed

the gash sewn back into a snarl
would last for years

I am a white girl gone brown to the blood color of my mother
speaking for her.

at five, *her* mouth pressed into a seam
a fine blue child's line drawn across her face
her mouth, pressed into mouthing english
mouthing yes yes yes
mouthing stoop lift carry

sweating wet sighs into the field,
her red bandana comes loose
from under the huge brimmed hat,
moving across her upper lip

at fourteen, her mouth painted,
the ends drawn up
the mole in the corner colored in darker larger mouthing yes
she praying no no no
lips pursed and moving

at forty-five, her mouth bleeding
into her stomach, the hole gaping
growing redder deepening
with my father's pallor
finally stitched shut from hip to breastbone
       an inverted V
       Vera
       Elvira

*I am a white girl gone brown to the blood color of my mother
speaking for her.*

    . . . . .

As it comes to be,
dark women enter
sitting in circles

I pass through their hands
the head of my mother painted in clay colors

touching each carved feature
swollen eyes and mouth
they understand the explosion, the splitting
open contained
within the fixed expression

they cradle her silence
nodding to me

La Güera[1]

It requires something more than personal experience to gain a philosophy or point of view from any specific event. It is the quality of our response to the event and our capacity to enter into the lives of others that help us to make their lives and experiences our own.

— *Emma Goldman*[2]

I am the very well-educated daughter of a woman who, by the standards in this country, would be largely considered illiterate. My mother was born in Santa Paula, Southern California, at a time when much of the coast and neighboring Central Valley was still farmland. Nearly thirty-five years later, in 1948, she was the only daughter of six to marry an Anglo, my father.

I remember all of my mother's stories, probably much better than she realizes. She is a fine storyteller, recalling every event of her life with the vividness of the present, noting each detail right down to the cut and color of her dress. I remember stories of her being pulled out of school at the ages of five, seven, nine, and eleven to work in the fields, along with her brothers and sisters; stories of her father drinking away whatever small profit she was able to make for the family; of her going the long way home to avoid meeting him on the street, staggering toward the same destination. I remember stories of my mother lying about her age in order to get a job as a hat-check girl at Agua Caliente Racetrack in Tijuana. At fourteen, she was the main support of the family. I can still see her walking home alone at 3 a.m., only to turn all of her salary and tips over to her mother, who was pregnant again.

The stories continue through the war years and on: walnut-cracking factories, the Voit Rubber company, and then the electronics boom. I remember my mother doing piecework for the plant in our neighborhood. In the late evening, she would sit in front of the TV set, wrapping copper wires into the backs of circuit boards, talking about "keeping up with the younger girls." By that time, she was already in her mid-fifties.

Meanwhile, I was college-prep in school. After classes, I would go with my mother to fill out job applications for her, or write checks for her at the supermarket. We would have the scenario all worked out ahead of time. My mother would sign the check before we'd get to the store. Then, as we'd approach the checkout, she would say—within earshot of the cashier—"Oh honey, you go head and make out the check," as if she couldn't be bothered with such an insignificant detail. No one asked any questions.

I was educated, and wore it with a keen sense of pride and satisfaction, my head propped up with the knowledge, from my mother, that my life would be easier than hers. I was educated; but more than this, I was "la güera"—light-haired and fair-skinned.

No one ever quite told me this (that light was right), but I knew that being light was something valued in my family, who were all Chicano, with the exception of my father. In fact, everything about my upbringing, at least what occurred on a conscious level, attempted to bleach me of what color I did have. Although my mother was fluent in Spanish, I was never taught much of it at home. I picked up what I did learn from school and from overheard snatches of conversation among my relatives and mother. She often called other lower-income Mexicans "braceros," or "wetbacks," referring to herself and her family as "a different class of people." And yet, the real story was that my family, too, had been poor (some still are) and farmworkers. My mother can remember this in her blood as if it were yesterday. But this is something she would like to forget (and rightfully), for to her, on a basic economic level, being Chicana meant being less. It was through my mother's desire to protect her children from poverty and illiteracy that we became anglicized. The more effectively we could pass in the white world, the better guaranteed our future.

From all of this, I experience, daily, a huge disparity between what I was born into and what I was to grow up to become. Because, as Goldman suggests, these stories my mother told me crept under my güera skin. I had no choice but to enter into the life of my mother. *I had no choice.* I took her life into my heart, but managed to keep a lid on it as long as I feigned being the happy, upwardly mobile heterosexual.

When I finally lifted the lid to my lesbianism, a profound connection with my mother reawakened in me. It wasn't until I acknowledged and confronted my own lesbianism in the flesh that my heartfelt identification with and empathy for my mother's oppression—due to being poor, uneducated, and Chicana—was realized. My lesbianism is the avenue through which I have learned the most about silence and oppression, and it continues to be the most tactile reminder to me that we are not free human beings.

You see, one follows the other. I had known for years that I was a lesbian, had felt it in my bones, had ached with the knowledge, gone crazed with the knowledge, wallowed in the silence of it. Silence *is* like starvation. Don't be fooled. It's nothing short of that, and felt most sharply when one has had a full belly most of her life. When we are not physically starving, we have the luxury to realize psychic and emotional starvation. It is from this starvation that other starvations can be recognized—if one is willing to take the risk of making the connection—if one is willing to be responsible to the result of the connection. For me, the connection is an inevitable one.

What I am saying is that the joys of looking like a white girl ain't so great since I realized I could be beaten on the street for being a dyke. If my sister's being beaten because she's Black, it's pretty much the same principle. We're both getting beaten any way you look at it. The connection is blatant; and in the case of my own family, the difference in the privileges attached to looking white instead of brown are merely a generation apart.

In this country, lesbianism is a poverty—as is being brown, as is being a woman, as is being just plain poor. The danger lies in ranking the oppressions. *The danger lies in failing to acknowledge the specificity of the oppression.* The danger lies in attempting to deal with oppression purely from a theoretical base. Without an emotional, heartfelt grappling with the source of our own oppression, without naming the enemy within ourselves and outside of us, no authentic, nonhierarchical connection among oppressed groups can take place. When the going gets rough, will we abandon our so-called comrades in a flurry of racist/heterosexist/what-have-you panic? To whose camp, then, should the lesbian of color retreat? Her very presence violates the ranking and abstraction of oppression. Do we merely live hand to mouth? Do we merely struggle with the "ism" that's sitting on top of our heads? The answer is: yes, I think first we do; and we must do so thoroughly and deeply. But to fail to move out from there will only isolate us in our own oppression—will only insulate, rather than radicalize us.

To illustrate: a gay white male friend of mine once confided to me that he continued to feel that, on some level, I didn't trust him because he was male; that he felt, really, if it ever came down to a "battle of the sexes," I might kill him. He wanted to understand the source of my distrust. I responded, "You're not a woman. Be a woman for a day. Imagine being a woman." He confessed that the thought terrified him because, to him, being a woman meant being raped by men. He *had* felt raped by men; he wanted to forget what that meant. What grew from that discussion was the realization that in order for him to create an authentic alliance with me, he must deal with the primary source of his own sense of oppression. He must, first, emotionally come to terms with what it feels like to be a victim. If he—or anyone—were to truly do this, it would be impossible to discount the oppression of others, except by again forgetting how we have been hurt.

And yet, oppressed groups are forgetting all the time. There are instances of this in the rising Black middle class, and certainly an obvious trend of such capitalist-unconsciousness among white gay men. Because to remember may mean giving up whatever privileges we have managed to squeeze out of this society by virtue of our gender, race, class, or sexuality.

Within the women's movement, the connections among women of different backgrounds and sexual orientations have been fragile, at best. I think this phenomenon is indicative of our failure to seriously address some very frightening questions: How have I internalized my own oppression? How have I oppressed? Instead, we have let rhetoric do the job of poetry. Even the word "oppression" has lost its power. We need a new language, better words that can more closely describe women's fear of, and resistance to, one another, words that will not always come out sounding like dogma.

What prompted me in the first place to work on an anthology by radical women of color was a deep sense that I had a valuable insight to contribute, by virtue of my birthright and my background. And yet, I don't really understand firsthand what it feels like being shitted on for being brown. I understand much more about the joys of it. Being Chicana and having family are synonymous for me. What I know about loving, singing, crying, telling stories, speaking with my heart and hands, even having a sense of my own soul comes from the love of my mother, aunts, cousins . . .

But at the age of twenty-seven, it is frightening to acknowledge that I have internalized a racism and classism, where the object of oppression is not only someone *outside* my skin, but the someone *inside* my skin. In fact, to a large degree, the real battle with such oppression, for all of us, begins under the skin. I have had to confront the fact that much of what I value about being Chicana, about my family, has been subverted by Anglo culture and my own cooperation with it. This realization did not occur to me overnight. For example, it wasn't until long after my graduation from the private college I'd attended in Los Angeles that I realized the major reason for my total alienation from, and fear of, my classmates was rooted in class and culture.

Three years after graduation, in an apple orchard in Sonoma, a friend of mine (who comes from an Italian Irish working-class family) says to me, "Cherríe, no wonder you felt so crazy in school. Most of the people there were white and rich." It was true. All along I had felt the difference, but not until I had put the words "class" and "race" to the experience did my feelings make any sense. For years, I had berated myself for not being as liberated as my classmates. I completely bought that they simply had more guts than I did to rebel against their parents and run around the country hitchhiking, reading books, and studying art. They had enough privilege to be atheists, for chrissake. There was no one around filling in the disparity for me between their parents, who were Hollywood filmmakers, and my parents, who wouldn't know the name of a filmmaker if their lives depended on it; and precisely because their lives didn't depend on it, they couldn't be bothered. But I knew nothing about privilege then. White was right. Period. I could pass. If I got educated enough, there would be no telling.

Three years after that, I had a similar revelation. In a letter to Black feminist Barbara Smith (whom I had not yet met), I wrote:

I went to a concert where Ntozake Shange was reading. There, everything exploded for me. She was speaking in a language that I knew, in the deepest parts of me, existed, and that I ignored in my own feminist studies and even in my own writing. What Ntozake caught in me is the realization that in my development as a poet, I have, in many ways, denied the voice of my own brown mother, the brown in me. I have acclimated to the sound of a white language which, as my father represents it, does not speak to the emotions in my poems, emotions which stem from the love of my mother.

The reading was agitating. Made me uncomfortable. Threw me into a week-long terror of how deeply I was affected. I felt that I had to start all over again, that I turned only to the perceptions of white middle-class women to speak for me and all women. I am shocked by my own ignorance.

Sitting in that Oakland auditorium chair was the first time I had realized to the core of me that for years I had disowned the language I knew best. I had ignored the words and rhythms that were the closest to me: the sounds of my mother and aunts gossiping—half in English, half in Spanish—while drinking cerveza in the kitchen. And the hands—I had cut off the hands in my poems. But not in conversation; still the hands could not be kept down. Still they insisted on moving.

The reading had forced me to remember that I knew things from my roots. But to remember puts me up against what I don't know. Shange's reading agitated me because she spoke with power about a world that is both alien and common to me: "the capacity to enter into the lives of others." But you can't just take the goods and run. I knew then, sitting in the Oakland auditorium (as I know in my poetry), that the only thing worth writing about is what seems to be unknown and, therefore, fearful.

The unknown is often depicted in racist literature as the darkness within a person. Similarly, sexist writers will refer to fear in the form of the vagina, calling it "the orifice of death." In contrast, it is a pleasure to read works such as Maxine Hong Kingston's *Woman Warrior*,[3] where fear and alienation are depicted as "white ghosts." And yet, the bulk of literature in this country reinforces the myth that what is dark and female is evil. Consequently, each of us—whether dark, female, or both—has in some way *internalized* this oppressive imagery. What the oppressor often succeeds in doing is simply *externalizing* his fears, projecting them into the bodies of women, Asians, gays, disabled folks, whoever seems most "other."

> call me
> roach and presumptuous
> nightmare on your white pillow
> your itch to destroy
> the indestructible
> part of yourself
> —Audre Lorde[4]

But it is not really difference the oppressor fears so much as similarity. He fears he will discover in himself the same aches, the same longings as those of the people he has shit on. He fears the immobilization threatened by his own incipient guilt. He fears he will have to change his life once he has seen himself in the bodies of the people he has called different. He fears the hatred, anger, and vengeance of those he has hurt.

This is the oppressor's nightmare, but it is not exclusive to him. We women have a similar nightmare, for each of us in some way has been both the oppressed and the oppressor. We are afraid to look at how we have failed each other. We are afraid to see how we have taken the values of our oppressor into our hearts and turned them against ourselves and one another. We are afraid to admit how deeply *the man's* words have been ingrained in us.

To assess the damage is a dangerous act. I think of how, even as a feminist lesbian, I have so wanted to ignore my own homophobia, my own hatred of myself for being queer. I have not wanted to admit that my deepest personal sense of myself has not quite caught up with my woman-identified politics. I have been afraid to criticize lesbian writers who choose to skip over these issues in the name of feminism. In 1979, we talk of "old gay" and butch and femme roles as if they were ancient history. We toss them aside as merely patriarchal notions. And yet, the truth of the matter is that I have sometimes taken society's fear and hatred of lesbians to bed with me. I have sometimes hated my lover for loving me. I have sometimes felt not woman enough for her. I have sometimes felt not man enough. For a lesbian trying to survive in a heterosexist society, there is no easy way around these emotions. Similarly, in a white-dominated world, there is little getting around racism and our own internalization of it. It's always there, embodied in someone we least expect to rub up against. When we do rub up against this person, *there* then is the challenge. *There* then is the opportunity to look at the nightmare within us. But we usually shrink from such a challenge.

Time and time again, I have observed that the usual response among white women's groups when the racism issue comes up is to deny the difference. I have heard comments like, "Well, we're open to *all* women; why don't they (women of color) come? You can only do so much . . ." But there is seldom any analysis of how the very nature and structure of the group itself may be founded on racist or classist assumptions. More important, so often the women seem to feel no loss, no lack, no absence when women of color are not involved; therefore, there is little desire to change the situation. This has hurt me deeply. I have come to believe that the only reason women of a privileged class will dare to look at *how* it is that *they* oppress, is when they've come to know the meaning of their own oppression. And understand that the oppression of others hurts them personally.

The other side of the story is that women of color and white working-class women often shrink from challenging white middle-class women. It is much easier to rank oppressions and set up a hierarchy than to take responsibility for changing our own lives. We have failed to demand that white women, particularly those who claim to be speaking for all women, be accountable for their racism.

The dialogue has simply not gone deep enough.

In conclusion, I have had to look critically at my claim to color, at a time when, among white feminist ranks, it is a politically correct (and sometimes peripherally advantageous) assertion to make. I must acknowledge the fact that, physically, I have had a *choice* about making that claim, in contrast to women of color who do not. It seems that we are first read by the color of our skin. I must reckon with the fact that for most of my life, by virtue of the very fact that I am white-looking, I identified with and aspired toward white values, and that I rode the wave of that Southern California privilege as far as conscience would let me.

Well, now I feel both bleached and beached. I feel angry about this—about the years when I refused to recognize privilege, both when it worked against me and when I worked it, ignorantly, at the expense of others. These are not settled issues. This is why this work feels so risky to me. It continues to be discovery. It has brought me into contact with women who invariably know a hell of a lot more than I do about racism, as experienced in the flesh, as revealed in the flesh of their writing.

I think: *what is my responsibility to my roots, both white and brown, Spanish-speaking and English?* I am a woman with a foot in both worlds. I refuse the split. I feel the necessity for dialogue. Sometimes I feel it urgently.

But one voice is not enough, nor are two, although this is where dialogue begins. It is essential that feminists confront their fear of and resistance to each other, because without this, there *will* be no bread on the table. Simply, we will not survive. If we could make this connection in our heart of hearts, that if we are serious about a revolution—better, if we seriously believe there should be joy in our lives (real joy, not just good times)—then we need one another. We women need each other. Because my/your solitary, self-asserting go-for-the-throat-of-fear power is not enough. The real power, as you and I well know, is collective. I can't afford to be afraid of you, nor you of me. If it takes head-on collisions, let's do it. This polite timidity is killing us.

As Lorde suggests in the passage I cited earlier, it is looking to the nightmare that the dream is found. There, the survivor emerges to insist on a future, a vision, yes, born out of what is dark and female. The feminist movement must be a movement of such survivors, a movement with a future.

September 1979
Berkeley, California

It's the Poverty

For Kim

You say to me,
"Take a drive with me
up the coast, babe
and bring your typewriter."

All the way down the coast
you and she stopped at motels
your typewriters tucked under your free arm
dodging the rain fast to the shelter
of metal awnings, red and white
I imagine them—you two
snorting brandy in those vinyl rooms
propping your each machine onto an end table.

. . . . .

This story becomes you.
A fiction I invent with my ears
evoking heroism in the first
description of the weather.

I say
my typewriter sticks in the wet.
I have been using the same ribbon
over and over and over again.
Yes, we both agree I could use
a new ribbon, but it's the poverty

the poverty of my imagination, we agree.
I lack imagination you say.

No. I lack language.
The language to clarify
my resistance to the literate.
Words are a war to me.
They threaten my family.

To gain the word to describe the loss,
I risk losing everything.
I may create a monster,
the word's length and body
swelling up colorful and thrilling
looming over my *mother;* characterized.
Her voice in the distance
unintelligible   illiterate.

These are the monster's words.

· · · · ·

Understand.
My family is poor.
Poor. I can't afford
a new ribbon. The risk
of this one is enough
to keep me moving
through it, accountable.
The repetition, like my mother's stories retold,
each time reveals more particulars

gains more familiarity.
You can't get me in your car so fast.

. . . . .

You tell me how you've learned
to write while you drive
how I can leave my droning machine behind
for all
you care.

I say, not-so-fast
not
so
fast.
The drone, a chant to my ears
a common blend of histories
repeatedly inarticulate.

Not so fast.
I am poorer than you.
In my experience, fictions
are for hearing about,
not living.

What Does It Take?

For Sally Gearhart upon the death of Harvey Milk

1
The martyrs they give us
have all been men
my friend, she traces her life
through them   a series of assassinations
but not one, not
one making her bleed.

This is not the death of my mother
but my father
the kind one/the provider
pressed into newsprint
in honest good will.

If they took *you*
I would take to the streets   scream   BLOODY MURDER.

But the deaths of our mothers
are never that public
they have happened before
and we were not informed.
Women do not coagulate into one
hero's death; we bleed
out of many pores, so constant
that it has come to be seen
as the way things are.

2
Waiting
my mother's dying
was not eventful.

Expecting it
I put a hole in my arm
no TNT blast
but a slow excavation
my nails, in silent opposition
digging down to the raw part
inside the elbow.

If they took *you*
I would take to the streets   scream   BLOODY MURDER.

What does it take to move me?
Your death
that I have ignored
in the deaths of other women?

Isn't the *possibility* of your dying
enough?

Anatomy Lesson

A black woman and a small beige one
talk about their bodies.
About putting a piece of their anatomy in their pockets
upon entering any given room.

When entering a room full of soldiers who fear hearts,
you put your heart in your back pocket,
the black woman explains. It is important, not to intimidate.
The soldiers wear guns, *not* in their back pockets.

You let the heart fester there. You let the heart seethe.
You let the impatience of the heart build and build
until the power of the heart hidden
begins to be felt in the room.
Until the visual absence of the heart
begins to take on the shape of a presence.
Until the soldiers look at you and begin to beg you
to open up your heart to them, so anxious are they to see
what it is they fear they fear.

Do not be seduced.

Do not forget for a minute that the soldiers wear guns.
Hang onto your heart.
Ask them first what they'll give up to see it.
Tell them that they can begin with their arms.

Only then will *you* begin to negotiate.

It Got Her Over

You're lucky you look the way you do. You could get any man.
Anyone says anything to you, tell them your father's white.
                                    —Michelle Cliff, *Claiming an Identity*
                                             They Taught Me to Despise[1]

1
To touch
her skin felt thick
like hide,
not like flesh
and blood
when an arm is raised
the blue veins shine rivers
running underground
with shadow depth, and tone.

No, *her* skin
had turned on her
in the light of things.
In the light of Black
women and children
beaten/hanged/raped/strangled
murdered in Boston/Atlanta
in California where redneck
hunters coming home
with empty white hands
go off to fill 'em
with Black Man

Her skin had turned in the light
of these things.
Stuck to her now
like a flat immovable paste
spread grey over a life.

Still,
it got her over
in laundromats
when machines ate her change
swallowed whole her dollar bill
when cops stopped to check what the problem was
Remember
I could be your daughter she used
looking up from the place on the sand
where two women were spread out, defiant
where he read, *the white one*
must be protected   that time
saving them both.

It got her over
when the bill was late
when she only wanted to browse not buy
when hunger forced them
off the highway and into grills
called "Red's" and "Friendly's"
coffee shops packed suburban
white on white, eyes shifting
to them   and away
to them   and away
and back again

then shifted into safety
lock inside their heads.

2
She had never been ashamed of her face.

Her lust, yes
Her bad grammar, yes
Even her unforgiving ways
but never, her face
recently taken to blushing
as if the blood wanted
to swallow the flesh.

Bleed through
          guilt by association
          complicity to the crime.
Bleed through
          Born to lead.
          Born to love.
          Born to live.

Bleed through

and flood the joint
with a hatred so severe
people went white
with shock and dying.

          . . . . .

No, she had *never* been ashamed of her face
not like this
grabbing her own two cheeks
her fingers pressed together
as if to hold between them
the thin depth of color.

See this face?

Wearing it like the accident
of birth.
    it was
a scar sealing up
a woman, now darkened
by desire.

See this face?

Where do you take this hate
to lunch?

How to get over this one.

Winter of Oppression, 1982

1
The cold in my chest comes from having to decide
while the ice builds up on *this* side
of my new-york-apt-bldg.-living window,
whose death has been marked
upon the collective forehead
of this continent, this shattering globe
the most indelibly.

Indelible. A catholic word I learned
when I learned that there were catholics
and there were not.
                            But somehow
we did not count the Jews
among the have-nots, only protestants
with their cold & bloodless god
with no candles/no incense/no bloody
sacrifice or spirits
lurking.

Protestantism. White people's religion.

. . . . .

First time I remember
seeing pictures of the Holocaust
was in the tenth grade and the moving pictures
were already there in my mind
somehow *before* they showed me

what I already understood
that these people were killed
for the spirit-blood
that runs through them.

They were like us in this.
Ethnic people with long last names
with vowels at the end or the wrong
type of consonants combined
a colored kind of white people.

But let me tell you
first time I saw an actual
picture glossy photo of a lynching
I was already grown & active & living & loving Jewish.
Black. White. Puerto
Rican.

And the image blasted
my consciousness
split it wide   I
had never thought   seen
heard   of such a thing
never even imagined the look
of the man   the weight
dead hanging swinging heavy
the fact   of the white people
cold bloodless
looking on.   It

had never occurred to me
I tell you   I

the nuns failed to mention
this could happen, too
how could such a thing happen?

. . . . .

Because somehow dark real dark
was not quite real
people killed
but some
thing not
taken to heart
in the same way it feels
to see white shaved/starved
burned/buried
the boned bodies stacked & bulldozed
into huge craters made by men
and machines
and at fifteen I counted 22
bodies only in the far left-hand
corner of the movie screen
& I kept running
through my mind

> *and I'm only one*
> *count one*
> *it could be me*
> *it could be me*
> *I'm nothing*
> *to this cruelty.*

. . . . .

Somehow tonight,
is it the particular coldness
where my lover sleeps with a scarf
to keep it out
that causes me to toss
and turn the events of the last weeks
the last years of my life
around in my sleep?

Is it the same white coldness
that forces my back up against the wall—
Choose. Choose.

I cannot
choose nor forget

how simple
to fall back
upon rehearsed racial memory.

I work to remember
what I never dreamed possible

what my consciousness could never
contrive.

Whoever I am

I must believe
I am not
and will never be

the only
one who suffers.

THE ROAD TO RECOVERY

Minds & Hearts

the road to recovering what was lost
in the war that never
announced itself

left no truly visible signs
no
ration cards
sailor boys
no
ticker tape

parades, no

road to recovering what was lost
in a war that never
pronounced correctly

always dead
missing
in action

prisoner of warring
minds & bleeding
hearts

No Born-Again Children

"Somebody in my family just died!
Now are you gonna stay dead or pull a Lazarus?"

Woman, if I could simply rise up
from this bed of doubt, miraculous and beaming,
I would.
       if I could,
       I would.

    . . . . .

You told me that when your brother saw the train coming
he didn't move. He was transfixed
intensely curious   a boy of twelve with a body of pure
speed and a death wish
he's ready to dump into the nearest river
or body that can swallow
it.

> *He opened you up, pink and hungry, too*
> *but for the tenderness in his fingers talking*
> *you into, coaxing you into*
> *turning cold and quiet into you.*

And taking the orange into your five-year-old fist
the boy coming at you again, you flung it out the window.

He stopped dead cold in his tracks.

. . . . .

I don't know why your brother died. I don't know why.
Was it the face of the orange, alive and bright, spinning
before his eyes? The vision of a girl
pushing life through the hole of doom
that bore you both?

It *was* a suicide, woman, a suicide we both refuse
daily with all our good brains and tenderness. Still,
you can see me in him, can't you?
Riveted onto that track
putting my cheek up against the size of a locomotive
just to see what it's like
just to taste how close it'll get before—
stone still & trembling I split
off that rail.

But I am not your brother. I will not die on you
no matter how you dare me
to reenact that tragedy
            like your momma dragging you down
            to the railroad tracks
            still hot from his suicide

      another child dead.

No, I will not die on you and yet, death keeps us
watching. We look
to each other for miracles
to wipe out a memory full of dead men and dying
women, but we can't save each other

from what we learned
to fear.

We can't.

There are no miracles.
No Lazarus.
No born-again children.

Only an orange flung out of a window
like a life line that bears repeating
again and again
until we're both
convinced.

You Call It "Amputation"

*Macalister's boy took one of the fish and cut a square out of
its side to bait his hook with. The mutilated body (it was alive
still) was thrown back into the sea.*
                        —Virginia Woolf, *To the Lighthouse*

You call it
"am pu tation"
but even after the cut
they say the toes still itch
the body remembers the knee,
                        gracefully bending.

She reaches down to find her leg gone—
the shape under the blanket dropping off
suddenly, irregularly.

It is a shock, Woolf says
*that by putting into words
we make it whole.*

Still, I feel the mutilated body
swimming in side stroke
pumping twice as hard
for lack of body, pushing
through your words
which hold no water
for me.

Glamorous

*For Amber Hollibaugh, upon the passing
of her friend Yve after a sudden stroke.*

I want to catch it while it's still fresh
and living in you, this talking like
you don't know what's gonna come outta your mouth
next. I watch the bodies pour
right out between those red lips of yours
and without thinking, they're changing me
without trying, they're transforming
before my eyes.

I told you once
that you remind me of my grandmother
the white one, the gypsy all dolled up
in a 1955 white Cadillac convertible
with Big Fins—she red deep behind the wheel,
her dyed bleached blonde flying.
At stop lights she'd be there
just waiting for some sucker to pull up,
thinking she was a gal of twenty.
She'd turn and flash him a seventy-year-old smile,
and press pedal.

Oh honey, this is you
in all your highway glory,
the glamour of your ways.

And without stopping
last night you talked about the places
in you, *thinking of your body*
that are lost to you, how we locate
that damage in our different parts
like a dead foot, you said,
how we run inventory, checking
on which show promise
of revival and which don't.

What I didn't tell you
was how my grandmother stopped
all of a sudden turned baby,
all of a sudden speechless
my momma giving her baths
in the tub, while I played nearby.
Her bare white skin slipping
down off those cold shoulders
piling up around her hips and knees,
slowing her down.

My grandma turned baby
and by the toilet I'd sit with her
she picking out designs in the linoleum
saying this one looks like a man
in a tub, scrubbing his back with a brush

and it did.

Heading East

We are driving this car on determination, alone.

The miles seem to repair us
convince us that we are getting somewhere
that we won't have another breakdown

we end up leaking into somebody's movie
trapped in a ghost town   shaniko, oregon   pouring rain

we dive under the car
                        expose its underside, our fingers
feeling into the machine for its sore spot

"I've got it," I scream
"I know where the hole is," our eyes fire each other's

thinking we have conquered the unknown
we patch up the lacerated hose with black tape.

     . . . . .

In this town of livery stable, turned museum
we roll out our bags onto the floor
of an abandoned caboose.

we *are* in somebody's movie

Two women stranded in a ghost town.
They are headed east.
They think they'll make it.

LO QUE NUNCA PASÓ POR SUS LABIOS

A Long Line of Vendidas

Para Gloria Anzaldúa, in gratitude

And in remembrance of my beloved friend,
Mirtha Quintanales (1948–2022)

SUEÑO: 15 DE JULIO 1982
During the long difficult night that sent my lover and me to separate beds, I dreamed of church and chocha. I put it this way because that is how it came to me. The suffering and the thick musty mysticism of the catholic church fused with the sensation of entering the vagina—dark, rica, full-bodied. The heavy sensation of complexity. A journey I must unravel, work out for myself.

I long to enter you like a temple.

MY BROTHER'S SEX WAS WHITE. MINE, BROWN

If somebody would have asked me when I was a teenager what it means to be Chicana, I would probably have listed the grievances done me. When my sister and I were fifteen and fourteen, respectively, and my brother a few years older, we were still waiting on him. I write "were" as if now, nearly two decades later, it were over. But that would be a lie. To this day in my mother's home, my brother and father are waited on by the women. I do this now out of respect for my mother and her wishes. In those early years, however, it was mainly in relation to my brother that I resented providing such service. For unlike my father, who sometimes worked as much as seventy hours a week to feed my face every day, the only thing that earned my brother my servitude was his maleness.

It was Saturday afternoon. My brother, then seventeen years old, came into the house with a pile of friends. I remember Fernie, the two Steves, and Roberto. They were hot, sweaty, and exhausted from an afternoon's basketball and plopped themselves down in the front room, my brother demanding, "Girls, bring us something to drink."

"Get it yourself, stupid," I thought, but held those words from ever forming inside my mouth. My brother had the disgusting habit on these occasions of collapsing my sister JoAnn's and my name when referring to us as a unit: his sisters. "Cher'ann," he would say, "we're really thirsty." I'm sure it took everything in his power *not* to snap his fingers. But my mother was out in the yard working and to refuse him would have brought her into the house with a scene before these boys' eyes that would have made it impossible for us to show our faces at school the following Monday. We had been through that before.

When my mother had been our age, more than forty years earlier, she had waited on her brothers and their friends. And it was no mere lemonade. They'd come in from work or a day's drinking, and las mujeres, often just in from the fields themselves, would already be in the kitchen making tortillas, warming frijoles or pigs' feet, albóndigas soup, and more. And the men would get a clean white tablecloth and a spread of food laid out before their eyes and not a word of resentment from the women.

The men watched the women—my aunts and mother moving with the grace and speed of girls who were cooking before they could barely see over the top of the stove. Elvira, my mother, knew she was being watched by the younger men and loved it. Her slim hips moved patiently beneath the apron. Her deep thick-lidded eyes never caught theirs as she was swept back into the kitchen by my abuelita's call of "Elvirita," her brown hands deepening in color as they dropped back into the pan of flour.

I suppose my mother imagined that Joe's friends watched us like that, too. But we knew different. We were not blonde or particularly long-legged or "available" because we were "Joe's sisters." This meant no boy could make any moves on us, which meant no boy would bother asking us out. Roberto, the Guatemalan, was the only one among my brother's friends who seemed at all sensitive to how awkward JoAnn and I felt in our role. He would smile at us nervously, taking the lemonade, feeling embarrassed being waited on by people he considered peers. He knew the Anglo girls they visited would never have succumbed to such a task. Roberto was the only recompense.

As I stopped to satisfy their yearning throats, their penises became animated in my head, for that was all that seemed to arbitrarily set us apart from each other and put me in the position of the servant and they, the served. I wanted to gun them all down, but swallowed that fantasy as I swallowed making the boy's bed every day, cleaning his room each week, shining his shoes and ironing his shirts for dates with girls, some of whom *I* had crushes on. I would "lend" him the money I had earned house-cleaning for twelve hours so he could blow it on one night with a girl because he seldom had enough money because he seldom had a job because there was always some kind of ball practice to go to. And as I pressed the bills into his hand, the car honking outside in the driveway, his double-date waiting, I knew I would never see that money again.

Years later, after I began to make political the fact of my being Chicana, I remember my brother saying to me, "*I've* never felt culturally deprived," which I guess is the term white people use to describe people of color being denied access to *their culture*. At the time, I wasn't exactly sure what he meant, but I remember in retelling the story to my sister, she responded, "Of course, he didn't. He grew up male in our house. He got the best of both worlds." And yes, I can see that truth now. *Male in a man's world. Light-skinned in a white world. Why change?* The pull to identify with the oppressor was never as great in me as it was in my brother. For unlike him, I could never have *become* the white man, only the white man's *woman*.

The first time I began to recognize clearly my alliances on the basis of race and sex was when my mother was in the hospital, extremely ill. I was eight years old. During my mother's stay in the hospital, my Tía Eva took my sister and me into her care; my brother stayed with my abuela; and my father stayed by himself in our home. During this time, my father came to visit me and my sister only once. (I don't know if he ever visited my brother.) The strange thing was I didn't really miss his visits, although I sometimes fantasized some imaginary father, dark and benevolent, who might come and remind us that we still *were* a family.

I have always had a talent for seeing things I don't particularly want to see and the one day my father did come to visit us with his wife/our mother physically dying in a hospital some ten miles away, I saw that he couldn't love us—not in the way we so desperately needed. I saw that he didn't know how and he came into my tía's house like a large lumbering child—awkward and embarrassed out of his league—trying to *play* a parent when he needed our mother back as much as we did just to keep him eating and protected. I hated and pitied him that day. I knew how he was letting us all down, visiting my mother daily, like a dead man, unable to say, "The children, honey, I held them. They love you. They think of you," giving my mother *something*.

Years later, my mother spoke of his visits to the hospital. How from behind the bars of her bed and through a tangle of intravenous tubing, she watched this timid man come and go daily, enacting the motions of being a husband. "I knew I had to live," she told us. "I knew he could never take care of you children." In contrast to the seeming lack of feeling I held for my father, my longings for my mother and fear of her dying were the most passionate feelings that had ever lived inside my young heart.

We are riding the hospital elevator. My sister and I pressed up against one wall, holding hands. After months of separation, we are going to visit mi mamá. My tía tells me, "Whatever you do, no llores, Cherríe. It's too hard on your mother when you cry." I nod, taking long deep breaths, trying to control my quivering lip.

As we travel up floor by floor, all I can think about is not crying, breathing, holding my breath. "¿Me prometes?" she asks.

I nod again, afraid to speak, fearing my voice will crack into tears. My sister's nervous hand around mine, sweating too. We are going to see our mother, mi mamá, after so long. She didn't die after all. She didn't die.

The elevator doors open. We walk down the corridor, my heart pounding. My eyes are darting in and out of each room as we pass them, fearing/anticipating my mami's face.

Then as we turn around the corner into a kind of lobby, I hear my tía say to an older woman.

"Elvira."

But this is not my mother, just skin and bone. An Indian, I think. Straight black and grey hair pulled back into a plain knot at her neck. I don't recognize her. This is not the woman I knew, her face made-up and her hair always a wavy jet black! I stay back until she opens her arms to me—this strange and familiar woman—her voice hoarse, "¡Ay mi'jita!" Instinctively, I run into her arms, still holding back my insides.

"Don't cry. Don't cry," I remember. "Whatever you do, no llores."

But my tía had not warned me about the smell, the unmistakable smell of the woman, mi mamá, el olor de aceite de olivo y jabón and comfort and home. "Mi mamá." And when I catch that smell I am lost in tears, deep long tears that come when you have held your breath for centuries.

There was something I knew at that eight-year-old moment that I vowed never to forget—the smell of a woman who is life and home to me at once. The woman in whose arms I am uplifted, sustained. Since then, it is as if I have spent the rest of my years driven by this scent toward la mujer.

With this knowledge so deeply emblazed upon my heart, how then was I supposed to turn away from la madre, la Chicana? If I were to build my womanhood on this self-evident truth, it is the love of la Chicana, the love of myself as a Chicana I had to embrace, no white man. Maybe this ultimately was the bitter difference between my brother and me. To be a woman fully necessitated my claiming the race of my mother. My brother's sex was white. Mine, brown.

Like a White Sheep I Followed

Sueño: 3 de julio

I am having my face made up, especially my eyes, by a very beautiful Chicana. The makeup artist changes me entirely for only five dollars. I think this is a very low price for how deep and dark she makes me look.

When I was growing up, I looked forward to the days when my skin would toast to match my cousins, their skin turning pure black in the creases. I never could quite catch up, but my skin did turn smooth like theirs, oily brown—like my mama's, holding depth, density, the possibility of infinite provision. Mi abuela raised the darkest cousins herself, she never loving us the way she molded and managed them.

To write as a Chicana feminist lesbian, I am afraid of being mistaken; of being made an outsider again, having to fight the kids at school to get them to believe that Teresita and I were cousins. "You don't *look* like cousins!" I feel at times I am trying to bulldoze my way back into a people who forced me to leave them in the first place,

who taught me to take my whiteness and run with it. *Run with it.*
Who want nothing to do with me, the likes of me, the white of me—
in them.

When was I forced to choose?

When Vivian Molina after two years of the deepest, richest
friendship, two years of me helping her through "new math," helping her not flunk once more—once was enough—and her so big
already, fat and dark-skinned. And beautiful, like family. When Vivian left me flat, I didn't know what happened, except I knew she was
beginning to smell like a woman and once, just before our split-up,
the neighbor-kid talked of Vivian growing hair "down there." I
didn't get it, except I knew that none of these changes were settling
right in Vivian. And I was small and thin, and light-skinned and I
loved Vivian which didn't seem to matter in the way teachers were
wondering if Vivian was going to make it through the year. So, one
day that year Vivian came to school and never spoke to me again.
Nothing happened between us. I swear nothing happened.

I would call her and plead, "Vivian, what did I do?" But she
never let on, except once when she nearly started to cry near the
water fountain in the school corridor when I asked her for the last
time and her eyes met mine finally and she said, I think or I'd like
to remember, "I'm sorry." And even if she didn't say that, exactly, I
know she said something that told me it couldn't be helped. It was
out of our control. Something she, a year and a half older and much
darker, knew before I knew, and like a white sheep I followed the
path paved for me.

Rocky Azuela was brilliant and tough. Got mostly A's in school, like
Carmen Luna, who was her second cousin in the same grade. They
were both wizards, but Rocky was sharper and mean in her sharp-
ness. "Antagonistic," the nuns would say, and she'd prove it in her
handwriting which slanted way off to the left which I admired greatly,

which the nuns found "incorrigible." When it came time for the Catholic high school entrance exams, we learned in May what track we would be in for the coming freshman year. To my amazement, I got into the "A" group—college prep. To my equal amazement, Rocky and her cousin were tracked into the "C" group—business and general education, where they teach you home economics and typing. Rocky could talk and write and compute circles around me, which didn't seem to compute on our entrance exams.

After we got into high school, the Irish and Italian girls became my friends. And separated by class(room), Rocky and I seldom spoke.

Years later, when I was already in college, I had come home for the weekend and went on a short run to the neighborhood supermarket for my mom. There, for the first time in at least three years, I ran into Rocky. She was pushing a shopping cart, and inside it was one of the most beautiful baby boys I had ever laid eyes on, jabbering and wide-eyed.

Rocky and I talked. It was clear we both still felt some connection from those grade-school days. When she turned to enter the checkout line, I wanted to stop her, not let her out of my sight again. But I hesitated, wondering what more we would have to say to each other after so many years apart. I let her go.

Driving home, I remembered that there had been rumors that Rocky had been pregnant at graduation.

It was my Mexican mother, not my Anglo father, who fixed on me the idea of getting an education. Meanwhile my Catholic grade school and high school years continued to suggest to me and my classmates that academic learning was the singular privilege of upwardly mobile gringas. "Without an education, you're nothing," my mother would insist. "Look at me. If only I could write better, I could get a different kind of job, I wouldn't have to do the kind of work I do." She was constantly criticizing this or that younger aunt or uncle or in-law who had what she did not—basic reading and writing skills—who still worked factory. It never occurred to her, or if it did, she never let on to us children, that race was a factor in reducing one's chances for success.

And in terms of rearing her three light-skinned chestnut-haired children, we in fact did not have to fear, like most of my cousins, racial discrimination. On the surface of things we could pass as long as we made no point of our Mexican heritage; as long as we moved my father's English surname through our lives like a badge of membership to the white open-door policy club.

"You get to choose." I remember Tavo's words, thrown at me across the kitchen table.

It is Boston, 1981, and Tavo is one of the few Chicano gay men I have met in this city. He tells me that he doesn't trust güeros; that we have to prove ourselves to him in some way.

"You see," he continues, "if at any time you decide to use your light-skin privilege, you can. You can decide you're suddenly not Chicana."

The latter, I cannot do, but once my light skin and good English saved me and my lover, a Black woman, from arrest. And I'd use it again. I'd use it to the hilt over and over to save our skins from violence.

But I *have* betrayed my people.

Rita Villareal and I used to go to the roller rink together. I never noticed how dark she was until my mother pointed this out to me, warning me against her. How her jet-black straight hair and coffee bean skin marked her as a different grade of mexicana. *Una india, de clase baja.* It was the first fight about race I ever had with my mother. When I protested, she said to me, "It isn't her color and I never tell you about your friends, but this girl is going to get you in trouble.

She's no good for you." Our friendship soon broke off, me keeping a distance from Rita. Later, she got into boys and booze. *Was my mother right?*

Looking back, I wonder maybe this was what Vivian had feared/ expected in me, my turning my back on her. Or maybe what separated us was something much more unspoken.[1] Even, in this remembered writing, I am left with the lingering sense of an impossible desire between us—one, which in the 1960s had no name we could own.

OUR MEXICAN EVE

By puberty, it seemed identity alliances were already being made along the rigid lines of race, as it combined with sex. And everyone— boy, girl, Anglo, and Chicano—fell into place. Where did I stand?

I did not move away from Raza because I did not love my people. I gradually became anglicized because I thought it was the only option available to me toward gaining autonomy as a person without being sexually ostracized.

I can't say that I was conscious of all this at the time, only that at each juncture in my development, I instinctively made choices that I thought would allow me greater freedom of movement in the future. This primarily meant resisting sex roles as much as I could safely manage, and this was far easier in an Anglo context than in a Chicano one. That is not to say that Anglo culture does not stigmatize its women for gender-transgressions, only that its stigmatization did not hold the personal power over me that my home (mexicano) culture did.

What may look like betrayal among Chicanas on the basis of race is deeply linked, I believe, to internalized sexism and misogyny. Chicanas begin to turn our backs on one another either to gain male approval or to avoid being sexually marked by men. The phenomenon is first observed in the schoolyard, long before it is played out with a vengeance within political communities. Chicanas' negative perceptions of ourselves as women finds its roots in nearly five centuries of Mexican history and mythology. It is further entrenched by a system of Anglo internal colonization, which long ago put Raza in a defensive posture against the dominant culture.

The sexual legacy passed down to Chicanas is one of betrayal, originating from the historical/mythic female figure of Malintzin Tenepal, the sixteenth-century Indigenous translator, tactical advisor, and enslaved mistress to the Spanish conquistador of México, Hernán Cortés. As bearer of his child, Malintzin (or Malinche)* is symbolically considered the mother of the mestizo (Mexican) people. But unlike La Virgen de Guadalupe, she is not revered as la Madre Sagrada, but rather slandered as la Chingada, meaning the "fucked one," and "la vendida," sellout to the white race.[2]

When Mexican independence from Spain is achieved in 1821, Malinche's previous iconic role in history takes a dramatic turn toward disdain. A politically motivated criollo† revisionist interpretation of the loss of the Indigenous México is paradoxically attributed less to Spanish antecedents and instead to Malinche's sexual and advisory relationship with Cortés. Female and Indigenous, she becomes the embodied symbol of betrayal. As such, the colonizer continues to inscribe his "master narrative" on the Mexican imagination, censuring Malinche for her historical/sexual "transgression," and, by extension, hold as suspect her entire sex.[3]

As a Chicana and a feminist, I must, like other Chicanas before me, examine the effects this narrative has on our racial/sexual identity and our relationship with one another; for there is hardly a Chicana growing up today who does not suffer under the name of "La Chingada." Even if she has never heard directly of the one-time Aztec princess, she knows what "chingar" means.

---

* Also referred to as Malinalli and Doña Marína.

† Ruling-class, Américan-born Spaniards.

In *El laberinto de la soledad*, the internationally recognized Mexican poet Octavio Paz explicates the misogynist term, arguing for the word's foundational place in the national Mexican consciousness. He states:

> The idea of breaking, of ripping open . . . When alluding to a sexual act, violation or deception gives it a particular shading. The man who commits it never does so with the consent of the *chingada*. . . . *Chingar* then is to do violence to another, i.e., rape. The verb is masculine, active, cruel: it stings, wounds, gashes, stains. And it provokes a bitter, resentful satisfaction.
>
> The person who suffers this action is passive, inert and open, in contrast to the active, aggressive and closed person who inflicts it. The chingón is the macho, the male; he rips open the chingada, the female, who is pure passivity, defenseless against the exterior world. The relationship between them is violent, and it is determined by the cynical power of the first and the impotence of the second.[4]

HER-STORY

The Aztec scribes had recorded that Quetzalcóatl, the Feathered Serpent god, would return from the east to redeem his people in the year One Reed. Destiny would have it that on that very day, April 21, 1519 (according to the Western calendar), Cortés and his men, fitting the description of the Quetzalcóatl, light-haired and bearded, landed on the shores of Vera Cruz.[5]

At the time of Cortés's arrival in México, the Aztec Empire already controlled much of Mesoamerica both economically, via tributes, and militarily. War was a religious requirement for the Aztecs, justified by the need to take prisoners offered in sacrifice to the sun god, Huitzilopochtli. Given the imperialist greed of the Aztecs, many

Mesoamerican peoples upon the arrival of the Spanish were eager to join forces with them to overthrow the empire. A case can be made that due to Aztec's systematic subjugation of much of the Mexican Indian population, they had decreed their own self-destruction.[6]

Along these lines, Chicana feminist theorist Aleida Del Castillo further contends that Malinche, as a woman of deep spiritual commitment, aided Cortés because she understood him to be Quetzalcóatl returned in a different form to save the peoples of México from total extinction. Del Castillo writes, "The destruction of the Aztec empire, the conquest of México and as such, the termination of her indigenous world" was, in Malinche's eyes, inevitable in order to make way for the new spiritual age that was imminent.[7]

Del Castillo and other Chicana feminists researching and reinterpreting Malinche's role in the conquest of México do not justify the imperialism of the Spanish. Rather, they attempt to create a more realistic context for, and less misogynist view of, Malinche's actions. The suspicion of female betrayal, of course, finds its origins in the Judeo-Christian biblical myth of Eve, whose sin (eating the apple from the tree of knowledge) resulted in the loss of paradise for all humankind. The story perfectly parallels the culpability Malinche is required to carry for the loss of an imagined paradisal pre-Hispanic Mexico.

TRAITOR BEGETS TRAITOR

In chronicling the conquest of Mexico by sword and cross, the Spanish passed onto mexicanos as legacy their own Spanish Catholic reading of Mexican events. Much of this early interpretation originated from Bernal Díaz del Castillo's eyewitness account—*Historia verdadera de la conquista de la Nueva España,* originally published in 1632. Still, what Díaz del Castillo's writings suggest about the Malinche's familial history resonates poignantly among many mexicanas and Chicanas to this day.

Díaz del Castillo notes that upon the death of Malinche's chieftain father, the young Aztec princess was in line to inherit his estate. When Malinche's mother remarries, however, she elects her son from her second marriage to inherit the wealth and sells her own daughter into slavery, effectively eliminating the competition.[8] According to Gloria Anzaldúa, there are writings in México to refute this account, but it was nevertheless recorded—or commonly believed—that Malinche was betrayed by her own mother.[9] This myth of the inherent unreliability of women and our natural propensity for treachery has been carved into the very bone of Mexican and Chicano collective consciousness. But, this is *pre*-Hispanic México and one is reminded that patriarchy is emboldened by capitalist incentives, even among Indigenous nations.

Traitor begets traitor.

Little is made of this first betrayal (mother-to-daughter). In a certain way Malinche's mother would only have been doing what we would interpret later as her Mexican wifely/motherly duty: *putting the male first.* Ask any mexicana mother about her children and she is quick to tell you she loves them all the same, but *the boys are different.*

Sometimes I sense that she feels this way because she wants to believe that through her mothering, she can develop the kind of man she would have liked to have married, or even have been. That through her son she can get a small taste of male privilege, since without race or class privilege that's all there is to be had. The daughter can never offer the mother such hope, straddled by the same forces that confine the mother. As a result, the daughter must constantly earn the mother's love, prove her fidelity to her. The son—he gets her love for free.

After ten years of feminist consciousness and activism, why does this seem so significant to me—to write of the Mexican mother favoring the son? I think because I had never quite gone back to the source. Never considered via a pre-conquest lens—*the brothers, they can do whatever they want . . . after all, they are men. In many ways, this prison shaped my rebellion.*

JOURNAL ENTRY: ABRÍL 1980

Three days ago, my mother called me long distance full of tears, loving me, wanting me back in her life after such a long period of separation. My mother's tears succeed in getting me to break down the edge in my voice, the protective distance. My mother's pleading "mi'jita, I love you, I hate to feel so far away from you" succeeds in opening my heart again to her.

I don't remember exactly why my heart had been shut, only that it had been very necessary to keep my distance; that in a way we had agreed to that, but it only took her crying to pry my heart open again.

I feel myself unriveting. The feelings begin to flood my chest. Yes, this is why I love women. This woman is my mother. There is no love as strong as this, refusing my separation, never settling for a secret that would split us off, always at the last minute, like now, pushing me to the brink of revelation, speaking the truth.

I am as big as a mountain! I want to say, "Watch out, Mamá! I love you and I am as big as a mountain!" And it is on the brink of this precipice where I feel my body descending into the places where we have not spoken, the times I did not fight back. I am descending, ready to speak the truth, finally.

And then suddenly, over the phone, I hear another ring. My mother tells me to wait. There is a call on my father's work phone.

Moments later, "It's your brother," she says. My knees lock under me, bracing myself for the fall. . . . Her voice lightens up. "Okay, mi'jita. I love you. I'll talk to you later," cutting off the line in the middle of the connection.

I am relieved when I hang up that I did not have the chance to say more. The graceful reminder. This man doesn't have to earn her love. My brother has always come first. Seduction and betrayal. Since I've grown up, no woman cares for me for free. There is always a price. My love.

What I wanted from my mother was impossible. Subtle as it may seem, it would have meant her going against Mexican tradition in a very fundamental way. You are a traitor to your race if you do not put the man first at all times. The potential accusation of "traitor" or "vendida" is what hangs above the heads and beats in the hearts of most Chicanas seeking to develop our own autonomous sense of ourselves, particularly through sexuality.

Even if a Chicana knew no Mexican history, the concept of betraying one's race through sex and sexual politics is as common as corn. As cultural myths reflect the economics, mores, and social structures of a society, every Chicana suffers from their effects. And we project the fear onto each other. We suspect betrayal in one another—first to other men, but ultimately and more insidiously, to the white man.

I don't sense within our culture the same fear of a man betraying our race. It is the woman who is the object of our contempt. We can't ultimately hold onto her, not in the cosmic sense. She who could provide us with the greatest sense of belonging is never truly ours, for she is always potential chattel for the white man—economically and sexually. As with so many of our mothers, my mother's relationship with white men made survival for her and her family possible.

It was Mr. Bowman who saved the day. Saved the day in Tijuana. Big white businessman Mr. Bowman. Not very good-looking, but did he need to be? Had money. A very good dresser, my mother claimed. The second wife, a mexicana—or was that his mistress? No recuerdo, pero this was a man to be counted on.

Cuando se murió mi abuelo, le dió a mi mamá the bucks for the funeral. Mi abuela never asking where it came from, "She didn't care how I got it." My mother says, "How did she think I got it? I was only a girl, hija, a girl."

By the time she started working at the Foreign Club, Boss Bowman and she were both older. He was no spring chicken, never, even in the early years, but by now she was close to eighteen and he thought, after all, it's about time.

The chauffeur, a mexicano, put them into the back seat of the big blue sedan and they all began their way down the coast toward Rosarito Beach. Mi mamá praying the entire way, praying "santo niño madre de dios san antonio" . . . you name it, she brought out every saint and holy person she could think of, but focusing, of course, on her patron, San Antonio. Running the rosary beads through her mind, she prayed, "San Antonio, por favor, ayúdame."

She had seen the chauffeur fill the tank with gas. They had all gone to the station together. She remembered that. She had seen him fill it up. But there they were, her praying between snatches of conversation, Big Bowman sitting next to her, pleased with himself, and the car starts sputtering and jerking to a stop.

They were out of gas. Smack in the desert. It was a day's journey back to town. No gas. No hotel. No Rosarito. No sex with Mr. Bowman.

That time the saints saved her.

"He never laid a hand on me. It wasn't that he didn't want to," she said, "but I was very lucky. If he would've wanted me, what could I do? But I was very lucky."[10]

So little has been documented as to the actual suffering Chicanas have experienced resisting or succumbing to the sexual demands of white men. The ways we have internalized the sexual entitlement and exploitation they have displayed against us are probably too numerous and too ingrained to even identify. If the Chicana, like her brother, suspects other women of betrayal, then she must, in the most profound sense, suspect herself. How deep her suspicions run will measure how ardently she defends her commitment, above all, to the Chicano male. As obedient sister/daughter/lover she is the committed heterosexual, the socially acceptable Chicana. Even if she's politically radical, sex remains the bottom line on which she proves her commitment to her raza.

We Fight Back with Our Families

Because heterosexism[11]—the Chicanas' imposed sexual commitment exclusively to the Chicano male—is proof of her fidelity to her people, the Chicana feminist attempting to critique the sexism in the Chicano community is certainly between a personal rock and a political hard place.

The Chicano discussion of sexism has been largely limited by heterosexual assumption: "How can we get our men right?" The feminist-oriented material that appeared in the late seventies and now into the eighties for the most part strains in its attempt to stay safely within the boundaries of Chicano—male-defined and often anti-feminist—values.

Over and over again, Chicanas trivialize the feminism advocated by the women's movement as being merely a white middle-class thing, having little to offer women of color. They cite only the most superficial aspects of the movement. For example, in "From Woman to Woman," Sylvia S. Lizarraga writes:

> Class distinction is a major determinant of attitudes toward other subordinated groups. In the U.S. we see this phenomenon operating in the goals expressed in the Women's Liberation Movement. . . . The needs represent a large span of interests—from those of capitalist women, women in business and professional careers, to *witches* and *lesbians*. However, the needs of the unemployed and working-class women of different ethnic minorities are generally overlooked by this movement.[12] (emphasis mine)

Although a legitimate critique of what could be called "bourgeoise feminism," this statement typifies the kind of one-sided perspective of the women's movement many Chicanas have given in the name of Chicana liberation. My question is, *whom* are they trying to serve?

Certainly not the Chicana who is deprived of some very critical information about a ten-year grassroots feminist movement where women of color, including lesbians of color (certainly in the minority and most assuredly encountering "feminist" racism), have been actively involved in reproductive rights (especially sterilization abuse), battered women's shelters, rape crisis centers, welfare advocacy, U.S. Third World Women's* conferences, cultural events, health clinics, and more.

Interestingly, it is perfectly acceptable among Chicano males to use white theoreticians—e.g., Marx and Engels—to develop a theory of Chicano oppression. It is unacceptable, however, for the Chicana to use white feminist sources to develop a theory of Chicana oppression.

Even if one subscribes solely to an economic theory of oppression, how can one ignore that over half of the world's workers are female who suffer discrimination not only in the workplace, but also at home and in all the areas of gender and sex-related abuse? How can we afford not to recognize that the wars against imperialism occurring both domestically and internationally are always accompanied by the rape of women of color by both white men and men of color? Without a feminist analysis, what name do we put to these facts? Are these not deterrents to the Chicana developing a sense of "species being"? Are these "women's issues" not also "people's issues"? It is far easier for the Chicana to criticize white women, who on the face of things could never be familia, than to take issue with a brother, an uncle, a father.

Even writings to ostensibly affirm Chicanas are often undermined by what I call the "stand-by-your-man-knee-jerk-phenomenon." For example, in speaking of María Hernández, "a feminist and leader in

---

* At the time of this writing, the US women of color movement defined ourselves as "U.S. Third World Women"; that is, internally colonized peoples within the industrialized capitalist country—the "First World" of the United States. It also put us in solidarity with the liberation struggles of people of color in what we now call the "Global South."

her own right," Alfredo Mirandé and Evangelina Enriquez, the editors of *La Chicana,* offer a typical disclaimer: "[Still] she is always
quick to point to the importance of family unity in the movement and
to acknowledge the help of her husband."[13] And yet we would think
nothing of the Chicano activist never mentioning the many "behind-
the-scenes" Chicanas who helped him!

In the same text, the authors fall into the too-common trap of
coddling the Chicano male ego (which should be, in and of itself,
an insult to Chicano men) in the name of cultural loyalty. Like the
Black Superwoman, the Chicana is forced to take on extra-human
proportions. She must keep the cultural home fires burning while
going out and making a living. She must fight racism alongside her
man, but challenge sexism single-handedly, all the while retaining
her "femininity" so as not to offend or threaten *her man.* This is what
being a Chicana feminist has meant in Chicano male-centric terms.

In recent years, however, deeply committed feminist Chicanas are beginning to make the pages of Chicano, feminist, and literary publications. This, of course, is a reflection of a fast-growing
Chicana/US Third World feminist movement. I am indebted to the
research and writings of Norma Alarcón, Martha Cotera, Gloria
Anzaldúa, and Aleida Del Castillo; the poetry of Bernice Zamora
and Alma Villanueva, to name several.[14] Their work reflects an
impassioned commitment to reclaim and center La Chicana, even
when it means criticizing our "brothers."

To be critical of one's culture is not to betray that culture. We
tend to be very righteous in our criticism and indictment of the dominant culture. And yet, we seem to suffer from the delusion that, since
Chicanos are so maligned from the outside, there is little room to
criticize those aspects within our oppressed culture that oppress us.

I remain amazed at how often self-identified "tercermundistas"
in the US—women and men—work to annihilate the concept and
existence of white supremacy, but turn their faces away from male

supremacy. Perhaps this is because when you start to talk about sexism the world becomes increasingly complex. The power no longer breaks down into neat hierarchical categories and the journey to unraveling it becomes a series of starts, stops, and detours. Since the categories are not easy to arrive at, the enemy is not easy to name.

It *is* true that some men hate women even in their desire for them. And some men oppress the very women they love. But unlike the racist, they allow the object of their contempt to share the table and marriage bed with them. The hatred they feel for women does not translate into separatism. It is more insidiously intracultural, like class antagonism. But different, because it lives and breathes in the flesh and blood of our families, even in the name of love.

In Toni Cade Bambara's novel *The Salt Eaters,* the curandera asks the question, *"Can you afford to be whole?"*[15] This line represents the question that has burned within me for years throughout my growing politicization. *What would a movement bent on the freedom of women of color look like?* In other words, what are the implications of looking not only *outside* of our culture, but *into* our culture and ourselves and from that place beginning to develop a strategy for a movement that could challenge the bedrock of oppressive systems of belief globally?

The one aspect of our identity that has been uniformly ignored by every existing political movement in this country is sexuality, as both a source of oppression and a site of liberation. Although the feminist and lesbian/gay movements have dealt with this issue, sexual oppression and sexual desire have never been considered specifically in relation to the lives of women of color (or for that matter, men of color). Politically, sexuality, race, and gender have usually been presented as oppositional to one another, rather than as part and parcel of a complex web of personal and political identity formation.

Female sexuality must be controlled, whether it be through the Church or through the State. The institutions of marriage and family, and compulsory heterosexuality[16] prevail and thrive under capitalism as well as socialism. Patriarchal systems of whatever ilk must be able to determine how and when women reproduce. For even after the revolution, babies must be made, and until they find a way of making them without us (which is not that far off into the future), women as (re)producers remain vital to the economy.*

In China, for example, due to overpopulation, married couples are now being mandated by the State to limit their children to one.[17] Abortions are not only available, but women are sometimes forced by family and friends to undergo an abortion or meet with severe economic recriminations from the State. In the US, the New Right's response to a weakening economic system, which they attribute in part to women's changing position in the family, is to institute legislation to ensure governmental control of women's reproductive rights. Unlike China, however, the New Right is "morally" opposed to abortion. The form their misogyny takes is the dissolution of government-assisted abortions for the poor, bills to limit teenage girls' right to birth control, and advocacy for the Human Life Amendment.[18] These backward political moves hurt all women, but especially women of color suffering economically.

The white patriarch's so-called benevolent protection of the family and the role of women within it has never extended to the woman of color. She is most often the victim of forced pregnancy and sterilization. She is always the last to choose how, when, if, and with whom she may reproduce.

Unlike most white people, with the exception of Jews (not all of whom are white), Third World people have suffered the threat of genocide since the coming of the first European expansionists. The

---

* Forty years after this initial writing, with evolving policies and understanding regarding distinctions between sex and gender identifications, transmen are now also giving birth.

family, then, becomes all the more ardently protected by oppressed peoples, and the sanctity of this institution is infused like blood into the veins of the Chicano. At all costs, la familia must be preserved: for when they kill our boys in their own imperialist wars to gain greater profits for American corporations; when they segregate us into ghettos, reservations, and barrios that ensure that our own people will be the recipients of our own frustrated acts of violence; when they sterilize our women without our consent because we are unable to read the document we sign; when they prevent our families from getting decent housing, adequate child care, sufficient fuel, regular medical care; then we have reason to believe—although they may be no longer technically lynching us in Texas—they intend to see us dead.

So we fight back, we think, with our families—with our women unconditionally pregnant, and our men, the indisputable heads. We believe the more severely we protect the sex roles within the family, the stronger we will be as a unit in opposition to the Anglo threat of institutional violence. And yet, our refusal to examine *all* the roots of the lovelessness in our families is our weakest link and softest spot.

Our refusal to deeply look at the relationships within our families—between husband and wife, lovers, sister and brother, father, son and daughter—leads me to believe that the Chicano male does not hold fast to the family unit merely to safeguard it from the death-dealings of the gringo. Living under Capitalist Patriarchy, he, too, wants to be able to determine how, when, and with whom his women—mother, wife, and daughter—are sexual. For without male-imposed social and legal control of our reproductive function, reinforced by the Church, and the social institutionalization of our roles as sexual and domestic servants to men, Chicanas might very freely *choose* to do otherwise, including being sexually independent *from* and/or *with* men. In fact, the forced choice of the gender of our sexual/love partner seems to precede the forced choice of the form (marriage and family) that partnership might take. As such, the two are indivisible in the oppression of women under patriarchy.

Homosexuality does not, in and of itself, pose a great threat to society. Male homosexuality has always been a tolerated aspect of Mexican/Chicano society, as long as it remains fringe and the men "manly." But lesbianism, in any form, and male homosexuality that openly avows both the sexual and emotional elements of the bond, challenge the very foundation de la familia.

The question remains: *Is the foundation as it stands now sturdy enough to meet the face of the oppressor?* I think not. There is a deeper love amongst our people that lies buried between the lines of the roles we play with each other. Family is *not* by definition the man in a dominant position over women and children. Familia is cross-generational bonding, deep emotional ties between opposite sexes and within our same sex. It is sexuality that may involve, but is not limited to, intercourse or orgasm. It springs forth from the ritual of shared confianza in our daily interactions. El beso en la mejilla and a blessing with every departure from the home. It is finding familia among friends where ties thick as blood are bonded in response to shared experiences of injustice. The strength of our families never came from domination. It has only endured in spite of it—like our women.

La Malinchista

Chicanos' refusal to look at our weaknesses as a people and a move-ment is, in the most profound sense, an act of self-betrayal. The Chi-cana lesbian bears the brunt of this betrayal, for it is she, the most visible manifestation of a woman taking control of her own sexual identity and destiny, who so severely challenges the anti-feminist Chicana and Chicano. What other reason is there for the virtual dead silence among Raza about lesbianism? When the subject is raised, the word is used pejoratively, as a way to censor any discussion of sexism in the movement. Describing the anti-feminism in El Movimiento of the late '60s, Sonia A. López writes: "The Chicanas who voiced their discontent with the organizations and with male leadership were often labeled 'women's libbers,' and 'lesbians.' This served to isolate and discredit them, a method practiced both covertly and overtly."[19]

The woman who defies her role as subservient to her husband, father, brother, or son by taking control of her own sexual destiny is purported to be a traitor to her race. Even if the defiant woman is not a lesbian, she is assumed to be one; that is, *una Malinchista*—a Mexican corrupted by foreign influences, threatening the integrity of the Mexican/Chicano nation.

Norma Alarcón elaborates on this theme of sex as a determinant of loyalty when she states:

> The myth of Malinche contains the following sexual possibilities: woman is sexually passive, and hence at all times open to potential use by men whether it be seduction or rape. The possible use is double-edged: that is, the use of her as pawn may be intracultural—"amongst us guys"— or intercultural, which means if we are not using her then "they" must be using her. Since woman is highly pawnable, nothing she does is perceived as choice.[20]

As such, the Chicana lesbian can be seen as a race traitor, being used by the white man, even if the man never lays a hand on her. *The choice is never seen as her own.* The Chicano politico decrees homosexuality is a white disease that he sinisterly spreads to Third World people, men and women alike. But, the lesbian carries the stigma of treason most virulently. Further, the Chicana lesbian who has relationships with white women may feel especially susceptible to such accusations, since the white lesbian is seen as the white man's agent. The fact that the white woman may be challenging the authority of her white father, and thereby could be looked upon as a potential ally, has no bearing on a case closed before it was ever opened.

The first dyke I remember was a girl in seventh grade called "Frank"—the way she liked it. She played the meanest game of four-square—built lean and solid as an eighth-grade boy, and smart too. And very, very clearly white. *Were all lesbians white?*

I remember thinking that I had never quite met a girl like Frank before—so bad and bold, somehow freer than the rest of us. She was an "army brat" and had lived many places, even in Europe. While all my Chicana friends were leaving me high and dry for the guys, this girl—although not particularly interested in me—represented a life beyond the tight group discussions of girls, locked arm in arm, where "chinga'o" and its multiple versions dropped like a slug in my gut with every utterance.

Even at twelve, I was still wondering if I could get pregnant slow-dancing with a boy, having picked up my knowledge of sex from these cryptic, closed-circled conversations. The desire I felt for women had nothing and everything to do with the vulgarity of intercourse; had nothing and everything to do with the naked dreams that rocked my bed at night. Somehow Frank connected with all this—as did the "funny" couple I had encountered secretly one hot summer afternoon several years before.

At the time we—my siblings and mom and I—were living in the Kenwood Hotel, a kind of drifter hangout, mostly SLOs,* down on Main Street in Huntington Beach, California, long before there was any development there. Just a few bars, a little drugstore, the Paddock restaurant, and a surfboard shop. My mom managed the Kenwood.

One day I was making my way down the long hallway to go play out on the big sundeck (I was eight years old) when I suddenly stopped short of the screen door. Some new tenants, who were not regulars, were out there. Hiding behind the screen door, I decided to observe.

---

* Single-living occupancy

One woman looked like a Marilyn Monroe type—fifties style. Her hair was brassy blonde and pressed into a kind of permanent wave. Her yellow sundress was very tight around her waist and low-cut. The other person next to her I knew was really a woman, although she looked mostly like a man: white dress shirt with sleeves rolled up, pack of cigs in her front breast pocket, black, men's trousers. She was a big woman, about twice the size of Marilyn, except her head was small—dark-haired and greased back.

Marilyn had her dress hiked up above her knees and between her thighs she had put an open jar of Skippy peanut butter. I watched as Marilyn dipped the knife into the jar, pulled out a thick glob of the brown mass, then ran her tongue along it luxuriously like she had all day to eat the stuff. She then gave it to her partner to lick from the same place. All I could think about were the germs that were being passed back and forth.

The next day, I learned that the "funny" women in room six had sneaked out in the middle of the night without paying. They had stolen the alarm clock too. My momma said she had lent them the clock, trying to give them the benefit of the doubt, "but never again."

Were all lesbians white? And decent ladies, Mexican?
Who was I in this?

A year later, we moved to San Gabriel and after-school would find me on Cathy García's couch, making out. I think mostly we put a sofa pillow between our faces so our lips wouldn't touch, but our bodies would get all wrapped up around each other. At eleven, Sandra was already "stacked" and, quite innocently, we would take the role of movie stars—she playing Deborah Walley and me, James Darren, lusting after each other. Cathy's young brown body seemed a miracle of womanhood to me, the pink bow of her brassiere always poking out from the opening of her too-small, white, Catholic school uniform blouse. I wanted Cathy and as long as she was interested, I'd throw myself on the couch with her and make out until my cheeks were sore.

The Mexican women in my life, a pain I don't want to get to.

It seems my life has always been a kind of catch-22. For any way you look at it, Chicanas are denied one another's fidelity. If women betray one another through heterosexism, then lesbianism is a kind of visible statement of our faithfulness to one another. But if lesbianism is white, then the women I am faithful to can never be my own. And we are forced to move away from our people.

As Gloria Anzaldúa once said to me, "If I stayed in Hargill, I would never have been able to be myself. I had to leave to come out as the person I really was." And if I had stayed in the San Gabriel, I would have been found for dead, at least the walking dead.

Journal Entry: primavera 1980

I don't know what happened to make me this way. I do fear for my life sometimes. Not that a bullet will hit my brain, but that I will forget to be afraid of the enemy. I dreamed last night of a hostility in me so great that on the job I put a pen through the skull of a white man.

I have felt like an outcast on my job lately. The new restaurant manager wants to fire me for my "politics."

I am a lesbian. In the dream, I love women to the point of killing for us all.

An old friend came to visit me yesterday. She is leaving her good husband for the wild love of a woman. We were both very sad together. Not for the separation from her husband but for so many years of separation from women.

Some people try to convince me that the secrets I hold about loving women do not put me in a position of threat to my life. You see, you can't see this condition—this posture of mind and heart and body—in the movement of my joints or on the surface of my skin. (And then again, sometimes you can.) But I know they are wrong.

I feel very threatened and very threatening.

My mother does not worry about me; she fears me. She fears the power of the life she helped to breathe into me. She fears the lessons she taught me will move into action.

The line of reasoning goes:

Malinche sold out Indigenous México by serving as courtesan and translator for Cortés whose offspring symbolically represent the birth of the bastardized mestizo/mexicano people. My mestiza[21] mother then is the modern-day Malinche marrying a white man, my father, to produce the güeros my sister, my brother, and I are. Finally, I—a half-breed Chicana—further betray my race by *choosing* my sexuality.

I come from a long line of vendidas.

I am a Chicana lesbian.

My being a sexual person and a radical stands in direct contradiction to, and in violation of, the Mexican woman I was supposed to be.

INOCENCIA MEANT DYING
RATHER THAN BEING FUCKED

Coming from such a complex and contradictory history of sexual exploitation by white men and from within our own race, it is nearly earth-shaking to begin to try and separate the myths told about us from the truths, and to examine to what extent we have internalized the lies.

Although intellectually I knew different, early on I learned that women were willing collaborators in rape. So over and over again in pictures, books, movies, I experienced rape and pseudo-rape as what sex was all about. Women want it. Real rape was dark, greasy-looking bad men jumping out of alleys and attacking innocent blonde women. Everything short of that was just sex; the way it is: dirty and duty. We spread our legs and bear the brunt of penetration, but we do spread our legs.

In my mind, inocencia meant dying rather than being fucked.

I learned these notions about sexuality not only from the society at large, but more specifically and potently from Chicano/mexicano culture. If the very act of sex—the penetration itself—implies female debasement and non-humanness, it is no wonder Chicanas often divorce ourselves from the conscious recognition of our own sexuality.

Even if we enjoy having sex, draw pleasure from feeling fingers, tongue, penis inside us, there is a part of us that must disappear in the act, separate ourselves from realizing what it is we are actually doing. We find ourselves sitting, as it were, on the corner bedpost, watching the degradation and violence some *other* woman is willing to subject herself to. And if we have lesbian feelings—want not only to be penetrated, but to penetrate—what perverse kind of monstrosity we must indeed be! Mentally, we leave our bodies to escape the painful recognition of this base physical/sexual self.

When I was about twelve years old, I had the following dream:
I am in a hospital bed. I look down upon my newly developing body. The breasts are large and ample. And below my stomach, I see my own penis, wildly shooting menstrual blood totally out of control. This, the image of the hermaphrodite.*

In another context, I could have seen this dream as a very sexually potent vision, reflecting a desire for integration of the male and female energies within me. But as a child, I am incapable of handling such information. Up to that point, I always knew that I felt the greatest emotional ties with females, but suddenly I was beginning to consciously identify those feelings as sexual. The more

---

* A more accurate naming is "intersex," language not widely available to my generation at the time.

potent my dreams and fantasies became and the more I sensed my own exploding sexual desire, the more I retreated from my body's messages and into the region of religion. Sexual fantasy and rebellion became "impure thoughts" and "sinful acts." By giving definition and meaning to my desires, religion became the discipline to control my sexuality.

I was raised within a very strict brand of Mexican, mixed with Irish, Catholicism. This was in many ways typical for many Chicano children whose parents are of my mother's generation and Catholic. We were taught by the Irish nuns to seek the love and forgiveness of the Father. But after confession, I went straight home to my Mexican mother, knelt before her, and asked pardon for my sins against her. It seemed the real test was to kneel down on the flesh and bones of your knees, to be relieved by lágrimas y por un besito en la cocina de la mamá.

The contradiction between what I experienced as a very female-centered and mestizo Catholicism and the punitive austerity of the Euro-American Catholic Church plagued me as a young adolescent. I remember once in the sixth grade, the nun was conducting a religion class on doubting the existence of God. In fact, I had been doubting for years if there truly was a god.

God had never actually once forgiven me, but my mother had.

I confess that it was during this class as the nun proceeded to describe the various forms of atheism that for some unspeakable reason I saw my life in a flash of revelation that filled me with horror. I pictured myself lying flat on my back on a kind of surgery table, and people—white-uniformed doctors—stood around my body, putting dreams into my head; the dream that made up my life—the people, the sensations, the emotions that gripped my heart. All these things were no more than figures in my imagination, thoughts that formed pictures of bodies that could not actually be touched. Love in this case was impossible. I was crucially and critically alone and powerless.

In fact, la Chicana *is* manipulated by a white god-father, the white president-father, the white priest and patrón, under whose jurisdiction she is nearly powerless in the dominant society. Was the vision no more than a foreshadowing of what oppression awaited me as an adolescent growing into womanhood? The vision became its own directive. In order not to embody *la chingada,* nor the perverse female version of the *chingón,* I would become pure spirit—bodiless. For what, indeed, must my desirous body look like if I were both *la chingada* and *el chingón?*

In my early adolescence, my fears moved me further and further away from the living flesh and closer and closer to the bodiless god; the confessions of box and curtain cloth; the perverse comfort I drew from the knowledge that the church would be standing there, just around the corner from the cemetery; that it would be expecting me—grand, square, predictable as stone; that the end of mass would find a palm placed in my hand. The sure knowledge of the spines of leaf bending into my grip.

The comfort and terror of powerlessness.

La niña chooses this time not to kneel in the pew. Having started for her knees, she breaks the bend, scooting back against the hard-boned wood of the pew bench: "O-my-god-I'm-heartly-sorry . . ."

No, the child chooses this time not to begin this way. Breaking the line, she says nothing. Waiting, she lets the visions come.

Y los diablos begin to parade before her. As common to her now as the space she'd grown to picture like a circle of flesh the size of communion host inside her ribcage—the place where she thought her soul to sleep. Thinking white, thinking empty, thinking quiet, clean and untouched. It was this spot she protected from the advancing intruders: blood-pumping, wild-eyed things. The parts of men, like animals rearing, ramming into anything that could swallow them. The parts of women, quartered, stripped, and shamed.

La niña shook the pictures from her mind, intervening before they could slip below and infect the sacred place inside her chest. She, the caretaker of her soul. The warrior. The watchdog, overburdened, beaten by now.

No resistance. Not this time. Not lifting her eyes, she only looked toward her hands, repeating to herself, "just look at your hands," repeating as the only language she would allow herself until words slipped from her altogether, until she knew only the touch of her red, cold hands against the wool thighs of her uniform skirt, until she knew only her body, without fire, her face dropped between her knees, her arms wrapped 'round her thin calves rocking, rocking, rocking.

Forgive us, Father, for how badly we need tenderness.

How does one describe a world where the mind twists like a rag dry of any real feeling? Only an absent inarticulate terror. A mouth hung open with no voice breaking through?

When I was nineteen, I lost my virginity. It was during those early years of heterosexual activity that the estrangement and anguished alienation I had experienced in puberty revisited me. In awakening to the touch of a man, my sexual longings for women, which I had managed to suppress since puberty, resurfaced. The sheer prospect of being a lesbian was too great to bear, as I fully believed that giving in to such desires would find me shot-up with bullets or drugs in a gutter somewhere. Further, although I *physically* found sex with men very satisfying, I couldn't quite look at what I was doing, having turned against my Church and my mother in the act. Instead I began to develop fantasies about it.

Like the white doctor visions of my childhood, I became in my imagination a dark and sinister priestess, her flowing robes of toads and sequins draped loosely over my naked shoulders. Her menacing laugh fell hungrily from my lips whenever I saddled up upon my boyfriend's lap, riding him.

But, the first time was different. Unexpected.

Not the first sex but the first time I felt that feeling, that surge of pure pleasure, coming out from behind my heart and through my open legs, gripping the bone of the boy wanting me, I fell into deep sobbing. I remembered I had felt this somewhere, sometime before. I had waited nearly ten years for its return—remembering when as a child, at first without touching myself, the pain that tugged gently at my ovaries (not maliciously, but only with an alive sense of their existence), the pressure I felt in my bowels, and the heat in my lower back—all commingled into a delicious kind of pleasure.

Today it has a name. At eleven, I only hoped the strange uncontrollable feeling would come back. It was an *accident* of pleasure. I wondered if other girls got this feeling too. If my sister, one year older, ever did. If it was a fact of growing up, like the thick red dirt smudge of blood that I had only months before found on my underpants. I would barely touch myself, except in the beginning when the feeling first occurred, my fingers instinctively moving down to the place where the slightest amount of pressure drew the sensation deep from out of the pit of my stomach and into my vagina in cool streams of relief. If I held my knees together tight enough to feel the lips puffed and throbbing between them, the feeling would sometimes replay itself in echoes of kindly, calling voices—momma voices—growing more and more faint as they departed.

Months later, my mother warned after I had spent some time locked in the bathroom that it was not good to push yourself too hard when you were trying to "go." She mentioned "piles," but not knowing what that was, I figured she knew about the pleasure, the pain, the pushing brought on and it was bad. It was years later before I ever reenacted my private bathroom ritual again.

Only occasionally, through high school, pretending it wasn't quite happening, I would sit with one foot under me, placing the wedge of the sole of my hard oxford school shoe up between my labia. For hours, I would allow myself at least this secret comfort through TV shows and homework late into the night, my sister on the other side of the dining room table.

At what point does the fear become greater than the flesh and the flesh of the fantasy prevail?

The more vividly the sinister priestess fantasies appeared to me, the more viciously I would fuck to obliterate them from my mind. I was always wanting sex: in cars, behind the bleachers of the neighborhood ballpark; my boyfriend and I breaking into the park office where he worked to use its floor. Somehow, I felt that if I fucked long and hard enough, I might begin to *feel* again.

Occasionally, I would go through days, sometimes a week, of reprieve from these preoccupations, but the relief would never last. Seemingly without my control, I would be in a conversation with someone and begin to feel as though I were being sucked down into a hole in the ground where I could always still *see* the person, but they would be shrinking further and further away from my hearing; the person's body framed by the lip of the tunnel I had fallen into, their mouth moving soundlessly. These visceral feelings of absence became the lens through which I saw most of my waking life, like a thin film between me and the people I longed to touch, to reach to for help.

> *we never spoke again, really*
> *after the time I pulled up in front*
> *of our mother's house, hands still*
> *on the wheel*
>
> *Sister, I need*
> *to talk with you and told her*
> *there was a devil on my tail*
> *riding me.*

I know she saw it clear as me
I know she'd seen it in my younger years
always creeping too close to her, like I was
some crazy infection,
and I guess I am, crazy
that catches.

In my "craziness" I wrote poems describing myself as a centaur: half animal/half human, hairy-rumped and cloven-hoofed, como el diablo, the symbols emerging from a deeply Mexican Catholic place. My recurring sense of myself outside the normal life and touch of human beings was again, in part, a kind of revelation: a foreshadowing of the marginal place, within my culture and in society at large, my sexuality was to eventually take me.

Sometimes a breakdown can be the beginning of a kind of breakthrough, a way of living in advance through a trauma that prepares you for a future of radical transformation. The third time I broke was many years after I had stopped seeing men. I had been out as a lesbian for a while and had examined, I thought, what this made me in the world at large, but I had never actually looked into the eyes of what this made me in the world of my then lesbian community. Since I was so busy making room simply to live a lesbian life safely—coming out to my family, friends, at school, in print, to my employers, etc., I had never wrestled with the reality of what being a *Chicana* lesbian meant.

All this changed, however, when I thought I saw in a lover, a woman, the chingón that I had so feared to recognize in myself: "the active, aggressive and closed person," as Paz writes, "who inflicts [the wound]."[22] I had met my match. I was forced to confront how, in all my sexual relationships, I had resisted, at all costs, feeling la chingada—which, in effect, meant that I had resisted fully feeling sex at all.

Nobody wants to be made to feel the turtle with its underside all exposed, just pink and folded flesh.

In the effort to avoid embodying la chingada, I became the chingón. In the effort not to feel fucked, I became the fucker, even with women, regardless of how benign my actions might have appeared on the outside. In the effort not to feel pain or desire, I grew a callous around my heart and imagined I felt nothing at all.

What I never quite understood until this writing is that to be without a sex—to be bodiless—as I sought to escape the burgeoning sexuality of my adolescence, my confused early days of active heterosexuality, and later my panicked lesbianism, means also to be without a race, a culture, a people. I never attributed my removal from physicality to anything to do with race or ethnicity, only sex, only desire for women. And yet, as I grew up sexually, my race, my mexicanismo (regardless of the shade of my skin), along with the genderqueer expression of my sexuality was being denied me at every turn.[23]

I was plagued with sexual contradictions. Lesbianism as a sexual act can never be construed as reproductive sex. It is not work. It is purely about pleasure and intimacy. How this refutes, spits in the face of, the notion of sex as productive, sex as duty! In stepping outside the confines of the institution of heterosexuality, I was indeed *choosing* sex freely.

The lesbian as institutionalized outcast.

During those years as an active feminist lesbian, I became increasingly aware of the fact that not only had my sexuality made me an outcast from Raza, but if I seriously listened to it, with all its specific cultural nuances, it would further make me an outcast from a very white and middle-class women's movement—a movement that I had run to for dear life to avoid the gutter of utter social ostracization I had feared was waiting for me elsewhere. With no visible Third World feminist movement in sight, it seemed to me to be a Chicana lesbian put me far beyond the hope of salvation.

TIRED OF THESE ACTS OF TRANSLATION

What the white women's movement tried to convince me was that lesbian sexuality was *naturally* different than heterosexual sexuality; that through lesbianism the desire to penetrate and be penetrated, to fill and be filled, would vanish; that retaining such desires was "reactionary," not "politically correct," and "male-identified"; and, that reaching sexual fulfillment with a woman lover would never involve any kind of power struggle. Women were different. We could simply magically transcend those old notions, just by seeking a kind of reciprocal emotional/spiritual union in bed.

The fact of the matter was that all these power struggles of "having" and "being had" were being played out in our own bedrooms. And in my psyche, they held a particular Mexican twist. White women's feminism did little to answer my questions. As a Chicana feminist my concerns were different.

As I wrote in 1982:

> What I need to explore will not be found in the lesbian feminist bedroom, but more likely in the mostly heterosexual bedrooms of Tijuana, South Tejas, L.A., or even Sonora, México. Further, I have come to realize that the values white feminists employ to define the erotic or what, to them, is legitimately expressed desire is bounded by race and class. Although we may share *aspects of* the psychosexual lives of Anglo/white-American women, their assumptions would have to be reexamined and translated to fit my people, in particular, the women in my family.
>
> And I am tired, always, of these acts of translation.[24]

Mirtha Quintanales corroborates this position and exposes the necessity for a Third World feminist dialogue on sexuality when she states:

The critical issue for me regarding the politics of sexuality is that as a Latina Lesbian living in the U.S., I do not really have much of an opportunity to examine what constitutes sexual conformity and sexual defiance in my own culture, in my own ethnic community, and how that may affect my own values, attitudes, sexual life and politics. There is virtually no dialogue on the subject anywhere and I, like other Latinas and Third World women, especially Lesbians, am quite in the dark about what we're up against besides negative feminist sexual politics.[25]

During the late 1970s and into the '80s, the separatist concept of women's culture among white radical lesbian feminists was in full swing. Womon's history, wommin's music, womyn's spirituality, and goddess worship became the vernacular of the day—all with the "man" left out of the spelling and the movement; and, all with the "white" modifier assumed, but unstated and unacknowledged.[26]

As cultural activist and scholar Bernice Johnson Reagon puts it: "We have been organized to have our primary cultural signals come from factors other than that we are women. We are not from our base, acculturated to be women people, capable of crossing our first people boundaries: Black, White, Indian, etc."[27]

Unlike Reagon, I believe that there *are* certain ways in which we have been acculturated to be "women people," and that there is therefore such a thing as "women's culture." This occurs, however, as Reagon points out, *within* a cultural context formed by race, class, geography, religion, ethnicity, and language.

JOURNAL ENTRY: JULIO 1981

Boston. Pouring summer rain. We are all immigrants to this town— una hermana de Chicago, una de Tejas, una de Puerto Rico, y yo, de California. And the four of us move out onto the porch under the beat and heat of the downpour on the roof above our heads. Cooling off from the evening of enchiladas.

I make up a little concoction of a summer drink: jugo de naranja, tequila, limón. Tossing in all kinds of ice cubes, "Try this," I say.

Y mis hermanas drink it up. Dos Chicanas y dos puertoriqueñas getting a little high from the food and the rain and the talk, hablando de nuestras madres.

Sitting out on the porch that night, what made me at home and filled me with ease where I forgot about myself in a fine and fluid way was not just that the Spanish sounds wrapped around the English like tortillas steaming in flour sacks, not just that we all had worked hard to get here from hard-working homes, not just that we understood the meaning of familia, but that we were women—somos mujeres.

This is what women's culture means to me.

It is understandable that many feminists opt for a certain kind of separatist solution as part of a liberatory strategy, especially those who have suffered tremendously via their close proximity to men (incest and domestic violence especially come to mind). Separatism among some sectors of the lesbian of color community also took place in the late 1970s, creating distance not only from men but also from white people, including white lesbians.

An argument can be made that every oppressed group needs to imagine through (re)visions of recorded histories and mythologies, applied in some way to living praxis, a world where our oppression does not seem the preordained order. Aztlán for Chicanos is a case in point. (See "Queer Aztlán" in this volume, p 271.) Perhaps the problem resides in believing in this ideal past or imagined future so thoroughly and single-mindedly that we miss or misinterpret the contradictions in our experience, and everyday inequities and injustices are ignored.

Compulsory heterosexuality and marriage—and men as the primary agents of those institutions—deeply influence our sexuality, but do so within the context of race, class, and ethnic identities. We can work to tumble patriarchal institutions so that when the rubble is finally cleared away we can see what we have left to build on, but we can't ask a woman to forget everything she understands about sex in a heterosexual and culturally specific environment nor tell her what she is allowed to think about it. Should she forget and not use what she knows to untie the knot of her own desire, she may lose any chance of ever discovering her own human (sexual and spiritual) potential.

Audre Lorde writes, "In order to perpetuate itself, every oppression must corrupt or distort those various sources of power within the culture of the oppressed that can provide energy for change."[28] She instructs, the erotic *is* a source of power for women and the distortion of women of color desire has been especially egregious.

FEEDING PEOPLE IN ALL THEIR HUNGERS

Current history has taught us that the effectiveness of liberation movements often depends on their ability to provide what, at least, feels like a spiritual imperative (I think here of the spiritually motivated calling of the civil rights movement). Spirituality that inspires activism and, similarly, politics that move the spirit—drawing from the deep longing for freedom—give meaning to our lives. Such a vision can hold and heal us in the worst of times.

Women of color have always known, although we have not always wanted to admit, our sexuality is not merely a physical response or drive, but holds a crucial relationship to our spiritual and psychological capacity. If our spiritual praxis has been linked in our oppression through patriarchal religions, it must also be linked in our liberation strategy. To date, no liberation movement has been willing to take on the task: to walk a freedom road that is both material and metaphysical, sexual and spiritual, while all along remaining attendant to the racial, ethnic, and cultural specificity of our struggle. Third World feminism is about feeding people in all their hungers.

In 1977, the Combahee River Collective wrote: "The most profound and potentially most radical politics come directly out of our own identity." They go on to say that they "are committed to struggling against racial, sexual, heterosexual and class oppression and see as [their] particular task, the development of integrated analysis and practice based upon the fact that the major systems of oppression are interlocking.[29]

Combahee's "Black Feminist Statement" speaks to the breadth and depth of US women of color oppression outlining a liberatory perspective, as Barbara Smith puts it, that "bring(s) the strands together."[30]

When I first encountered Combahee's work in 1978, three things especially impacted me: first, the lesbian visibility of its authors; second, their expressed solidarity with other women of color; and third, a concern for what might be considered the *psycho-sexual* oppression of women of color. The statement asserts: "We are all damaged people merely by virtue of being Black women."[31]

The appearance of these sisters' words *in print,* as lesbians of color, suddenly made it viable for me to put my Chicana *and* lesbian self in the center of our movement. I no longer had to postpone or deny any part of my identity to make revolution easier for somebody else to swallow. I had heard too many times that my concern about specifically sexual issues was divisive to the larger struggle or wasn't really the "primary contradiction" and, therefore, not essential for revolution; that to be concerned about the sexuality of women of color was an insult to women in the Third World literally starving to death.

But the only hunger I have ever known was the hunger for sex and the hunger for freedom and somehow, in my mind and heart, they were related and certainly not mutually exclusive. If I could not use the source of my hunger as the source of my activism, how then was I to be politically effective?

Finally, I encountered a movement, first voiced by Black women, which promised to deal with the oppression that occurred *under* the skin as well (and by virtue of the fact that that skin was female and colored); because the damage that has been done to us sexually and racially has penetrated our minds as well as our bodies. The existence of rape, genital mutilation, sterilization abuse, and violence against lesbians has bludgeoned our entire perception of ourselves as female beings.

One of the major components of Black feminism is that women of color embody the coalition essential for revolution and that each form of oppression is part and parcel of the larger political strategy of capitalist and racist patriarchy.

Radical Feminism makes a compelling argument that patriarchy—men's oppression of women (and the control over our reproduction)—is the root of, and paradigm for, all other oppressions. And, as true as that may be, the concept of the "simultaneity of oppression" to which Third World feminism subscribes speaks to the absolute connective tissue between *all* systems of oppression that has kept the human body and spirit enslaved from time immemorial.

What women of color suffer in our families and relationships is, in some way, inherently connected to the rape of women in our neighborhoods, the high suicide rate of Native Americans on reservations, attacks on Black gays and disabled people in New York City bars, and the war in El Salvador. Whether one death is sexually motivated and the other the result of US imperialism, women of color are always potential victims.

Each movement, then, that tries to combat an aspect of women of color oppression offers an organized contributory strategy for change that women of color cannot afford to ignore. The difference now is that as we begin to organize and create our own programs and institutions, we are building a political base so that we will no longer have to fall prey to the tokenism and invisibility we have

encountered in other movement work. Without the political autonomy of oppressed groups, there is not an even playing field and coalition politics are a bankrupt notion.

But organizing ourselves is no easy task. The homophobia of
heterosexual sisters and the racism among us cross-culturally are
two major obstacles toward our being a unified movement. To begin
with, we are profoundly ignorant about one another's cultures, traditions, languages, particular histories of oppression and resistance,
and the cultural adaptations our peoples have had to make in the
face of total cultural obliteration. But even this would only be a matter of education, had our prejudices against one another only penetrated our minds, and not also our hearts.

Quite simply, the oppressions suffered by women of color, especially as we have internalized them, hold the greatest threat to our
organizing successfully together, intra-culturally as well as cross-culturally. I think what is hardest for any oppressed people to understand
is that *the sources of oppression form not only our progressive radicalism,
but also our pain.* Therefore, they are often the places we feel we must
protect unexamined at all costs. On a daily basis, we have learned to
take the race hatred, the class antagonism, the shame of our desires
and use them as weapons against ourselves and our kind.

*In the wee hours of the morning my lover and I fight. We fight and cry
and move against each other and a torrent of pain. The pain doesn't stop.
We do not shout at midnight. We have learned to keep our voices down.
In public. In the public ear of the building where we try to build a home.
We fight quietly, urgently.*

*The latina mother who lives below us—who catches sight of us in
the hall and turns her pale cheek away, whose eyes are the eyes of my
enemy—is pounding on the ceiling. Again. A frantic hateful beating
below us, under our bed.*

She knows we are up, up to something. She hates us. And my lover's eyes staring back at me are red like apples from tears. The pounding—more vicious—continues. La vecina wants to remind us. She is there with her husband, her children in the next room. Decent people sleep at this hour.

My lover says, "We are two women. We have no right to care so much about each other that the pain could keep us up."

"Those women or whatever they are," she describes us to the lady next door the next morning.

If they hurt me, they will hurt me in that place.

What might our relationships with one another look like if we did not feel we had to protect ourselves from those with whom we truly believe we share common cause? How might desire and spirit be expressed differently?

Mirtha Quintanales, en una carta:

> There is something I feel for you or with you or from you that I experience with no one else, that I need and crave, that I never get enough of, that I do not understand, that I am missing at this very moment . . . perhaps it's spiritual openness, two souls touching, love that transcends the boundaries of materiality, ordinary reality and living.[32]

The right to love expressed in a freed cultural tongue is what this essay seems, finally, to be about. I would not be trying to develop some kind of Chicana feminist theory if I did not have strong convictions, urgent hunches, and deep racial memory that la Chicana would *not* betray a sister, a daughter, una compañera in the service of "the man" and his institutions if somewhere in the chain of historical events and generations, we were shown a path to love ourselves.

The visibility of lesbians of color choosing our sexual partners against the prescribed cultural norms and our examining the political implications of such a choice can provide the political space necessary for heterosexual women of color to begin to ask themselves some profound and overdue questions about their own acts of loving, their own deseo. The lesbian of color brings sexuality with all its raggedy edges, oozing wounds, and liberatory desires into the light of day.

I once had a very painful conversation with my mother—a conversation about moving away from her. I am the only person—male or female—among my relatives who ever left home for good without getting married first. My mother told me that she felt in some way that I was choosing my "friends" (she meant lesbian lovers) over her.

She said, "No one is ever going to love you as much as I do. No one." We were both crying by then and I responded, "I know that. I know how strong your love is. Why do you think I am a lesbian?"

Silence. But I felt in the air that it was the silence of an unspeakable recognition. Of understanding, finally, what my being a lesbian meant to me. I had been "out" to my mother for years, but not like this. When we name this bond among Raza women, Chicana feminism emerges.

To refuse to allow the Chicana lesbian the right to the free expression of her own sexuality, and her politicization of it, is in the deepest sense to deny one's self the right to the same; for there will be no change among heterosexual men and there will be no change in heterosexual relations, as long as people of color communities keep lesbians and gay men political prisoners among our own people. Any movement built on the fear and loathing of anyone is a failed movement. The Chicano Movement is no different. No one else can or will speak for us. We must be the ones to define the parameters of what it means to be—and love—la Chicana.

> For you, mamá, I have unclothed
> myself before a woman

have laid wide the space between my thighs straining
open the strings held there taut and ready
to snap.

Stretching my legs and imagination so open
to feel my whole body cradled
by the movement of her mouth, the mouth
of her thighs rising and falling, her arms
her kiss, all the parts of her open
like lips moving, talking
me into loving.

I remember this common skin, Mamá
oiled by work and worry.
Hers is a used body like yours
that carries the same scent of silence
I call it home.

The first women I loved were the women of my race.
Me fui muy lejos de mi pueblo en busca
del amor de una mujer,
pero ahora . . . ahora
regreso a mi pueblo
a la mujer mestiza
Xicana
Indígena

March 1983
Brooklyn, New York

RiverPoem

En el sueño mi amor me pregunta
—¿Dónde está tu río?
and I point to the center of my chest.

I am a river cracking open.
Before,
all my parts were just thin tributaries,
lines of water like veins running barely beneath the soil
skimming the bone surface of the earth
sometimes desert creek
sometimes city-wash
sometimes sweat sliding
down a woman's
breastbone.

Now I can see the point of juncture,
and I open its banks
to let
the river run.

Feed the Mexican Back into Her

para mi prima-hermana

What I meant to say to her as she reached
around the cocktail glass to my hand, squeezing it
saying, *it makes no difference to me.*

what I meant to say
it must
make
a difference
       but then I did say that
       and it made no difference,
       this difference between us.

What I meant to say to her is I dreamed we were children.

I meant to tell her
how I took her thin brown hand in mine
and led her to the grocery store—the corner one,
like in LA on Adams Street,
where I remember her poor and more mexican than ever,
we both were.

I meant to remind her
of how she looked in her brother's hand-me-downs—
the thin striped tee shirt, the suspenders holding
up the corduroy pants literally
"in suspension" off her small frame.
I meant to sit her down and describe

for her the love, the care with which I drew the money
from my pocket—my plump pink hand, protective,
counting out the change.
I bought tortillas, chiles verdes.

I meant to say,
"Teresita, mi'jita, when we get home, I'll make you a meal
you'll never forget."

Feed the Mexican back into her.

I meant to tell her
how I thought of her as not brown at all, but black—
an english-speaking dark-girl,
wanting to spit the white words out of her,
be Black angry.
I meant to encourage.

Teresita
There is a photograph of us.
At seven, you are skinny at the knees
where the brown wrinkles together black,
my hand like a bright ring around yours
we are smiling.

In the negative, *I* am dark
and profane / *you* light & bleached-boned
my guts are grey & black coals glowing.

I meant to say,
it is this fire you see coming out from inside me.
Call it the darkness you still wear on the edge

of your skin
the light you reach for
across the table
and into my heart.

And Then There's Us . . .

for LaRue and Elvira

Nobody would believe it to look at us
how our families'
histories
converge.

Two women on opposite south
ends of the continent
working cotton for some man.

Nobody would believe it.

Their backs
and this country collapsing
to make room
for us together.

Querida compañera

Para Papusa Molina, en respuesta

*"...fue como rencontrar una parte de mi misma que estaba
perdida, fue el reafirmar mi amor por las mujeres, por la mujer, por mi raza, mi lengua, el amor que me debo, a mí misma."*
              —una carta de mi compañera, mayo 1982

> ¿qué te puedo decir?
> in return
>
> stripped
> of the tongue
> that could claim lives
> de otras perdidas?
>
> la lengua que necesito
> para hablar
> es la misma que uso
> para acariciar
> tú sabes.
>
> you know the feel of woman
> lost en la boca
> amordazada
>
> it has always been like this
> profundo y sencillo
> lo que nunca pasó por sus labios

but was
utterly
utterly
heard.

THE LAST GENERATION

1985–1992

The Last Generation

Prose & Poetry
by Cherríe Moraga

Cover of *The Last Generation*, published in 1993 by South
End Press. Cover art, *Mis Madres*, copyright © 1986
by Estér Hernández

Debe haber otro modo . . .
Otro modo de ser humano y libre
Otro modo de ser.

—Rosario Castellanos

To honor the legacies
of Audre Lorde
and César Chávez.

And for the yet unborn.

Prophecy of a People

Introduction, 1992

> *"Pray for others."*
> *This is what the elders taught her.*
> *"Praying for yourself is only one prayer."*

The Last Generation is written as a prayer at a time when I no longer remember how to pray. I complete this collection of writings in 1992, five hundred years after the arrival of Cristóbal Colón. Its publication reflects a minor Mexican moment in an otherwise indifferent world literary history. Colón's accidental arrival to these lands, on the other hand, was an event of catastrophic consequence to the world, literary and otherwise. Still, in my mind, the two events are somehow intimately connected—the violent collision between the European and the Indigenous, the birth of a colonization that would give birth to us as Raza, and to this writer and writing.

In 1524, just three years after the Spanish conquest of the Aztec Empire, the Náhuatl sages, the tlamatinime, testified before the missionary friars in defense of their religion. "Our gods are already dead," they stated. "Let us perish now." Their Mesoamerican codices lay smoldering in heaps of ash.

I write with the same knowledge, the same sadness, recognizing the full impact of the colonial "experiment" on the lives of Chicanos, mestizos, and Native Americans. Our codices—dead leaves unwritten—lie smoldering in the ashes of disregard, censure, and erasure. *The Last Generation* emerges from those ashes. I write it against time, out of a sense of urgency that Chicanos are a disappearing tribe, out of a sense of this disappearance in my own familia.

At my fortieth birthday party, my tíos and tías sit talking around the dinner table. Most are in their late seventies now, and I notice their whitening hair and frail bodies, their untiring dignity. I relish the sound of their elegant and common Spanish, the subtlety of their humor and the vividness of their recovered memories, their cuentos. Watching them, I know lo mexicano will die with their passing. My tíos' children have not taught their own children to be Mexicans. They have become "Americans." And we are all supposed to quietly accept this passing, this slow and painless death of a cultura, this invisible disappearance of a people. But I do not accept it, I write. I write as I always have, but now I write for a much larger familia.

The poems here span a period of about seven years, beginning with my return to Aztlán (California) in 1985 from a five-year self-imposed exile in the Northeast. The essays are all more recent, written within the first three years of the last decade of the twentieth century, beginning with the loss of the Sandinista election in early 1990 and ending with the quincentenary in 1992. After a long period of silence, I had imagined I had given up the essay as genre, until the political urgency of the times—the Gulf War, the collapse of the Soviet Union, Indigenous peoples' international campaigns for sovereignty, the hundreds of thousands of deaths of gay people, women, and people of color from AIDS and breast cancer, the United States' complicity in the civil conflicts in El Salvador and Guatemala, the 1992 Los Angeles Uprising, and the blatant refusal by the United States to commit to environmental protection at the Earth Summit in Brazil—called me to respond.

History is advancing at an unprecedented speed. A writer-friend tells me, "Everything we write nowadays is outdated before we've finished." I have to agree. Still, history is always stumbling, always limping a few steps behind prophecy. And it is prophecy that drives this writing—not my personal prophecy, but the prophecy of a people.

The date is October 17, 1989. I am returning home from work, traveling across the San Francisco–Oakland Bay Bridge. The Union Oil 76 sign reads 4:53 p.m. My eyes scan the city skyline, ever amazed (shocked) by its growing enormity, and then I think, in seconds, the whole thing could go. I don't know why I think this, but eleven minutes later, pulling into my neighborhood block, a 6.9 earthquake shakes the Bay Area.

It's all just a sign of the times and every writer is a prophet if she only opens her heart and listens. The journey of this writing is as much a journey into the past as it is into the future, a resurrection of the ancient in order to construct the modern. It is that place where prophecy and past meet and speak to each other. Although I cannot pretend their wisdom, I see my task as that of the ancient Mesoamerican scribes: to speak to these cataclysmic times, to expose the "dream world" of individualism, profit, and consumerism. Truth must be expressed in "Flower and Song" (Flor y Canto—in Xochitl, in Cuicatl), in metaphor, the sages professed. So, these are not essays as much as they are poems and these are not poems as much as they are essays. Possibly the distinction no longer matters. As Audre Lorde writes, "Poetry is not a luxury. It is a vital necessity of our existence."[1]

This picture book I write is a drawing made of words—sometimes elegant, most times raw, always in earnest. The stories have a lot to do with Chicano culture and Indian people and homosexuals and half-breeds and women loving and hating women. They are a queer mixture of glyphs, these writings, but they shape the world I know at the near-turn of this century.

December 1992
San Francisco, CA

The Last Generation

I am the space occupying the middle of the sofa.

The sofa in the same front room that was off limits to us as children. They, this family of cousins, had a den. Children belonged in the den. (Was the "den" an invention of the fifties?) Front rooms were just that: rooms in the front, never altered by human contact, except on Christmas Eve when half of the expansive room was filled with a tree, the tip of which always had to be sawed off by my Tío Manuel, the father of the family. The one with the wide belly and the rough hands of a man, a worker, a man who worked with his hands.

We, on the other hand, were not a family like this family because we did not have a father like that father nor a den. We had a father with soft pink hands and a front room that was used every day of the week by everyone in the family. A front room separated from the dining room by an ironing board and two huge sacks of laundry, one of which I remember always contained neatly rolled little burritos of sweet-smelling wet starched cotton. And there was, of course, the TV in its ever-popular pivotal position—all the furniture, whether peopled or not, posed expectantly in view of the tube.

"You should be an engineer" my mother would boast. I was the only one in the family who had the required sensitivity and know-how to maintain that perfect balance between channel dial and clothes-hanger antenna, creating a picture with snow kept at a one-inch maximum level. I was also told I should be a chiropractor or a lawyer. The first, when I would straddle my mother's thin hips and press her back to the floor, her wailing in relief. The second, when I began to exhibit the first glimmerings of political consciousness and my protests sent most of the family, with the exception of my ever-faithful big sister, away from the table with indigestion. Vietnam atrocities splattered like red chile over the nopalitos.

But what I really wanted to be was a musician. That was the only other time kids were allowed in my tíos' front room. Piano lessons. Once a week, a stranger in a dark suit who was rumored to have the breath of an old goat came to give my cousins lessons. I couldn't vouch for the breath because the closest I got to him was about ten feet away, when I squeezed myself between the wall and the back of the sofa to get firsthand for free what my cousins were paying for.

Bad breath or not, how I envied those small hands sheltered by the hot weight of the man's as he stretched and coaxed and begged a response from my cousins. But their hands were as dead as lead and mine were itching to fly and sing and dance across that keyboard. So after a few months, my tía said it was like throwing money down the toilet, and the piano stood silent again. Silent and grand. Its lid, a mouth stretched wide wide open ready to sing or moan or howl in rage, but today . . .

This Christmas it appears more bored than anything else, tired of this life and this family. A great black yawn in the corner whose purpose in life has been reduced to providing an extra seat for company on Christmas. A new generation of cousins, legs dangling in even descending patterns from its bench: black patent leather, Adidas tennis shoes, white baby high-tops. A sea of Christmas wrapping beneath them.

And I am the space occupying the middle of the sofa.

I never became a musician or a lawyer or a chiropractor for that matter. Neither did my cousins. They made babies. And I wonder for a moment about creativity. They created babies. But when? When was the act of creation? At conception? At the moment of impregnation? During the hours spent in labor waiting for the new life to expel itself? Or is it the daily toil that makes up the creation? Then creativity is the hours spent wiping dirty nalgas, washing and folding laundry, cleaning mocos off forever running noses, changing wet bedding.

I am the space occupying the middle of the sofa.

Since I have no children I am worse than an inept musician. My hands have been so busy touching things, getting themselves on as much as fast as they could, that I have nothing to show for my life. No babies. No little feet dangling from the piano bench with just my curl of baby toe, like my father's.

I am disappearing into this couch. I envy them, my cousins—the men—their trim morena wives: patient, pregnant, steadily middle-class, and climbing; to what? Their almond-eyed children who will never hear from their parents' mouths the meaning/memory of that chata face, that high rooster'd chest. But my tío remembers, and tells me, the sponge, the childless timeless one, everything.

Cornering me in the hallway:

"We were the Indians that built the San Gabriel Mission."

"I thought you were all dead," I say, egging him on.

"It was all our land," he continues. "This entire valley. We owned from here to . . ."

He draws a wide swath of Tongva* territory with the broad back of his truck driver hand.

"All the way up into those mountains."

I barely reach his belly (that's the kind of Indian I am) and I bend my neck way back to take in the whole breadth of him and his pride compressed into the three minutes we share in the hallway waiting for the bathroom.

"Where did Ceci go?" I hear my sister call from the kitchen. I am now in the den where most of the viejos are, including my orphan father. The one who stole the Mission from the Spanish (and from the Indians enslaved by the Spanish) without a dime to show for it.

Rebecca is doing a little dance. She is my father's granddaughter. There is no sign of her grandmother, la mexicana, having entered the picture. The grandchildren, they're the ones who turn up with the grandfather's eyes, a pale blue in a flurry of light lashes. Rebecca has wrapped herself in her mother's red wool scarf and is performing a two-and-a-half-year-old version of Jingle Bells for her tamales-fed, sleepy-from-too-much-kids-and-beer captive audience. My dad lays a heavy arm around my shoulder. "She sure is somethin'. Isn't she, daughter?"

"Yeah, Dad. She sure is."

"Clap!" my niece commands. "Clap!" And we all comply, me and this brood of spouses the women in my family have taken on. All good men. Quiet men. They accept my presence among them because I am without a man but old enough to have known a few.

And I feel just like the piano in the next room, a great big yawn in the middle of the sofa.

---

* More commonly known as "Gabrieleños" at the time of this first writing, the Tongva people were not recognized as the aboriginal nation of the Los Angeles basin by the state of California until 1994.

My family is beginning to feel its disintegration. Our Mexican grandmother of ninety-six years has been dead two years now and la familia's beginning to go. Ignoring this, it increases in number. I am the only one who doesn't ignore this because I am the only one not contributing to the population.

My line of family stops with me. There will be no one calling me Mami, Mamá, Abuelita . . .

I am the last generation put on this planet to remember and record.

No one ever said to me, you should be a writer someday. But I went ahead and did it anyway.

Like most things, I went ahead and did it.

THE ECOLOGY OF WOMEN

En Route para Los Angeles

For Vienna

i.
After a while it comes down to a question
of life choices not a choice between you/or her
this sea town/or that bruising city
but about putting one foot in front of the other
and ending up somewhere
that looks like home.

Salinas is not home,
although the name is right
and the slow curve of road 'round the fence
where farmworker buses are kept imprisoned overnight
outhouses trailing
stinking after them.

I am always en route *through* that town,
but managed five years en Nueva York
where the name doesn't sound right
even spanglicized
it's cold yanqui blue bruised.

Your body couldn't be the land
only made me want it more
'cause indoors everything could be México
if I closed my eyes and imagined
the hot breath beneath the blankets in winter
rivers of apartment sweat in summer

was that country I had abandoned
with my womanhood awakened.

ii.
On the grapevine of the interstate
I first turned my back on my los angeles
my head to a future missed america/
mexican legacy.

Now I return
nodding off a greyhound
dreaming of you and the trail
of small deaths behind me.

Are you a dreamer, too?

It is a kind of dying, this parting
one we imagine freely chosen
in the way one chooses a wife
how far apart
to   space
the   children.

iii.
Nightly before I left you
I dreamed of dying
not my own, but others loved
and abandoned.

Figured it the woman I beat dust tracks to find,
figured that lover covered in wounds
was calling me in my sleep.

But it was you
running through my cupped palms
as I brought you to my lips
you I mourned
with the gone you never get
a chance
to say good bye.

I thought somebody somewhere
wants me to get wind of this
que el camino real is full
of these rude awakenings
unto death.

Girls Together

For Vienna (again)

It was a poem that curled the girls'
knuckles 'round chain-link
white bone splitting
through clenched brown fists. It was
a poem

that held the two women in the grip
of a rhetoric they found
both their grown mouths shaping
voices thin
as november air.

"I thought you had my back!"
It was a poem

that enveloped
their tiny brooklyn-blocked world
made love to their innocence
and fresh sharp-stabbed
sense of betrayal.

"They was girls together"*
trying to do the impossible—
love.

---

* Toni Morrison's *Sula.*

It was a poem
that forgave them
their failure.

The Ecology of Woman

Why hold a grudge against a place, a country?
—Ana Castillo, *The Mixquiahuala Letters*

1. MEXICO CITY, 1985

The room is huge. Three double beds. Slow season in la capital.
Rain.

Once friends filled the room momentarily. Not exactly friends, but
faces she recognized, faces that spoke a language whose signs she'd
learned to interpret through years of northern city dwelling. Each a
sponge holding in her liquid balm. One with a weight familiar to her
weight she let fall fully down on top of her and slept a deep night's
dream under such a cobija.

Una cobija. Por favor, necesito más cobijas.

She looked up the word in advance to get the right thing, the singu-
larly exact thing she needed, *más cobijas. Estoy enferma tengo calen-
tura y un frío ... Señora, por favor, ¿me trae más cobijas?*

The hotel maid con la cara de su Tía Pancha brings the girl a thin
blanket from the hall closet, a serape frayed all around its edges. She

crawls under, drawing it up to her chin along with three bedspreads, stripped naked from their springs in the damp of the evening.

So ashamed to be ill before Doña Pancha, Pancha is not her mother, but pities the young woman *pobrecita niña viajando sola* through the same eyes that see the girl's skin a stone grey-white like the sheets she's washed of too many souls wrestling with the pesadillas of the loveless.

But Cecilia has gone this far to keep her illness to herself, to be away from the mother. This far to a country where there are no longer living relations, only dead relics of a past she imagines to bring her succor. *Socorro.* Virgins of miniature dimension who weep real tears for daughters wedded to la miseria of the hungry mouths between their legs.

. . . . .

Days later. Midnight window moon. Cecilia shuns the mirror of all those she has ever seen naked. She won't think of them here. She blows out the shape of each one's name on the face of the glass and their reflection clouds as the smog of the city settles into a frozen stillness overnight.

Still México does offer a mirror of sorts—the amusement park version. Her flesh distorted into proportions impossible to inhabit: güera/norteamericana/pocha/gringa/turista/hembra/sola/hembra/huérfana/hembrahembrahembra

2. Zihuatanejo
I let him touch my nipple I don't know why I let him sit by me on that beach and gently stroke my right nipple back and forth back and forth

with no clear purpose except he wanted to make love and as I hadn't in
ten years with a man and I was lonely to put something solid between my
legs I let him stroke my nipple back and forth back and forth hardening...

—Halo. Te vi ayer. Siempre he tenido, no sé por qué, desde que
era niño . . . una atracción por las mujeres vellosas—for this was
foreplay, after all, though it would be hours before he'd disappoint
her with his body.

When it is over, the boy will walk her to a corner to catch a cab.
—Nos vemos mañana en la playa—he says and she slams the
door against the prospect, already knowing morning will find her
bags packed, leaving the shape of that boy, she would like to have
reduced her own incongruous body into its neat contour of high
breastbone, that flat belly, lean hips, tucked snugly into bathing suit,
she covertly coveting his secret.

But there is no secret. With soundless drop, all is revealed, no sub-
tlety of suggestion. No wonder. Except his.
—¿Es que 'stas casada?
—No.
—¿Tienes novio?
—No.
—¿Vives con alguien?
—No. No. No.
—Bueno. Es que te gustan las mujeres. Dicen que a las mujeres muy
vellosas les gustan las mujeres.

And she remembers where she is. México. After the revolution.

For a moment she sees herself as he sees the body that refuses the
staid line, the circle of independent unruly strands stroking each

nipple, the eruption of coarse dark wires at the swell of her belly, the soft fur that coats her legs from thigh to ankle glistening gold from so much sol y brisa salada.

Sí, soy una mujer velluda.
Sí, soy.
Y sí, a mí me gustan las mujeres.

That night she heads back to her hotel, walking the beach alone. Men with rifles and uniforms sit on rocks contemplando el mar and the decent job they got. It was worth the trek over las sierras where primos pick at the dirt for a root. Here they guard turistas from unwanted guests like the boy whose scent she still carries.

I am a woman walking the beach solita.

She suspects they know where she's been. They decide her fate: *otra gringa who will give it up pa' nada.* They exchange glances, the soldier and she exchange words, a few. She is lonely and longs for the good conversation of a woman.

> *He has a gun he really has a gun*
> *not just in his pants*
> *but strapped over his shoulder.*

She walks on holding her back stiff against the barrel placed there.

Although she showered with the boy, she does so again, stretching across cool hotel sheets. The fan overhead lapping gusts of tepid air, sponging water from her flesh. She is oddly satiated, though he never gave her the satisfaction of having to do nothing but throw back her hands and scream out her own pleasure.

No, she was different.

The touch of her hand too confident in its fingered hold of ribcage, its square grasp of thigh and buckling buttocks. These were the hands of a woman who took charge, so he rolled onto his back and she rode him as she did all those lazy cowboys of her past.

After removing the evidence of the boy, she allows the ease of the company of women to enter her dream of the child she'll have. It is a girl, a daughter to be sure. She imagines the tender flesh-seed growing inside her. The one who will call her mami and forgive her the calling of her own mother's name for the last time.

3. México Returned

When the blood dyes
the sheets red in the bed
of an orphaned Mexico City
she feels no loss.

It was a dream awakened.

For three days, she gives birth
to her own motherless
menses.

Just Vision

Your cosmic or third eye is a synthesis of your two eyes. Neither left nor right views, just vision.

—El Centro Campesino Cultural,
                   "Footsteps of the Creator"

I once imagined
my bones and muscles were made
of steel and rotors
and I could do it
stretch/leap/spin
throw myself
across any barrier/obstacle:
wide and turbulent seas of snapping dragons;
fiery pools of naked uplifted arms—
sinners awaiting
their salvation;
oceans stiff and still as mud,
pressed flat between
two pieces of city

just to get to the other side,
just to keep the two halves of myself
from cracking
down
wide
open
through the center of my skull.

But I have seen that mass

of brain and blood, the splitting
has already occurred.

There is a faint line of fault
driven like a stake into the spot
where once was the third eye
seeking both sides to everything
keeping each eye,
left and   right
from wandering
off too   far.

Poema como Valentín
(or a San Francisco Love Poem)

An artist friend
once showed me how to see

color as a black & white phenomenon.

Look. See that broad-faced, glistening leaf?
Look. See where it is white, a light
magnet to the sun?
Look. See where it is black?

> The eye narrows
> into a pinpoint focus
> of what was never
> really green
> only light condensing
> into darkness.

You could paint a portrait this way,
seeing from black to white.

Her mouth would still
be rose and round
but less tired of explaining
and as I pressed mine to hers
it could remember no mouth
evenly vaguely reminiscent

no mouth with this particular blend
of wet and warm in the darkest
and fullest place that sustains me
while all the world of this city weeps

beneath a blanket of intercepted
light.

Reunion

For "cousin"

In your Oakland apartment
I bring fruta
I recall the color yellow
the walls, the banana
something else . . . a flower
a deep rose yellow
and the fine-haired delicacy of kiwi

we laugh
at their tender resemblance
to testicles never to touch
our ruby lips
except sliced with strawberry
and sour green
apple

you cut with efficiency
I watch
the bowl of fruit shrink
between us
silver spoons colliding
we shovel out the remains
I faintly remember

your apology
vaguely

your reference to a past
where we parted
ways

I don't remember
words

only the drive up to your house
my old neighborhood
that black & white memory.

Dreaming of Other Planets

my vision is small
fixed
to what can be heard
between the ears

the spot
between the eyes
a wellspring opening
to el mundo grande

relámpago strikes
between the legs I open
against my will
dreaming

of other planets I am
dreaming
of other ways
of seeing

this life.

New Mexican Confession

Upon reading Whitman fifteen years later. Jemez Springs, 1988.

1.
There is great joy in the naming of things
that mean no more than what they are.
Cottonwood in winter's nakedness,
frozen black skeleton against red rock
canyon walls converging
onto this thin river of water
and human activity:

> Los Ojos Bar
> Hilltop Hotel and Café
> the grain and feed shop.

These were the words denied me in any language:

> piñón
> cañón
> arroyo

except as names on street signs,
growing up in california sprawl,
boundaries formed
by neat cement right angles.

2.
Like a poet
I have come here to look for god
but make no claim of finding—
the quest, a journey
of righteous and humble men

strangers to their bodies
cartographers to the contour of foreign flesh
a border between nature and its lover,
man.

I am a woman
who walks by the motherhouse
of the sisters of the precious blood
sleeping beneath the snow
and can as easily see myself there
my body sleeping beneath the silent
smell of fresh pressed linen,
the protection of closed doors
against the cold
against the foul breath 'n' beer
talk of Alaskan pipe-liners passing through

against the vibrant death this land is seeing . . .

Who do they pray for? Do they pray for this land?

The sister ventures out into the cold of noon
to play the campanas. They sound of tin,
a flat resonance as I pass
not an even twelve strikes but a sporadic
three strikes here
another two—rest—again three
and I imagine she calls me as I always feared
to join her in her single bed
of aching abstinence.

I am the nun
as I am the Giusewa woman
across the road
who 300 years ago
with mud and straw and hands
as delicate as her descendant's
now scribbling on dead leaves,
walled up the Spanish religion
built templos to enclose his god
while the outer cañón enveloped
and pitied them all.

3.
My sin has always been to believe
myself man, to sing a song
of *my*self that inhabited everyone.

I fall to sleep contemplating the body of the poet
Whitman at my age, 100 years ago
and see his body knew the same fragility,
the desire to dissolve the parameters of flesh
and bone and blend with the mountain
the blade of grass
the boy.

I *bleed* with the mountain
the blade of grass
the boy
because my body suffers in its womb.

The maternal blood that courses this frozen ground
was not spilt in violence, but in mourning.

I am everyman more than man.
This is my sin—

this knowledge.

WAR CRY

War Cry

lo que quiero es tierra
si no tierra, pueblo
si no pueblo, amante
si no amante, niño
si no niño
soledad
tranquilidad
muerte

tierra.

Ni para El Salvador

I am a woman nearing forty without children.
I am an artist nearing forty without community.
I am a lesbian nearing forty without partner.
I am a Chicana nearing forty without country.

And if it were safe, I'd spread open my thighs
and let the whole world in
and birth and birth and birth life.
The dissolution of self/the dissolution of borders.

But it is not safe.
Not for me
Ni para El Salvador.

So we resist and in resistance, hope is born.
An art conceived in hope.

Dreams die, crash and die.
I have known the death of a love that I had once believed
would ferment a revolution. I still seek that love, that
woman writer in me who is worth her salt, who is relentlessly hopeful, who can create a theater, a poetry, a song
that dares to expose that very human weakness where we
betray ourselves, our loved ones, even our own revolution.

We Have Read a Lot
and Know We Are Not Safe

                                            Oakland, 1987

A black and white film is our love-making
foreign
very serious
subtitled.

I can barely discern your face
between the venetian blind slats of evening streetlamp
shafts of particled air piercing this womb
of bed and nightstand
half-drunk cups of coffee magazines
books curled into the shape of palms.

You fold back your page of print,
tuck the sheet around my thighs
"But this is not Nicaragua," you tell me.
Still, it is some other place
where we've learned to fear
for our lives.

                    . . . . .

In this dark movie
where we find ourselves touching
the thin shield of my flesh hardens
against the tumult, quiet revolution
you pronounce in language
coded for my comprehension—

"You are not so different from anyone else,"
and I don't understand your meaning
and I do

y me ofreces el pecho
to give the mother pleasure
to give the daughter courage
and I know we are children y ancianas at once
and this is not a game we play with each other.

We are here to help the other change and survive
amid the gunshot blasts outside our iron-barred window.

Tonight there is no peace in each other's arms,
sometimes there is but tonight . . .
tonight we make love against the darkness
a delicate-fingered ritual of discovery—

Can I stir her back to life
with so much death surrounding us?

La Despedida

> In pilgrimage to El Santuario de Chimayó,
> Nuevo México

El Santuario de Chimayó is a shrine dedicated to "El Señor de Esquipulas," a large dark figure of the crucified Christ, whose Indigenous origins can be traced to the same santo in Guatemala. Peregrinos visit the shrine daily with supplications. In the back of the church is a candlelit womb-shaped chamber with an earthen hole in the floor at its center. From there supplicants dig out a rich red earth that is said to contain great curative powers.

i. Chimayó

I am not a believer
only a seeker
of the spirit as manifested in acts
of MAN,

Cynical of all that is not holy
grasped between bleeding palms
burning crosses
tortured tongues of muted fire.

I enter, peregrina
this stone circle of heat,
the Angel of Death, my companion
not in search of the divine
but of the word made flesh—
retablos that testify to el milagro

of familial devotion:
"Querido Señor, bring mi hijo home safe."
Vietnam remembered.
Cancerous tumors dissolved.
Broken hearts healed.
The last, my own pitiful wish.

And its earth mouth opens to us all.

Soy la santa
five feet of human
dimension and heart.
I birth electric
from the flames de los fieles.
Their burnt ofrendas singe
my cracked desert lips.
Agua Sagrada
lágrimas stain
my ashen cheeks.

I remember Guatemala and therefore, I weep.

ii. Cochiti* Mesa

Peregrina, I enter her forest,
leaves pressing underfoot.
I am riveted by the sight,
this Angel of Death
before me.

---

* The pueblo Cochiti (K'úutiim'é) are descendants of the Anasazi of Nuevo
México.

Mirrored in her huge deer eyes
I have neither vagina nor pigment politicized.
She frightens me in her immense
animalness, such brutal naked strength
outside the law of men.

The forest floor supports us
heaves and sighs beneath our broken
weight.

Tierra bendita
ruega por nosotras
ruega por nosotras
ruega
            por nosotras.

The dust of her hoof and flight powdering mine,
she is gone.

iii. Oakland, Califas

Under your raised arm
I return
to sleep animal cheek against animal breast,
y los angelitos do not sleep with us, protecting
the Angel of Death, my nightly companion.

Angelita, remember
that woman you sought
that essence that you claimed—
"mi Cecilia, deer-runner girl"

ya no existe.

True, I once rolled my head
toward the sweet music
your calling my name
ce-ci-i-i-i-l-ya
three syllables, one chord of meaning
spoken with the confidence
that the bearer would indeed turn her face to you
her wondrous moon-like
face she would turn the miracle of her mouth
to you and all that you had ever wanted
would be mirrored in the ageless
animal eyes, pero
¡Y-A-A-A-A N-O-O-O-O!

In some Native tongues the word for lonely
is not knowing who you are.
You no longer call my name
and I am no longer
you whom you sought to know.

I remember and therefore I weep.

Proposition

It is very simple
between us
woman to woman
you must leave to return
again in another form
not woman

so we
without fear
of the fathers
can make a country of our bed.

Art in América con Acento[1]

March 7, 1990

I write this on the one-week anniversary of the death of the Nicaraguan Revolution.[2]

We are told not to think of it as a death, but I am in mourning. It is an unmistakable feeling. A week ago, the name "Daniel" had poured from nicaragüense lips with a warm liquid familiarity. In private, doubts gripped their bellies and those doubts they took finally to the ballot box—doubts seeded by bullets and bread: the US-financed Contra War and the economic embargo. Once again, a sovereign nation is brought to its knees. A nation on the brink of declaring to the entire world that revolution is the people's choice betrays its own dead. US imperialism makes traitors of us all, makes us weak and tired and hungry.

I don't blame the people of Nicaragua. I blame the US government. I blame my complicity as a citizen in a country that, short of an invasion, stole the Nicaraguan revolution that el pueblo forged with their own blood and bones. After hearing the outcome of the elections, I wanted to flee the United States in shame and despair.

I am Latina, born and raised in the United States. I am a writer. What is my responsibility in this?

Days later, George H. W. Bush comes to San Francisco. He arrives at the St. Francis Hotel for a $1,000-a-plate fundraising dinner for Republican Pete Wilson's gubernatorial campaign. There is a protest. My camarada and I get off the subway. I can already hear the voices chanting from a distance. From a distance, I can't make out what they're saying, but they are Latinos and my heart races, seeing so many brown faces. They hold up a banner. The words are still unclear but as I come closer closer and closer to the circle of my people, I am stunned. "¡Viva la paz en Nicaragua!" it states. "¡Viva George Bush! ¡Viva UNO!" And my heart drops. Across the street, the "resistance" has congregated—less organized, white, young, middle-class students.

¿Dónde está mi pueblo?

A few months earlier, I was in another country, San Cristóbal, Chiapas, México. The United States had just invaded Panamá. This time, I could stand outside the United States, read the Mexican newspapers for a perspective on the United States that was not monolithic.

In the Na Bolom Center Library I wait for a tour of the grounds. The room is filled with norteamericanos. They are huge people, the men slouching in couches. Their thick legs spread across the floor; their women lean into them. They converse. "When we invaded Panama . . ." I grow rigid at the sound of the word "we." They are progressives (I know this from their conversation). They oppose the invasion, but identify with the invaders.

How can I, as a Latina, identify with those who invade Latin American land? George Bush is not my leader. I did not elect him, although my tax dollars pay for the Salvadoran Army's guns.[3] We are a living breathing contradiction, we who live en las entrañas del monstruo, but I refuse to be forced to identify. I am the product of invasion. My father is Anglo; my mother, Mexican. I am the result of the dissolution of bloodlines and the theft of language; and yet, I am a testimony to the failure of the United States to wholly anglicize its mestizo citizens.

I wrote in México, "Los Estados Unidos es mi país, pero no es mi patria." I cannot flee the United States, my land resides beneath its borders. We stand on land that was once the country of México. And before any conquistadors staked out political boundaries, this was Indian land and in the deepest sense remains just that: a land sin fronteras. Chicanos who carry the memory of our Native counterparts recognize that we are a nation within a nation. An internal nation whose existence defies borders of language, geography, race, who since 1848 have been displaced from our ancestral lands or remain upon them as indentured servants to AngloAmerican invaders.

Today, nearly a century and a half later, the Anglo invasion of Latin America has extended well beyond the Mexican/American border. When US capital invades a country, its military machinery is quick to follow to protect its economic interests. This is Panamá, Puerto Rico, Grenada, Guatemala, and onward. Ironically, the United States' gradual consumption of Latin America and the Caribbean is bringing the people of the Americas together. What was once largely a Chicano/mexicano population in California is now guatemalteco, salvadoreño, nicaragüense. What was largely a Puerto Rican and Dominican "Spanish Harlem" of New York is now populated with mexicanos playing rancheras and drinking cerveza on their one Sunday off. Every place the United States has been historically involved militarily has brought its offspring, its orphans, its homeless, and its workers to this country—Vietnam, Cambodia, the Philippines.

Third World populations are changing the face of North America. By the twenty-first century our whole concept of "America" will be dramatically altered, most significantly by a growing Latino population whose strong cultural ties, economic disenfranchisement, racial visibility, and geographical proximity to Latin America discourages any facile assimilation into AngloAmerican society.

Latinos in the United States do not represent a homogenous group. Some of us are Native-born whose ancestors precede not only the arrival of the AngloAmerican but also of the Spaniard. Most of us are immigrants, economic refugees coming to the United States in search of work. Some of us are political refugees, fleeing death squads and imprisonment; others come fleeing revolution and the loss of wealth. Finally, some have simply landed here very tired of war. And in all cases, our children had no choice in the matter.

US Latinos represent the whole spectrum of color and class and political position, including those who firmly believe they can integrate into the mainstream of North American life. The more European the heritage and the higher the class status, the more closely Latinos identify with the powers that be. They often vote Republican. They stand under the US flag and applaud George Bush for bringing "peace" to Nicaragua. They hope one day he'll do the same for Cuba, so they can return to their patria and live a North American–style consumer life. Because they know that in the United States, they will never have it all. They will always remain, to some degree, "other."

As a Latina artist I can choose to contribute to the development of a docile generation of would-be Republican "Hispanics" loyal to the United States, or to the creation of a force of disloyal americanos who subscribe to a multicultural, multilingual, radical restructuring of América. Revolution is not only won by numbers, but by visionaries, and if artists aren't visionaries, then we have no business doing what we do.

I call myself a Chicana writer. Not a Mexican-American writer, not a Hispanic writer, not a half-breed writer. To be a Chicana is not merely to name one's racial/cultural identity, but also to name a politic, a politic that refuses assimilation into the US mainstream. It acknowledges our mestizaje—Indian, Spanish, and African.

After a decade of "hispanicization" (a term superimposed upon us by Reagan-era bureaucrats), the term Chicano assumes even greater radicalism. With the misnomer "Hispanic," AngloAmerica proffers to the Spanish surnamed the illusion of blending into the "melting pot" like any other white immigrant group. But the Latino is neither wholly immigrant nor wholly white; and here in this country, brown don't melt. (Puerto Ricans on the East Coast have been called "Spanish" for decades and it's done little to alter their status on the streets of New York City.)

The generation of Chicano literature being read today emerged from a grassroots social and political movement of the sixties and seventies that was definitively anti-assimilationist. It responded to a stated mandate: art is political. The proliferation of poesía, cuentos, and teatro that grew from El Movimiento was supported by Chicano cultural centers and publishing projects throughout the Southwest and every major urban area where a substantial Chicano population resided. The Flor y Canto poetry festivals of the seventies and the literally grassroots teatro that spilled off flatbed trucks into lettuce fields in the sixties are hallmarks in the history of the Chicano cultural movement. Chicano literature was a literature in dialogue with its community. And as some of us became involved in feminist, gay, and lesbian concerns in the late seventies and early eighties, our literature required further expansion to reflect the multi-issued and complex nature of the Chicano experience.

The majority of published Chicano writers today are products of that era of activism, but as El Movimiento grew older and more established, it became neutralized by middle-aged and middle-class concerns, as well as by a growing conservative trend in government. Most of the gains made for farmworkers in California were dismantled by a succession of reactionary governors and Reagan/Bush economics. Cultural centers lost funding. Many small press Chicano publishers disappeared as suddenly as they had appeared. What was once a radical and working-class Latino student base on university campuses has become increasingly conservative.

A writer will write. With or without a movement.

Fundamentally, I started writing to save my life. Yes, my own life first. I see the same impulse in my students—the dark, the queer, the mixed-blood, the violated—turning to the written page with an insistent passion, a drive to avenge their own silence, invisibility, and erasure as living, innately expressive human beings.

A writer will write with or without a movement; but at the same time, for Chicano, lesbian, gay, and feminist writers—anybody writing against the grain of Anglo misogynist culture—political movements are what have allowed our writing to surface from the secret places in our notebooks into the public sphere.

In 1990, el pueblo chicano—with artists and writers as emissaries—is not much better off than we were in 1970. We have an ever-expanding list of physical and social diseases affecting us: AIDS, breast cancer, police brutality. Censorship is becoming increasingly institutionalized, not only through government programs, but through transnational corporate ownership of publishing houses, record companies, etc. Without a movement to foster and sustain our writing, we risk being swallowed up into the "Decade of the Hispanic" that never happened. The fact that a few of us may be doing better than we imagined has not altered the nature of the beast. He remains blue-eyed and male and prefers profit over people.

Like most artists, we Chicano artists would like our work to be seen as universal in scope and meaning and to reach as large an audience as possible. Ironically, the writing capable of reaching the hearts of the greatest number of people is the most culturally specific because in that specificity, a human story is told. The European-American writer understands this because it is *his* version of cultural specificity that is deemed universal by the literary establishment. In the same manner, universality in the Chicana writer requires the most Mexican and female sensibility we can conjure. Our task is to write what no one is prepared to hear, for what has been written of us thus far in barely a decade of consistent production is a mere bocadito. Raza writers, who for the most part are first-generation college educated, are still learning the art of transcription, but what we will be capable of producing in the decades to come, if we have the cultural/political movements to support us, could make a profound contribution to the social transformation of these Américas. The challenge, however, is to remain as culturally specific and culturally complex as possible, even in the face of mainstream seduction to do otherwise.

Let's not fool ourselves, the European-American middle-class writer is the cultural mirror through which the literary and theater establishment sees itself reflected, so it will continue to reproduce itself through new generations of writers. On occasion New York publishes our work, as it perceives a growing market for the material, allowing Chicanos access to national distribution on a scale that small independent presses could never accomplish. (Every writer longs for such distribution, particularly since it more effectively reaches communities of color.) But I fear that my generation and the generation of young writers that follows will look solely to the Northeast for recognition. I fear that we may become accustomed to this very distorted reflection, and that we will find ourselves writing more and more in translation through the filter of AngloAmerican censors.

I would like to believe that in the richest and most inspired junctures of Chicano works, our writer-souls might turn away from the Northeast of American letters and toward the Southwest of a México Antiguo. That is not to say that contemporary Chicano literature does not wrestle with current social concerns, but without the memory of our once-freedom, how do we imagine a future?

I still believe in a Chicano literature that is hungry for change; that has the courage to name the sources of our discontent both from within our raza and without; that challenges us to envision a world where poverty, crack, and pesticide poisoning are not endemic to people with dark skin or Spanish surnames. It is a literature that knows that god is neither white nor male nor reason to rape anyone. It is an art of "resistance," resistance to domination by AngloAmerica, resistance to assimilation, resistance to economic and sexual exploitation. An art that subscribes to integration into Mainstream-America is not Chicano art.

All writing is confession. Confession that breathes its release in the space between a stanza or reveals itself behind the transparent mask of a character. True and necessary works admit our vulnerabilities, our weakness, our tenderness of skin and fragility of heart; our overwhelming desire to be relieved of the burden of ourselves in the body of another, to be forgiven of our aloneness in communion with a mystical god or in the common work of a revolution. These are human considerations that the best of writers presses her finger upon. The wound ruptures and heals.

One of the deepest wounds Chicanos suffer is separation from our Southern relatives. Gloria Anzaldúa calls it a "1,950-mile-long open wound,"[4] dividing México from the United States, "dividing a pueblo, a culture." This "llaga" ruptures over and over again in our writing—Chicanos in search of a México that never wholly embraces us.

"Mexico gags," poet Lorna Dee Cervantes writes, "on this bland pocha seed."[5] This separation was never our choice. In 1990, we witness a fractured and disintegrating América, where the Northern half functions as the absentee landlord of the Southern half and the economic disparity between the First and Third Worlds drives a bitter wedge between a people.

I hold a vision requiring a radical transformation of consciousness in this country, that as the people-of-color population increases, we will not be just another brown faceless mass hungrily awaiting integration into White-America, but that we will emerge as a mass movement of people to redefine what "America" is. Our entire concept of this nation's identity must change, possibly be obliterated.

We must learn to see ourselves less as US citizens and more as members of a larger world community composed of many nations of people and no longer give credence to the geopolitical borders that have divided us, Chicano from mexicano, Filipino American from Pacific Islander, African American from Haitian, Native America from its southern relations. Call it racial memory. Call it shared economic discrimination. Chicanos call it "Raza." Be it quechua, cubano, or colombiano, it is an identity that dissolves borders. As a Chicana writer that's the context in which I want to create.

I am an Américan writer in the original sense of the word—of an América con acento.

LA FUERZA FEMENINA

Credo

En frente del altar de mi madre
burning beads de lágrimas cling to the frozen face of glass,
flame quaking in the wake of the meeting of mothers.

Tenemos el mismo problema,
the one says to the other
sin saber the meaning.

Each, their youngest daughter
a heretic
a nonbeliever.

But when you raised the burning
bush of cedar
our faces twin moons in the black night
I believed and dreamed
my body stripped naked
like the virgin daughter splayed
upon your altar.

Not that you, my priestess
would wrench from me
el corazón sangrante
but to feel your hand heavy
on that raised hill of flesh

my breast rising
like a pyramid
from the sacred
walls of this templo,
my body.

Blood Sisters

I remember a love once germinated outside the womb.
No blood ties that knot and strangle the heart,
but two soul sisters instantly joined
pressing wound against wound in tribal solemnity.

The first already broken open, beginning to scab.
The other, the braver—the young yielding lamb
performing the ritual with any object
capable of cutting flesh.

She:
I dig at it — esta herida vieja
remind it to bleed
this time with your name upon its lips

She:
obsidian, hermana
you, the dark mirror that splits
my breast

Love has always been a sacrificial rite,
the surrender of one's heart to a merciless mother-god
who never forgave us our fleshy mortality
our sin of skin and bone, our desire
to meld them into miracles
of something   not woman.

If

If in the long run
we weep together
hold each other
wipe the other's mouth
dry from the kiss pressed there
to seal the touch
of spirits separated
by something as necessary
as time

we will have done enough.

En busca de la fuerza femenina[1]

I have just returned from the CARA Exhibit (Chicano Art: Resistance and Affirmation, 1965–1985). I had asked Ricardo to come with me, somehow knowing he was the spirit-brother to take; the one with whom to witness our past in order to reconstruct a future. Ricardo Bracho: twenty-two years old today, Chicano poet, and gay.

And we felt such pride upon entering the gallery from the sight of the very first image: "¡VIVA LA RAZA!" it proclaimed. The "VIVA" spread across the canvas in bold black splashes, the enflamed red Chicano eagle rising. "Orgullo" was the word that kept rising up in my chest, expanding in my throat until it spilled out from my lips. "I'm so damn proud," I say. To witness a living art, an art molded out of our brown and multifarious lives.

The exhibit opened to a world of color, like the México I had just returned from days before. There was no shyness, no inhibition, no Anglo beige. Ponemos el color dondequiera—like the colors that paint the courtyard walls of San Cristóbal, like the richest colors at the hour of a Oaxacan sunset; like the light landing onto la buganvilla, onto the curve of Tarascan nose and cheekbone, onto the huipil of Zapotec women. I experienced there in the artwork the same México, its Indian territory emblazoned upon graffitied walls, pressed into the creased edges of José Montoya's "drapes," gestating in Yreina Cervántez's exposed wombs of Native mothers. And the Earth quakes, remembering . . .

I didn't know I was lonely. I had forgotten. I had forgotten I was without a country. I had forgotten I had lost a language. For a moment until I saw the word "CHICANO" in bold orange and red letters on Van Ness Avenue in downtown San Panchito, Aztlán and my territory was righteously reclaimed by my sister and brother artists.

And yet, something was missing. Artist Rupert Garcia noted the same when he said that the show did not immediately inspire him to pick up the paintbrush. It did, however, inspire me to pick up the pen. I was going to write, "the pain, to pick up the pain." That, for me, was what was missing: an honest portrait of our pain.

After resistance and affirmation, where do we go? Possibly to a place of deeper inquiry into ourselves as a people. Possibly, as we move into the next century, we must turn our eyes away from racist Amerika and take stock of the damages done us. Possibly the greatest risks yet to be taken are entre nosotros, where we write, paint, dance, and draw the wound for one another in order to build a stronger pueblo. The women artists seemed disposed to do this, their work often mediating that delicate area between cultural affirmation and criticism.

What was missing in this exhibit was the rage and fuerza of women, the recognition that the violence of racism and misogyny has distorted our view of ourselves. What was missing was a portrait of sexuality for men and women independent of motherhood and machismo: critical images of the male body as violador and also vulnerable, and of the female body as the site of woman-centered desire. There was no visible gay and lesbian response to our chicanidad that would challenge institutionalized and mindless heterosexual coupling; no breakdown and shake-up of La Familia y La Iglesia; no portrait of our isolation, of machismo as monstruo, of la Indígena erased and muted in the body of la Chicana.[2]

Sometimes when I write, I feel I am drawing from the most

silent place in myself—a place without image, word, shape, sound—
to create a portrait of la mechicana before the "fall," before shame,
before betrayal, before Eve, Malinche, and Guadalupe; before the
occupation of Aztlán, la llegada de los españoles, the Aztecs' War
of Flowers. I don't know what this woman looks like exactly, but I
know she is more than the bent back in the fields, more than the
assembly-line fingers and the rigid body beneath him in bed, more
than the veiled face above the rosary beads. She is more than the
sum of all these fragmented parts.

As Chicana artists, our efforts to imag(in)e what has never
been portrayed is a deeply spiritual quest. Like every male artist—
Chicano, Anglo, or otherwise—we women artists also look for god
in our work. We too ultimately seek the divine in the beauty we
create. Sometimes that beauty is merely a portrait of mutilation in
color or language. This is something Frida Kahlo understood. For
the road to the female god is wrought with hatred, humiliation, and
heartbreak.

How did we become so broken?

El mito azteca

*Según la leyenda, Coatlicue, "Madre de los Dioses," is sweeping on top
of the mountain, Coatepec, when she discovers two beautiful feathers.
Thinking that later she will place them on her altar, she stuffs them into
her apron and continues sweeping. But without noticing, the feathers
begin to gestate there next to her womb and Coatlicue, already advanced
in age, soon discovers that she is pregnant.*

*When her daughter, Coyolxauhqui, learns that her mother is about
to give birth to Huitzilopochtli, God of War, she is incensed. And, along
with her siblings, the Four Hundred Stars, she conspires to kill Coatlicue
rather than submit to a world where war would become God.*

*Huitzilopochtli is warned of the planned matricide by a hum-
mingbird and vows to defend his mother. At the moment of birth, he*

murders Coyolxauhqui, cutting off her head and completely dismembering her body.

> *Breast splits from chest splits*
> *from hip splits from thigh*
> *from knee from arm and foot,*
> *her parts bleeding down the face*
> *of the Serpent Mountain,*
> *Coyolxauhqui is banished to the darkness to become the moon,*
> *la diosa de la luna.*[3]

In my own art, I am writing that wound. That moment when brother is born and sister mutilated by his fear. He possesses the mother, holds her captive, because she cannot refuse any of her children, even her enemy son. Here, mother and daughter are pitted against each other and daughter must kill male-defined motherhood in order to save the culture from misogyny, war, and greed. But el hijo comes to the defense of patriarchal motherhood, kills la mujer rebelde, and female power is eclipsed by the rising light of the Sun/ Son. This machista myth is enacted every day of our lives, every day that the sun (Huitzilopochtli) rises up from the horizon and the moon (Coyolxauhqui) is obliterated by his light.

Huitzilopochtli is not my god. And although I revere his mother, Coatlicue, diosa de la muerte y la vida, I do not pray to her. I pray to the daughter, la hija rebelde. She who has been cast out, the mutilated sister who transforms herself into the moon. She is la fuerza femenina, our attempt to pick up the fragments of our dismembered womanhood and reconstitute ourselves. She is the Chicana writer's words, the Chicana painter's canvas, the Chicana dancer's step. She is motherhood reclaimed and sisterhood honored. She is the female god we seek in our work, la mechicana before the "fall."

And Huitzilopochtli raises his sword from the mouth of his mother's womb and cuts off his sister's head, tossing it into the night sky. Coyolxauhqui, moon-faced goddess, is banished into darkness; y nuestra raza enters the ever época de guerra.

Pero de vez en cuando la luna gets her revenge.

SIX MINUTES OF DARKNESS

Just a week ago, I returned from a two-month stay in México, the last day of which found me on top of a pyramid in Tepotzlán, an hour outside of Mexico City. At 1:26 p.m. the sky fell to complete darkness as the moon eclipsed the sun. "Tonatiuh cualo"—el sol fue comido por la fuerza femenina de la luna. And el conchero who led the ceremonia in full Aztec regalia de pluma y piel believed it an ominous sign, this momentary and sudden loss of light, this deep silent feminine darkness. The quieting of the pájaros; the retreat of the ground animals into their caves of night. And he prayed to the gods to return the light. And I prayed with him, brother that he is, brother who never recognizes his sister in prayer, brother who fears her power, as mother and daughter and wife and lover, as he fears the darkening of the light.

But we women were not afraid, accustomed as we are to the darkness. In public, we mouthed the shapes of his words that mourned the loss of light, and in secret we sang praise to:

She Who went unacknowledged,

She Who remains in shadow,

She Who has the power to eclipse the sun's light.

Coyolxauhqui, the moon, reduced in newspapers to the image of a seductress, flirtatious coquette, merging in coitus with the sun. Later, we women, lesbianas from all parts of América Latina, would offer sacrifice, burn copal, call out her name. We, her sisters, would pay tribute to la luna—keep the flame burning, keep destruction at bay.

In those six minutes of darkness, something was born in me. In the darkness of that womb of silence, of that female quietude, a life stirred. I understood for the first time the depth and wonder of the feminine, although I confess I have been awed by it before, as my own female face gazes upon its glory and I press my lips to that apex in the women I love.

Like the others, I welcomed the light upon its return. El canto del gallo. Probably that was the most amazing of all—el segundo amanecer. The female passed on y dió a luz a un sol nuevo. As the light took the shape of the sky again, el conchero stood on top of the pyramid mountain and announced the end of El Quinto Sol, y los quinientos años de una historia sangrienta that saw to the near-destruction of the Indigenous peoples of México. And from the ashes of destruction, a new era is born: El Sexto Sol: La epoca de la conciencia humana.

The day after the eclipse, I called my mother from San Francisco to tell her I had arrived home safely. And without planning to, when describing the eclipse I told her, "Ahora conozco a Dios, Mamá." And I knew she understood my reverence in the face of a power utterly beyond my control. She is a deeply religious woman, who calls her faith "católica." I use another name or no name at all, but she understood that humility, that surrender, before a sudden glimpsed god. Little did she know god was a woman.

I am not the churchgoer that my mother is, but the same faithfulness drives me to write: the search for Coyolxauhqui amid all the disfigured female characters and the broken men that surround them in my plays and poems. I search for a whole woman I can shape with my own Chicana tongue and hand.

A free citizen of Aztlán and the world.

La Ofrenda

UN CUENTO

Strange as it may seem, there is no other way to be sure. Completely sure. Well, you can never be completely sure but you can try and hold fast to some things. Smell is very important. Your eyes can fool you. You can see things that aren't there. But not smell. Smell remembers and tells the future. No lying about that.

Smell can make your heart crack open no matter how many locks you have wrapped 'round it. You can't see smell coming, so it takes you off guard, unaware. Like love. That's why it can be your best friend or worst enemy depending on the state of your heart at the time.

Smell is home or loneliness. Confidence or betrayal. Smell remembers.

Tiny never went with women because she decided to. She'd always just say, "I follow my nose." And she did and it got her ass nearly burned plenty of times, too, when the scent happened to take her to the wrong side of town or into the bed of the wife of someone she'd wish it hadn't in the morning.

She hated to fight. That was the other problem. She never stuck around for a fight. "The only blood I like," she'd say, "is what my hand digs out of a satisfied woman." We'd all tell Tiny to shut her arrogant mouth up and get her another drink.

Cristina Morena, who stood in front of me in the First Holy Communion line. Then, by confirmation, Tiny'd left most of us girls in the dust. Shot up and out like nobody's business. So Cristina, who everyone called Tina, turned to Tiny overnight and that's the name she took with her into "the life." Given her size, it was a better name to use than Cristina and certainly better than mine, Dolores. Dottie, they used to call me years later in some circles, but it never stuck, cuz I was the farthest thing from a freckled-faced bony-kneed gabacha. Still, for a while I tried it. Now I'm back to who I was before. Just Lolita. Stripped down. Not so different from those Holy Communion days, really.

When we were kids, teenagers, Tiny and I came this close to "doing it" with each other. This close. I don't know what would've happened if we had, but I couldn't even've dreamed of doing it then. Yeah, I loved Tiny probably more than I loved any human being on the face of the earth. I mean I loved her like the way you love familia like they could do anything—steal, cheat, lie, murder and you'd still love them because they're your blood. Sangre. Tiny was my blood. My blood sister. Maybe that's why we didn't do it back then. It'd be like doing it with your sister. Tiny was my sister like no sister I've ever had and she wanted me and I left her because she'd rather pretend she didn't and I was too stupid to *smell* out the situation for what it really was. I kept watching what was coming outta her damn mouth and there wasn't nothing there to hear. No words of love, commitment, tenderness. You know, luna de miel stuff. There was just her damn solid square body like a tank in the middle of my face with tears running down her cheeks and her knees squeezed together like they were nailed shut on that toilet, her pants like a thick rubber band wrapped down around her ankles and I ran from her as fast as my nalgas could take me.

"Fuck fuck chinga'o, man, fuck!"

"Tina . . ." I can barely hear myself.

"Tiny. The name's Tiny."

"What're you doin' in there?"

"I'm crying, you joto. That's what you want, isn't it? To see the big bad bitch cry? Well, go get your rocks off somewhere else."

"I don't have rocks."

"In your head you do, pendeja!"

But I never loved anyone like I loved Tiny. No body. Not one of those girls from the Westside that spread their legs for me and my smooth-talking. There was blood on my hands and not from reaching into those women but from Tiny's hide. From my barrio's hide. From Cha Cha's Place where you only saw my ass when the sophisticated college girls had fucked with my mind one too many times. That's something Tiny would have said. We weren't meant to be lovers, only sisters. But being a sister ain't no part-time occupation.

"Lolita Lebrón." That's what they used to call me at Cha Cha's. Of course, they didn't even know who Lolita was until I came in with the story about her with the guys and the guns taking on the whole pinche US Congress. They'd say, "Hey, Lolita, how goes the revolution?" And then they'd all start busting up and I'd take it cuz I knew they loved me, even respected what I was doing. Or maybe it was only Tiny who respected me and all the others had to treat me right cuz of her. Tiny used to say her contribution to La Causa was to keep the girlfriends of the Machos happy while they were out being too revolutionary to screw.

But it was me she wanted. And I needed my original home girl more than I needed any other human being alive to this day. Growing up is learning to go without. Tiny and me . . . we grew up too fast.

"Do you think Angie could want me?"
So there we are, too many years later, me sitting on the edge of her bed, playing with the little raised parts of the chenille bedspread while my sister there is taking off all her damn clothes, tossing them onto the bed, until she's standing bare ass naked in front of me.
    "Look at me."
    I can't look up.
    "Lola."
    I'm still playing with the balls on the bedspread.
    "Look at me. C'mon I gotta know."
    "Tiny give me a break, man, this is too cold. It's fuckin' scientific, no one looks at people this way."
    "You do."
She was right. So, I check her out. There I am staring at her with my two good eyes, the blue one and the brown one and I knew she wanted my one hundred percent true and honest opinion; that she could count on me for that since we were little, so I sat there looking at her for a long time.
    "C'mon, man, does it hafta take so long? Jus' answer me."

The blue and the brown eye were working at this one, working hard. I try to isolate each eye, see if I come up with different conclusions depending on which eye and which color I'm working with. Figure one is the European view, the other the Indian.
    Tiny goes for her pants, "Fuck you."
And then I smell her, just as she reaches over me. Her breast brush-

ing my shoulder, a warm bruised stone . . . something softening. I inhale. Grab her arm.

"No, wait. Let me look at you."

She pulls back against the dresser, holds the pants against her belly, then lets them drop. She's absolutely beautiful. Not magazine beautiful, but thirty-three years old and Mexican beautiful. The dresser with the mirror is behind her. I know that dresser. For years now, it didn't change, but Tiny . . . she did. The dresser is blonde. "Blonde furniture," very popular among mexicanos in the fifties. We are the children of the fifties. But the fifties have gone and went and in the meantime my Cristina Morena went and changed herself into a woman. And in front of this blonde dresser is brown Cristina. Cristina Morena desnuda, sin a stitch on her body and she looks like her mama and my mama with legs like tree trunks and a panza that rolls round into her ombligo como pura miel. And breasts, breasts I want to give back to her, compartirlos con ella para que nos llenen a los dos.

"Well . . . ?" she asks.

And it had never occurred to me that we had grown up. The hair below the hill of her belly is the same color as her head. A deep black. Denso. Oculto como un nido enterrado. Un hogar distante, aguardándome.

It didn't stop there. She needed me to touch her, that's all. Is that so much to ask of a person? Angie and her wouldn't last long. Tiny didn't let her touch her. She never let any of 'em touch her.

"Never?"

"Never."

"I don't get it. What do you do then?"

"I do it *to* them."

"But I mean do you . . . you know."

"Get off? Yeah. Sure."

"How?"

"Rubbing. Thinking."

"Thinking. Thinking about what?"

"Her. How she's feeling."

"You ever think about yourself?"

"No one's home."

"What?"

"I don't gotta picture, you know what I mean? There's nobody to be. No me to be. Not that way in the bed, anyway."

So, I put my hands inside her. I did. I put them all the way inside her and like a fuckin' shaman I am working magic on her, giving her someone to be.

"Fuck fuck chinga'o, man, fuck!"

"Shut up," I say.

"What?"

"Don't say shit."

"But . . ."

"Shhhhh." I press my fingers against her lips. "Don't say nothing, Tiny." Open your mouth and speak me something else.

She smells like copal between the legs. Tiny, Tina who stood in front of me in the First Holy Communion line, smells like fucking copal

sweet earth sap
oozing outta every pore
that dark bark tree
flesh kissed
I couldn't kiss her, only between the legs
where the mouth there never cussed
where the lips there never curled
into snarls, smoked cigarettes, spit
phlegm into passing pale stubbled faces

mouthing dagger
dyke
jota
mal
flor
I kissed her where she had never spoken
where she had never sang
where . . .

And then we are supposed to forget. Forget the women we discover there between the sheets, between the thighs, lies, cries. But some things you don't forget
smell.

I close my eyes and I am rubbing and thinking rubbing and thinking rubbing and remembering what this feels like, to find my body, una vega anhelosa, endless llano de deseo.

¿Dónde 'stá ella que me regaló mi cuerpo como una ofrenda a mí misma?
Ella
Lejana.
Una vez, mía.

I open my eyes, desaparecida.

I would've married Tiny myself if she would've let me. I would've, I swear to it. But I was relieved when she put on her pants and told me to get out. I was relieved because I wouldn't have to work for the rest of my life loving someone. Tiny.

But I *was* willing to stay. This time I wasn't going nowhere. I mean, where was there to go, really? The girl was family and I knew her. I knew her and still loved her, so where was there to go? You spend your whole life looking for something that's just a simple matter of saying, "Okay, so I throw my lot in with this one." This one woman y ya!

Tiny knew she wouldn't last that long.

She was already telling me in her thirties how tired she was, fighting. And then I read it, right there in the *LA Times*. All these women, lesbians who never had babies, getting cancer. They never mention Tiny's name, but Tiny was there, among the childless women, among the dead.

I thought, what's *this* shit? Women don't use their breasts like biology mandates, and their breasts betray them? Is this the lesbian castigo? AIDS for our brothers, cancer for us? Hate thinking like this, hate thinking it's all a conspiracy to make us join the fucking human race.

. . . . .

I burn copal.
Her name rising up with the smoke,
dissolving into the ash morning sky.
Her flesh softening like sap
over rock, returning liquid
to the earth. Her scent inciting
memory.

I inscribe my name, too.
Tattooed ink in the odorless flesh of this page.

I, who have only given my breast
to the hungry and grown,
the female and starved
the women.

I, who have only given my breast to the women.

THE BREAKDOWN
OF THE BICULTURAL MIND

Mestizos, children of violence,
neither slaves nor masters.

—Chilam Balam

Red

I have been at an amusement park.

On my way home, I stop to buy something at a small tiendita. There is a thin young girl working the register. It is a family store. This is her home. Other family members are nearby. She tells me the purchase costs three hundred, but I am confused. Does she mean three hundred dollars, cents, pesos? She keeps changing the amount and I keep apologizing, thinking at one point she means pesos, then realizing three hundred pesos is nothing, then realizing I am not in México, but possibly Puerto Rico where the currency is dollars. Then I see that the girl is merely trying to cheat me.

For some reason, my response is to take out paints and give the family a chance to use them. The father sits at the opposite end of the table from the son. They begin to paint. All is the color red. As the father works, his paints spill like blood all over the table. I realize now how hard it has been for the family. The man is very thin, frail, sickly. As he bleeds onto the page, the red runs. The boy manages to keep most of his drawing unstained by the father's. I see the son protecting his painting, shielding it from the father's with his forearm. His picture is very neat. There is the image of a flower. When the drawing is done, the boy has disappeared and the father retreats to the next room, but the old man is still visible and within earshot.

227

Now the older sisters are at the table. The young girl joins them. I see her painting. It is pages and pages of blood red writing. She did not draw, but wrote her story in images of words. I spy the word "testicles," and I know on some level the story has to do with the father's pain. After finishing her painting, the girl is very shaken.

I take her under my arm, bring her to the couch. I hold her and tell her, "We're going to read what you've painted out loud, so that you can get it off of you, so that you can be free of his pain." (I am conscious of speaking softly so that the father does not hear, but he is aware of our presence.) The older sisters say they must go, that they can't bear to hear the story.

I understand.

And as I press the girl next to me, I begin to read aloud . . .

Peloncito

there is a man in my life
pale-man born infant
pliable flesh
his body remains a remote
possibility

in secret it may know many things
glossy newsprint female thighs
spread eagle wings
in his flying imagination

soft shoe
he did the soft shoe
in the arch that separated the living
from dining room
miller trombone still turns his heel
and daughter barefoot and never pregnant
around and around and around

soft-tip
penis head he had
a soft-tipped penis that peeked out
by accident one kitchen cold morning
between zipper stuck and boxer shorts
fresh pressed heat lining
those tender white-meat loins

wife at the ironing board snaps:
"what're you doing, joe, what're you doing?"
he nervously stuffs the little bird back

it looked like *Peloncito*
the bald-headed little name
del pajarito de mi abuelita

Peloncito
a word of endearment
never told to the child/
father/ yellow bird-man/
boy

If a Stranger Could Be Called Family

There are men in my life.

Inconsequential, I reason.
Their histories silenced between the sheets
of frozen intercourse who lie in the morning
about who came to their bed last night
what dark stranger's drink did he taste upon his lips
he won't tell.

Unlike the wife, he has no stories
only memories glossed and nostalgic:
the loving mother
the absent, but distinguished father.

Now once
there was the glimpsed image
of a trolley car blur of San Francisco technicolor
twelve-year-old boy sitting with little sister
decently dressed depression years,
not a word outta him from Judah to Market.

"He'd never speak to me," the sister complained.
It was *her* story, she the protagonist in search
of a brother a father a man
his boy shoulders folded
into the broad leaves
of a book.

Now an old man
whose middle age I've forgotten,
he tells a few stories once in a blue
though he's never learned the Mexican art,
grandchildren fidgeting restlessly
in straight-backed chairs.

His older, more generous offspring patiently wait out
the long lapses in memory the punch line
slipping precipitously
from the crease in his mouth.
The old man, he tries.
We patronize
apologize.

But once
there was a story
not a story exactly, but a picture
he remembered the naked legs of a man
in a bathrobe
and a word he had awoken to in the morning,
"uncle"
and there would be many many "uncles"
to follow
long lines of them
faceless
behind the bolted door
of his mother's bedroom.

If a stranger could be called family, what was family worth?

Today
on visit to his hometown
San Francisco
we roll by Geary Theater.
He remembers it 1930s
mother in her silk kimono
exotic in the vestiges of her vaudeville days.
The son waxes nostalgic like an old lover
a young suitor.

"She was nothing special,"
the back-seat wife whispers
"I don't think they ever put her on the stage even."
She was nothing nothing
what little legacy we orphans
my father and I have
shattered.

I point to the small theater across the street.
It is nothing nothing special,
but there I will tell *their* stories
lies, nostalgia, and the whole ball of wax
because we all got a story
we all   each one
got a story
to tell.

I Was Not Supposed to Remember

1
the pure
unadulterated scent
of geraniums
the whiff of perfume
not grown
from a bottle 'n' mother's wrists 'n' just a dab
behind each ear
I was not supposed to remember her ears
like mine, the earlobe without lobe really
the mole that marked her
mine.

I was not supposed to remember being she
the daughter of some Indian somebody somewhere
an orphaned child somewhere
somebody's cast-off half-breed I wasn't
supposed to remember the original rape.

I wasn't supposed to remember
the timbre of my whitedaddy's
whimper, his unnamed *something*
I was never to see myself
reflected in the cold
blue steel frightened
fluttering
of his look-away eyes.

I was not intended
to marry that man.

I am a woman, childless
and I tell my stories to other
childless women and somehow
the generations propagate
and prosper
and re-member pre-memory,
re-member rose gardens
thorn-pricked thumbs
digging into well-watered
LA basin soil kissing
the edge of steaming
black-top.

How is it I remember dirt when I grew up on asphalt?
How is it dirt means so much to me?
What is there to remember in a tree?
a tree
thoroughly tree

I, thoroughly hybrid/mongrel/mexican/yaqui-oakie girl.

"Yaquioakie" holds all the world I knew as it shaped my abuela's mouth, calling in my breed-brother and full-bred primo—sandy wool y pelos de indio—bent over bowls of albóndigas soup.

Mongrel is the name that holds all the animal I am.

2

My legs split open, straddling the examination table,
she tells me "your fibroid ain't no watermelon
just the size of a small navel orange"
and I consider this sphere of influence
steadily growing behind my own navel
little satellites of smaller fibroids floating
inside its citric orbit.

I imagine the color/the taste of fruit/the bitterness
of peel and pleasure.
There *is* pleasured familiarity
as she moves her dark safe-sexed-gloved hand
up inside me—a lesbian gesture.
I, a lesbian monster.

She recommends hormones.
"Have you always been this hairy?"
"Yes," I say, I remember
 since I became a woman
with hair in all the wrong places.
Does that make a woman
or a lesbian
or an animal?

Which brings me back to the mongrel
and the hybrid sheep-goat I saw in a magazine once
with pitiful pleading eyes
trying to bust out of her genetically altered face.

And I saw my face in her
no matter how much I am loved

no matter how much woman I am
no matter how many women hold
and suckle me

I am mirrored in those pitiful
lonesome
product of mutation
eyes.

Half-breed

the difference between you and me
is as I bent over strangers' toilet bowls,
the face that glared back at me
in the tedium of those waters
was not my own, but my mother's
brown bead
floating in a soon pool
of crystalline whiteness

she taught me how to clean
to get down on my hands and knees
and scrub, not beg

she taught me how to work,
not live in this body

my reflection has always been
once removed.

It's Not New York

It is a chinese diner that serves grey
american hamburgers, garlic-spread bread, pale
chicken'n'rice soup,
watered-down ice tea.
We have it all.

The homegirl and I eat
and sit cross-eyed from each other
vinyl-checkered tablecloth beneath our elbows, we wave
forks she, a spoon and we talk like this could be any city
where my bed waits for me could be a thousand miles away.
It doesn't matter.

Pouring rain outside the restaurant plate glass.
I have to prove this to her, make her
turn and look the other way, see
the rain through the glare of taxi-cab headlights.
It could be New York. It's not.
And she sees and agrees.
Rivers of gutter rain.

This is joy.

It has the name and look of her,
her black eyes, my childhood eyes staring back at me
and nothing in our mutual LA sub-urban pasts prepared
us for this moment of neon-rippled reflection
off store-front windows, brake lights swimming in pools
of black liquid, umbrellas competing

for headroom on sidewalks.

Theater surrounds us.
We talk and talk and all
is complete. The circle of her moonface
holding vigil to mine. If we touch hands,
it is not a plea but an electric acknowledgment:

I was there, too.
The long hot drives home from Fresno to LA,
the half-breed cousins mexican mothers
thinking spanish talking spanglish teaching english
to their children. The two of us
bony-elbowed grace in the back of the station wagon
57 buick, the fleshy backs of our arms
sticking like bandaids
we pull away from each other,
giggle and slide back in again.

I see you, homegirl, behind the gas station,
bruised kneecap against my chest, you got me down!
Your hands, brown cuffs of flesh around my wrists, I twist
and squirm, I twist and squirm,
the crab grass itching my back.

Tougher always tougher than me
your face softens and when you bend to kiss me,
I don't turn away.

Indian Summer

Barely midday and the sun has already moved behind the cedar tree. Watering time so tomato leaves won't burn from direct light, so the soil don't soak up the liquid life like so much sponge.

I watch her through my window. She got a way with that hose and hoe. She got a way of turning country on me. She a big girl. No nonsense. Wielding that liquid tongue like she the fertility goddess herself.

"You act like you own it," I shout out to her.
"What?"
"That garden."
"No, baby. I'm only a squatter. Squatter's rights is all it is, but I intend to assert them."
I love that kind of talk. It'd be hard to be without that talk.

She's got the hose now wrapped 'round her naked shin, twisted up between her legs, mud splattered around her ankles and those tired-ass sandals. I'll be wiping up their tracks again once she comes back inside.

"You can't stay here."
That's the first thing out of her mouth as she puts one muddy paw inside the front door. I like living like this, always on the edge of her throwing me out.
"Why now?"
"Cuz I'm getting too attached, that's why. The garden's growing. The tomatoes are on the verge of ripening and you're gonna leave me anyway, so get out now."
She's not even mad, even grinning a little bit, mud smudges just above the left side of her lip. She's a wild whitegirl.

"It's only for a month," I bargain.

"You won't even be here to see the tomatoes turn." She's pouting.

"I regret that," I say.

"Regret. Right." She's working herself into a serious pout now. I grab her by the hip, slide my hand into the back pocket of her jeans shorts.

"Sit down." I pull her onto my lap. She puts her face inside the hollow of my neck. This is the dance we do.

"Let's bury it," she says.

"What?"

"This 'relationship' routine. All you desperate wounded butches who can't make up your damn minds. I'm tired of it."

She's got a hold of her ankle now and is wiping the mud from it with a saliva-tipped finger.

I want that finger in my mouth, that mud.

I start to my feet, she slides off of me.

"You can't stay here," she says. "I warn you."

The Grass, Not Greener

In dreams
that take me away from you
we are a different two
women, mestizas traveling in the land
that is at once ours and stolen
and we live daily in the moment of that
highway robbery
on each side, a desert claimed
and disturbed.

I confess my dreams look like this,
what is not outside our mutual morning
window of shipyard, loading dock, warehouses
of corrugated aluminum roof.

I cannot stay here forever.
But will you take me with you? you ask.

My life and yours is a prayer.
I live it daily as the last one
said before parting into another world
whose terrain we can only guess.
I imagine the grass, not greener
only the earth, more yielding to a Native daughter's
step and dance.

Today I think of leaving you, I won't.
Because today is a grey August San Francisco morning
that tricks us into winter feelings. And one does not leave

in winter when flesh assumes the texture of covers
dense and delicate where the curve
and simple weight of one breast folded into the arc
of rib cage is sufficient to keep me
hours longer still not moving
into this deceptive day.

If I could love you as a mother
I would be the best of lovers.
Preparing your morning tea, I dream
of the woman you want to be.
I see her take shape in the thickening
of your hands, peasant hands.
We grow middle-aged together.

But in eyes the color of sea
you sail away.
I stand on the shore's edge,
its desert sands rise to envelop me.

I wave goodbye eternally.

The Breakdown of the Bicultural Mind[1]

Like many other prophetic leaders of nativistic movements,
be they Moses or Malcolm X, the intensity of the vision seems
to be fired by the internal conflict coming from a culturally
mixed parentage.

—William Irwin Thompson,
Blue Jade from the Morning Star

No Moses, No Malcolm

I read all I can for a clue, to come up with some thread of connection, some sense of how my mixed-blood identity has driven me to politics, protest, and poetry—of why I awaken at three o'clock in the morning, a heaviness over my heart. *Who is sitting on my chest?*

I don't pretend the importance of gods or revolutionary leaders—only know that even "great men" are weak within. I read of Quetzalcóatl—the story of the man, not the god, destined to relive, as Thompson writes, "the primal act of rape which brought his soul into the world." He compulsively reenacts that history through sexual indulgences, subsequent penance, and submersion into the fire of transformation. And like the phoenix rising, Quetzalcóatl is reborn to become the morning star.

I read and I remember.

At nineteen, I first heard the story of the "mulatto," as my friend called him. A jazz musician she knew who was born a black smudge into an otherwise lily-white family. The family never spoke about it. He was never told he was Black, but figured it out, like a perverse prophecy fulfilled, in a life in and out of prison, drugs, and jazz clubs.

And then one night, alone in his apartment and thrashing so bad inside, he went, without thinking, into the bathroom and filled the tub with scalding hot water. At the moment he submerged his body, long legs and back, then face into the water, he remembered. He remembered being no bigger than the alabaster length of his mother's arm as she dropped him suffocating into the liquid flame. So the story goes, the next day the man sold all that he owned, including his precious saxophone, but kept his car to live and sleep in, never moving it. One morning they found him in it, gassed to death. Sometimes one lifetime is not enough to repair the damage.

The story stuck. Twenty years later and I'm still thinking about it. This mixed-blood scenario that ends in suicide, that ends in rebirth. *What fiery pit awaits us, we new breed of twenty-first-century mestizo? Into what shapes shall we be transformed?*

I reread my own writings of a decade ago and see the same struggles. Then I was no less the mixed-blood Mexican, la mestiza's mestiza than I am today. The difference now is that I understand that my writer's journey is not strictly wedded to my individual story—the marriage of my US-born Mexican mother of Sonoran roots to my San Francisco–born white father. That story alone does not explain my dreams, my nightmares, my insistent Chicanismo, complicated and contradictory as it is. There is something older, something I remember and live out again and again in the women I love, the family I make, the poems and characters I create.

Thompson goes on to write, "we are more than we know." There is consolation in this—that there may be a more powerful impetus than my mere forty-year-old biography to explain this unyielding need to relive the imperial rape, to understand what's been stolen, the loss . . . the truth.

> *We are no Moses, no Malcolm,*
> *no Queztalcóatl,*
> *but we are all our own gods.*
> *And our liberation won't happen*
> *by some man leading the way*
> *and parting the sea for us.*
>
> *We are the red and bleeding sea,*
> *we women.*

WE INVENT OURSELVES

Lifting off the runway, I don't really feel I am leaving home until I spy the moon, a San Francisco dawn's full moon, descending into the skyline. She speaks to me of longevity, a sister-guide in an otherwise lonesome horizon. I've come to recognize the city's topography of peninsula and bay and eastside hills, the Golden Gate heading north buried beneath fog caps. I know the history of those dotted islands; of now empty prison cells and Asian immigrant processing camps; the cruel welcomings, and forever land grabs.

My Spanish surname is chiseled into a tombstone on the breast-bone of Mission Dolores tiles laid into Indian dirt. There are whole city blocks carrying that name and we (whatever "we" I am with at the moment) invariably fantasize coming in the middle of the night, stealing the signs and leaving the streets nameless and unoccupied. It is a Chicana lesbian dream, like the moon, grander than city planner visions with blueprints and conquistador maps.

I have loved all kinds of women in all kinds of towns. Last night an old writer friend, a Southern woman, tells me over a meal of fried okra and chicken and polenta—"Polenta's no more than grits, just a fancy name for grits." But this is a new San Francisco restaurant in what-*used*-to-be Black Filmore, so it's polenta from now on.

I tell her, spooning the last of that upscale yellow mush into my mouth, "We've known a lot of women, Dorothy. Why is it so hard to write of what we know about women?"

And much of what I know, I admit, is about race.

In fact, I have never had a race-less relationship. Somehow I have always attributed this to being mixed-blood, but I wonder if anyone has in this country. Maybe children—before the color of societal power and preference is brutally painted into their lives. Or maybe only wealthy whites, imagining they have nothing to protect or defend. Maybe only they enjoy the luxury of "colorblindness." And then there are those literally em(bed)ded with one another— their own culture, their own vernacular, their own neighborhood, their own kin; perhaps they can forget race relations momentarily until America tells them different and daily.

And it does so, different and daily.

As deeply as I have feared the creative potential of my infinite female darkness, feared my Mexican muteness, feared my bottom- less rage reflected in a brown-skinned lover, I have feared the mirror of my passivity, my orphanhood, my arrogance and ignorance in the white women I have loved. It is not a pretty picture.

I have at times experienced some Black women as cold as any white woman in their gringa chauvinism, and I have seen Latinas as spineless as any man in their disloyalty to women. I have been both agringada and spineless and this is not a confession. It is an unholy testament to my unwavering faith in lesbians to name from the bed those battles being waged on the street—along with the profound hope that those insights might matter to the world.

We light-skinned breeds are like chameleons, those lagartijas with the capacity to change the color of their skins. We change not for lack of conviction, but lack of definitive shade, its interpretation dependent upon the eyes of others outside of us. I recognize this as privilege and onus at once.

My lovers have always been the environment that defined my color. With a Black lover in apartheid Boston I was seen as a white-girl in the passenger seat of her car, when a white man rammed us off the road in a rage over the portrait of miscegenation he *thought* he saw. When we two moved to Brooklyn, we became Ricans reflecting the full spectrum of color, in our puro Latino apartment building. In México, we were both Cubans. With my brown girl-friends we be brown girls sitting on brownstones. We be family. Among Native women in the States, I'm a half-breed who looks like every other breed Indian—colored mixed with cowboy. Among Indígenas in México, I am güera, ladina, extranjera, and not to be trusted. Among Chicanas, I am everybody's cousin Carmen. Whitegirls change my shade to a paler version. People think I'm Italian, Jewish. In bed, I sizzle brown indifference, brown in dif-ference. On downtown Main Streets, I disappear effortlessly into the gray of sidewalks. Nobody notices, except me. For that reason, I got to be choosy 'bout who I hang with—everybody so conta-gious. I pick up their gesture, their joke, their jive, their caribeña Spanglish and homegrown machisma.

I am la Malinche of multiple tongues.

"We invent ourselves," a mixed-blood Hawaiian friend tells me. "I create whole biographies of the Black childhood I never had. Give me enough time with you," she says. "I'll invent a Mexican one, too."

BLACK FAMILIA

> *The dark woman looking in through the glass*
> *is as frightened as I am.*
> *She is weeping. I will not let her in.*

I remember Pacific Ocean Park in the fifties. She was a girl my age, my size—maybe we were six or seven years old. We stood packed in line for the "Wild Car" ride. I remember her darkness, her difference, her thick hair corralled into three perfectly plaited pigtails. I didn't understand the third one. *Why was it there?* My mother always twisted my buster brown straightness into two limp fountains spilling out from behind each ear, temples stretched to breaking point. *So tight a hairdo, it could last for weeks.* I didn't know about little black girls' hair and how their mothers sat them between their knees, greasing and separating and combing each section into that exact symmetry. *So tight a hairdo, it could last for weeks.* I didn't know how thick hair could be until I grew up and felt its sure density supporting my chin as we two slept.

There was a time when I truly believed I could never live without Black women in my life—without uptown city buses, without Vienna's fedora-feathered dreads, her femme fatality sliding up next to me. We peer out onto a street-soaked Harlem. She, a small-town-colored-girl-import; me, "Spanish," the way Black folk called Latinas. But somehow we managed to make home in Harlem, her talking its talk in girls' bars and boys' clubs, with girls and boys always eyeing us dancing together, envying. Or so we liked to imagine; the best of us, a seamless fit.

I had imagined I could never live without that. That her. That life. But then, it seemed, I did learn to live without—something calling me away—until Audre died and I remembered that singular biography denied me.

I dial New York, call Barbara,* hear my name echoed back to me familiar.

"We were so young," she says. *And Black*, I think.

A decade ago all I knew was Black familia. Audre was our dark womanhood wrapped around dark womanhood in subways and on street corners. We coloredgirls kissing under rain-soaked umbrellas; up 'til 4 a.m. in uptown jazz clubs; plotting kitchen table revolution in the basement of a midtown Church.

I had a Black family once. What happened to that?
Like my Mexican childhood, my Puerto Rican dreams.
What happened to all those women I made history with?

In December 1985, I left New York to return home to California. It was one of the hardest decisions I ever had to make because I loved my life and my loving in Nueva York and I was not so sure Califas would welcome me. As a Chicana. As a lesbian. As a writer.

What had been missing for me in New York was utterly impossible to explain to anyone there because in the mid-1980s, Chicanas were simply invisible.

And no one knew to miss us, except me.

You Wanted a Real Mexican, You Got It

The first colored woman I slept with wasn't colored at all, but darker than me in her anger, in her resolve; and, I tasted on her immigrant tongue resting speechless upon mine a sister of tragic dimension. How she envied me my education, my seamless face, my freedom. The taste was bitter and mother-Mexican familiar.

---

* Barbara Smith is a feminist writer and activist, who, along with Audre Lorde and I, cofounded Kitchen Table: Women of Color Press in New York City in the early 1980s.

I wanted more.

My first Chicana lover was the smoothness of the clay pots she dragged from home to home, making home out of anything, stolen milk crates, heavy tamales of woolen Indian blankets. She was a childless woman like me; childless as Carlos Castañeda's "Don Juan" describes, without holes in her body. Still, like those Mexican pots, she had a wide-open mouth, ready to devour everything surrounding her. This was Chicana lesbian, I discovered. And I had never been so in love.

I thought I met a lesbian once, in an Indian woman from the south of Oaxaca who sat three tables away from us at a club in the capital city. As the salsa band plays, I watch the woman in a short mannish haircut watch us, a table of US Latinas, as Sabrina takes her girlfriend out to dance. When they return to the table, the waiter brings us another round, courtesy of the woman three tables away. We invite her to join us. She is already drunk and her tears well up and flow down effortlessly as she recounts to my comadre, Myrtha,* the story of her passage here to this city of ricos and government officials and poverty.

She speaks of a recent death, the murder of a family member. And with the same despair, she speaks of the sudden cutting of her trenza. A government program had brought her here, hundreds of miles away from her village, and filled her pockets with pesos and her belly with mescal. She cries, and eyeing Sabrina's Indian trenza and Indígena features, keeps wanting to understand who we all were. We try to explain, but she only cries all the more as the full moon passes into view through the zócalo window.

She tells us that at that very moment she is missing her village's ceremonia to the moon. I mention the moon's Indian name "Coyolxauhqui." She stares at me. It is the first time she has looked at me all

---

* Myrtha Chabrán, a Puerto Rican feminist poet and independentista who remains a beloved friend.

evening. "How do you know that?" she asks. "You are white."

And I look over to Myrtha whose watery eyes have held the woman's for over an hour. She smiles back at me, sadly.

"She's right," I say later. "In her world, I'm just white."

It was Myrtha who told me on a particularly gloomy Berkeley afternoon, "You don't know what it feels like to always be perceived as Third World, to see in everybody's eyes that disdain, that despre-cio." And yet, we move around these ancient Mexican sites from Palenque to Monte Albán like long lost sister-companions. Una puertorriqueña y una chicana, we speak in wordless code to each other. We are without nationality in the deepest sense, even though they only ask me and the Germans for passports on this local bus full of mexicanos and Myrtha. She doesn't mention it, her hand rest-ing on mine. Neither do I.

And suddenly I remember the lover I had left, weeks earlier, on the sandy streets of a Mexican Caribbean beach town, and the one distinct time I made love with her and shook. Shook from the tequila still poisoning my veins, shook from how boldly her gringa-ameri-can eyes stripped me of my Chicana cultural bravado, shook from how shamed and naked I felt. And I remember vaguely, because I was so drunk, the trip across to the island, her holding my back as I threw up in a bag. I remember her getting us to the hotel in a cab. I remember her hand always guiding my back, and I remember again throwing up all that bitterness, all that self-hatred, all that disgust at my whiteness, my hunger to be part of that memory, that México. And I called her "sister," too. With a voice I use only for my own blood-sister's name, as I worked my hand and tongue inside of her, trying to find a place to rest all that homesickness.

In 1986, I wrote a play, *Giving Up the Ghost,* in which a Mexican woman says of her young Chicana lover, "Sometimes I think with me that she only wanted to feel herself so much a woman that she would no longer be hungry for one." Today, in my own voice I would add, "I only wanted to feel myself so much a Mexican . . ." but I am always hungry and always shamed by my hunger for the Mexican woman I miss in myself.

I would have left sooner if it hadn't been for the smell of albóndigas in her kitchen, the sticky desert taste of nopalito behind her ears, the texture of that thick rope of hemp hair I twisted into my fist, holding her hamaca and swaying beneath me.

I would have left her if her Spanish had been less than perfectly provincial, her repertoire of rancheras lacking, her knowledge of brujería anything but respectfully restrained.

I would have left her for a woman less Mexican if México had not been so forgotten in me. Instead, I stayed and stayed and stayed until her México no longer mattered so much, became an island thoroughly remote and unreachable.

Soy de lo europeo y de lo indígena. Most Mexicans can claim the same, but it's the gringo that riddles me with shame. Why, exactly? My white family was kept apart from me, not because of its conquests, but its failures.

She Won't Let Go

I grew up judging the white side of my family very harshly. Our one family of white cousins were abandoned children, fed from giant-sized peanut butter jars, while we Mexican cousins ate homemade warm tortillas with a clean embroidered tablecloth under our elbows. There was the story one of those white cousins told of how her mother—my father's only and younger sister—would punish her daughter by locking her in a room where she had to piss and shit in coffee cans. And I remember my sister, at five, after a week's stay at my aunt's house, never wanting to return there. She became frightened of the dark, of closed closet doors.

After my paternal grandmother's death, I think I saw my aunt perhaps no more than a handful of times. My father never expressed an interest in visiting her or her family, although my mother regularly encouraged him to do so. She found it impossible to understand the distance between them since we saw her familia—aunts, uncles, first and second cousins—daily. My dad simply seemed indifferent to the idea.

Still, one meeting with my aunt stands out in my mind. After at least a twenty-year hiatus, we meet at a Chinese restaurant. She has just received word that she may have cancer. She fears she is dying and wants to repair any damages done. We are not her children. We have nothing to forgive in her, except her twenty-year absence, fully knowing my father is equally responsible.

I am the last to arrive at the restaurant. My mother, father, sister, and aunt have already ordered drinks and appetizers. As I enter, I spot her first. She looks as I remembered her, only a little older, thicker, tougher. But she was always tough, tougher than her brother, the preferred and protected one. She reminds me of a dyke. She is not a dyke, but she must spy something queer in me as I approach the table, smiling.

"You are your grandma Hallie," she says to me after the second drink. "You've got my mother's spirit. Did you know that?" No, I didn't know that any more than I knew the woman herself. But I am hungry to know, as my sister is. So, the stories begin . . . stories that had been censored by my father. Stories of my grandmother's wild ways, her five marriages, the last to a homosexual; of her adopted daughter never to be heard from again. My grandmother was a wild woman in a white Cadillac with white skin and white bleached hair. But to my five-year-old mind, she was merely a strange wrinkled lady with long red painted fingernails that she used like a tortilla to push her food onto her fork. She was white, and therefore foreign. And now, over a generation later, her daughter tells me I carry her character. Later, I would learn of my grandmother's vaudeville days; her work as a stage actress through FDR's Works Progress Administration during the 1930s Depression. I learn to put the pieces together. She was an independent woman, my white grandmother, a woman with an artist's hunger for love and limelight.

Once, my aunt appeared to me in a dream. I cannot see her face, because she stands behind me, holding me, her arms around me like a straightjacket. I panic. She won't let go. I wake up, heart pounding.

In another dream, my aunt is a waitress slapping hash onto a grill and tossing plates onto customers' tables. My Mexican aunts and my mother are nearby. They sit hunched around a low table. They are whispering secrets. They appear very dark and conspiratorial, like brujas. This gathering is a holy coven. I stand between this circle of witches and my working-class aunt. She throws a hand on her hip, wipes her brow with the back of the other.

"These Mexicans," she says, "are so damn crazy!"

My cousin David appears. He is brown and beautiful, indifferent to the world of women around him. He does not have to choose. He remains aloof and elegant in his Mexican masculinity. I envy him.

She will not let go.

My aunt died this year, not of the cancer she had feared ten years earlier, but of a stroke. She died quietly and tragically a few months after she had retired from forty-plus years working as a nurse and supporting seven children who have known drugs and alcoholism and gunshot wounds more intimately than any of us Mexicans. My girl-cousin, the one who suffered those early "lockups" was the one who was at her side, holding her mother's square freckled hand (my father's hand) until the moment of her passing.

My white aunt comes to visit me as many of the women in my family have, uninvited through my bedroom door. She will stay until she is given the respect due her. She will stay until she has changed from a faceless entity straightjacketing my every movement into a woman of real flesh and bones and name. My aunt's maiden name is Barbara Slatter and I am here to make peace with her in the white women I have loved, in the white woman I am—that hard-ass hash-slinging whitegirl I learned to fear on the other side of the family, on the other side of me.

TALKIN' BREED TALK

> It is best for them (Anglos) when we (Chicano/as) are light-skinned, but better still when Chicano/as are half-white and half-Chicano/a. That places half-breeds closer to Anglo language and culture. But these false privileges many recognize for what they are, a token, a maldición.
>
> —Emma Pérez, "Sexuality and Discourse:
> Notes from a Chicana Survivor"[2]

Emma's got it right. In the illusion of privilege resides the curse, the "maldición." *If my thoughts could color my flesh, how dark I would turn.* But people can't read your mind, they read your color, they read your womanhood, they read the women you're with. They read your walk and talk, your stand in this world. And then the privileges begin to wane and the choices become more limited, more evident.

Call me breed. Call me trash. Call me spic beaner dyke jota bulldagger o malflor. Call me something meant to set me apart from you and I will know who I am. Do not call me "sister." I am not yours.

Do I write this to my brother who has chosen, against me, who he will be in this lifetime? He does not perceive his white manhood as a choice. To him it is the natural evolution of a light-skinned mixed-blood son of a white man. But Ester's son, Jacobo, doesn't feel this way; Lola's son, Tim, doesn't feel this way and writes it blue-veined into his skin—"¡Viva la Raza!" It is a life-long mark of identity, of loyalty to his mother and to the dark side of his mestizaje.

Only my sister understands. JoAnn tells me, "Nobody I know talks about this, Ceci, about being mixed. Nobody else has to prove who they are, who they aren't." Of our one-hundred-plus cousins, she and I are the only ones working with la Raza. I know full well that my mestizaje—my breed blood—is the catalyst of my activism and my art. I have tasted assimilation and it is bitter on my tongue. Had I been born a full-blood Mexican, I sometimes wonder whether I would have struggled so hard politically to stay a part of la Raza.

Sueño: 18 febrero 1990

I see in the distance a herd of calf-children traveling in packs with their white lesbian mothers. They are half animal/half human. They are goat-people, young calves with the expressions of injured children. One has the buttocks of a human, but it is fur-covered like an animal. They are me.

After they pass, I approach a table where one of the mothers is selling wares. I am eating cheese and she tells me I must stand away from the table, something about the mixing of elements (the cheese I am eating with what she is selling). I inquire about the half-breed children. She informs me that there is one father for all of them and they have turned out this way due to a mixing of bloods—too many with one father.

I want to chastise the women for their irresponsibility, but the thought passes through my mind that possibly there is another meaning here, inside the bodies of these deformed ones. The creation of a new species (half human/half animal). Maybe they are the hope of the future, these mixed beings who will bridge a world of opposition, reunite the human with the natural world.

And I am not alone in this dreaming. Recently, Marsha Gómez (Choctaw/Chicana/Cajun) told me of her dream like mine. In it, she is raped by a lion and becomes pregnant. She is outraged until she realizes that she is the one named to bear the new species—half beast/half she. She tells me how much the dream disturbed her.

"I don't want to be the fuckin' Virgin Mary of the next generation."

"Me neither," I say. "Me neither."

As mixed-blood women, we are the hybrid seed Marsha carried in the dream and the mothers of a new generation. We are the products of rape and the creators of a new breed. We are Malinche's children and the new Malinches of the twenty-first century. We are breeds talkin' breed when the whole world's turning breed at unprecedented rates, while Third and Fourth and First Worlds collide and collapse into one another.

Make no mistake, we continue to live under the imperialist narrative of the Rapist Father and he is white and the Violated Mother and she is not. In spite of the personal stories to the contrary, the political and economic conditions of miscegenation, to this day, occur within the larger framework of white supremacy, forced migration, patriarchy, and transnational capital. And miscegenation's children wrestle, in one way or another, with the consequences.

I am not that rare breed of mixed-blood person, a Jean Toomer, who writes, as Alice Walker said of *Cane*, "to memorialize a culture he thought was dying."[3] I am that raging breed of mixed-blood person who writes to defend a culture that I know is being killed. I am of that endangered culture and of that murderous race, but I am fundamentally loyal only to one. My mother culture, my mother land, my mother tongue, further back than even she can remember.

My father said it himself, speaking of the WhiteMan, "We are our own worst enemies."

Remembering Navajo Nation

I have witnessed speechless beauty here, in this nation of Dineh. My insignificance enters me amid the antiquity of these red rock canyons. I have no desire to return or go forward. There is nowhere to arrive, only this journeying . . .

I remember Phoenix. My cousin, Carlos, and my Tía Tencha: that dying breed of Mexican cowboy and his mother. My aunt of eighty-three years is speechless. She can't recall English or Spanish words, just can't seem to bring them to the surface of her tongue. The facts: dates, names, places. She falters . . . "Desde que se murió mi viejo . . . ," forgetting who is her "viejo." At times her son, forty years younger, assumes the old Indio's shape and voice. She looks to him to finish her lines.

He waits. She suffers.

Rainclouds form over Navajo Nation.

The sky darkens. We wait.

The sun will break through these clouds.

My companion mistakenly keeps calling Carlos my "brother," although he is a brother of sorts. More than my own. The queer son, like me, desperately clinging to history. The family anthropologist searching out raíces from the bowels of Mission churches in a Sonora that once hardly knew the word "gringo."

We are the childless ones, he and I. I do find a brother in the passion he exudes when pulling out death certificates and reproduced photos of what could be Indian, could be Arabe, could be "old country" great-great-grandmothers. He names them: Refugio, Paula, Victoria, braids stretched across seamless foreheads, skin stretched across chiseled cheekbones, hazel eyes buried into them. Conversing with my cousin, I search his words, his excited moving mouth.

The Spanish surnames spill from his tongue . . . Figueroa, Mendibles, Rodriguez . . . I swallow, hesitate. I ask.

"And the Indians? Did you find out anything about our Indian blood?"

"Oh there must have been some," he says. But no mention, no unnamed bisabuelo. Still, the dark faces appear and disappear in photographs with no Native claim, no name.

The road is red in Arizona, a river of red clay. I am surrounded by red and spin it green in poetic imagination. What are the names of these trees that hover like sentinels by the river's weed banks? *El agua es el mismo color del barro de Chimayó; el color del sagrado.*

I remember la curandera, Elena's words, "You have so much air, Ceci. Walk the earth with bare feet. Feel the ground."

I remove my shoes. I walk. I want this mud to stain me red from the soles up. My toes turn purple with the chill of the creek, bleed rose red into the clay.

No wonder Marsha became a potter, a worker of clay, a sculptor. No wonder she studied how to shape fingered earth into canyon walls reaching toward rain god skies.

No wonder, half-breed sister, half-sister.

We are a mongrel nation, and yet this ground is testimony to the purity of the sacred. Water and earth blend, turn the river mud red, and it refreshes no less through the open pores of flesh and palm.

Open palm.

When did our real ancestors arrive here?
Before Olmec heads and Maya gods?
Before gods?

I am a trespasser. I do not need signs to remind me. My immigrant blood is a stain I carry in the fading of my flesh each winter.

But I am made of clay. All our ancestors know this. It is no myth, but wholly evident in the slow dissolving of my skin into the red road of this river. Where will you take me, immigrant, Indian, and orphaned?

All is familia: ancestor and future generations. The tree branches out, bears fruit. The cañón grows dark and I dream of dying.

Not violence, but a slow and peaceful return to the river.

QUEER AZTLÁN

It's the land.
You cannot own the land.
The land owns you.

—Dolores Keane from "Solid Ground"

Meditation

the third eye

never cries

it knows

I Don't Know the Protocol

I fly along these backroads. I want to keep consuming miles under the spin and bump of my tires. I don't ever want to arrive—anywhere. But I stop when I see the stiff hide of bone and meat. I pull over onto the gravel that shoulders a frost-grey pasture.

As I approach the deer, I already know she has been dead since nightfall. Dawn found her this way, stone-still, no trace of blood, but there is the telltale foam spilling from her lengthened tongue. Is it a tongue or a piece of raw meat she has regurgitated?

I am afraid to look at the face of her recent, so recent, death. Why am I afraid?

I don't know the protocol. I have only read about this in books. I have only heard about tobacco and offerings to deer who sacrifice themselves to the hunt. This reckless hunter abandoned her, did not consume her flesh. Her flesh must be so bitter. Are all prey turned bitter by the bullet, the speeding car, the butcher's hatchet?

I know she is no dumb animal. I pray stupidly, wafting her with sage smoke, sprinkling tobacco at hoofs, forehead, foaming mouth. I don't know the protocol and I wonder if my actions are a mockery to a knowledge missing from me now.

But I pray for her and all of her kind who will be offered up to this season of white Texans in American-made pickup trucks, rifles riding horizontal behind their heads, deer bleeding out of open-bed U-Hauls. The hunters congregate in packs like animals. But unlike animals, they plot, create ritual, drink coffee, eat donuts, pat each other's flannel-covered shoulders, and think they will live forever.

Rattle and flute sounds rise up from the dashboard. It is a "Yaqui Deer Dance." I don't know why I chose it; why it called me from the shelf in San Anto; why I don't know where tobacco belongs on a dead deer.

Our Lady of the Cannery Workers

*June 1992. In Watsonville, California, a town of Mexican
cannery and agricultural workers, a woman reported that la
Virgen de Guadalupe had appeared to her near the county
park lake where her son had drowned a few years earlier.
Nearby, a tree took on la Virgen's form in its bark.*

Para Celia

1
Returning from Watsón
the road, a forest of fleeting
visitations, la Madre Creadora
in every standing sequoia
every virgin oak.

Ehécatl follows me
reminds me to listen to the stillness
observe its subtle and sudden apparition
in pine-scented breezes
copal dancing smoke
in icy San Francisco winds whipping
open bedroom
windows, sudden slamming
doors —
> *Who entered just then,*
> *taking leave of their senses?*
the pinwheel descent
of an aging
oak leaf.

2

Guadalupe
a tattoo emblazoned
into dark bark flesh.
The same slight inclination
of shrouded head, the same
copper rose shade
imprinted en la tela
de Juan Diego's
prayer.
  Tonantzín
  te traigo flores.

Pilgrims hold mirrors to the sun.
Beams of light ricochet
in all directions.
blinding
coastal gloom,
factory shut-downs
migra raids.
  Ahora, ¿la ves?
  Sí.
  Dios te salve, María.

La guadalupana
vestida de blanco
counsels the faithful,
  "Let go de su coraje."
The chain link,
a sagging fortress of protection.

I work my swollen knuckles

into its rusting wire
rosary beads
of pink, turquoise glass
carved pine wood
drape from curling polaroids.
Make-shift retablos hang
by a thread
of Christmas ribbon.

3
There is one who refuses
the catholic words;
buries small ties of tobacco
at the four corners.
She is Diego's living descendant,
her prayer, an artist's anger
righteous
and unforgiving.

If la virgen appeared to me,
what would she look like?
Not cannery worker
pero pintora?

Sequoia Virgen, I see you
in every crevice
of burnt bark flesh.
Sus ramas se abren
two thick thighs
of female
eruption.

You grow old and tall
you fall
you turn
to seed.

Queer Aztlán—The Re-formation of Chicano Tribe,[1] 1992

How will our lands be free if our bodies aren't?
—Ricardo Bracho

At the height of the Chicano Movement in 1968, I was a closeted, light-skinned, mixed-blood *Mexican*American, disguised by my father's adoptive Anglo last name. Since I seldom spoke of it publicly, few people questioned my Anglo credentials. But my eyes were open and my throat thirsty as I drank in images of students my age, of vatos and viejitas, who could have been primos or tías or abuelitas raising their collective fist into a smoggy East Los Angeles skyline.

Although I could not express how at the time, I knew I had a place in that Movimiento that was spilling out of barrio high schools and onto police-barricaded streets just ten minutes from my tree-lined working-class neighborhood in San Gabriel. What I didn't know then was that it would take me another ten years to fully traverse that ten-minute drive and to bring all the parts of me—Chicana, lesbiana, half-breed, and poeta—to the revolution, wherever it was.

My real politicization began, not through the Chicano Movement, but through the bold recognition of my lesbianism. Coming to terms with that fact meant the radical restructuring of everything I thought I held sacred. It meant acting on my woman-centered desire and against anything that stood in the way of it, including my church, my family, and, what I had come to believe was, my "country." It meant acting in spite of the fact that I had learned from my Mexican culture and the dominant culture that my womanhood was, if not despised, certainly deficient and hardly worth the loving of another woman in bed. But act I did, because not acting would have meant a kind of death by despair.

That was twenty years ago. In those twenty years I have traversed territory that extends well beyond the ten-minute trip between East Los Angeles and that Mission town of San Gabriel. In those twenty years, I experienced the racism of the women's movement, the elitism of the gay and lesbian movement, the homophobia and sexism of the Chicano Movement, and the invisibility of US Latinos in progressive Latin American solidarity movements. I also witnessed the emergence of a national Chicana feminist consciousness, along with a literature, art, and activism to support it. I've seen the growth of a lesbian-of-color movement, the founding of an independent national Latino/a lesbian and gay men's organization, and the flourishing of Indigenous people's international campaigns for human and land rights.

A quarter of a century after those school walkouts in 1968, I can write at the age of forty that I have found a sense of place among la chicanada. It is not always a safe place, but it is unequivocally the original familial place from which I am compelled to write, which I reach toward in my audiences, and which serves as my source of inspiration, voice, and lucha. How we Chicanos define that struggle has always been the subject of debate and is ultimately the subject of this essay.

A QUEERER AND MORE FEMINIST NATION

"Queer Aztlán" had been forming in my mind for over three years and began to take concrete shape a year ago in a conversation with poet Ricardo Bracho. We discussed the limitations of "Queer Nation," whose leather-jacketed, shaven-headed white radicals and accompanying white-centrism were an alien(nation) to most lesbians and gay men of color.[2] On the opposing spectrum of radicalism was Chicano nationalism, which even into the nineties has not accepted openly gay men and lesbians among its ranks. Ricardo half-jokingly concluded, "What we need, Cherríe, is a *Queer* Aztlán." Of course. A Chicano homeland that could embrace all its people, including its jotería.*

Everything I read these days tells me that the Chicano Movement is dead. In Earl Shorris's *Latinos: A Biography of the People*, the author insists that the Chicano himself is dead. He writes, "The Chicano generation began in the late 1960s and lasted about six or eight years, dying slowly through the seventies."[3] He goes on to say that Chicanismo has been reduced to no more than a "handshake practiced by middle-aged men." Chicano sociologists seem to be suggesting the same when they tell us that by the third generation, most Chicanos have lost their Spanish fluency, and nearly a third have married non-Latinos and have moved out of the Chicano community. Were immigration from México to stop, they say, Chicanos could be virtually indistinguishable from the rest of the population within a few generations. What is not mentioned is race and racism, i.e., the lighter the skin, the easier the assimilation. Painting a broad stroke portrait of Raza, much of this may be true, but it doesn't account for those third and fourth generations who remain in, or return to, their communities (by zip code and/or in their political and cultural engagement). Looking forward perhaps, "Chicano community" may be defined by something more intentional than street address and economic class.

Still, I mourn the dissolution of a recognized coalesced active/activist Chicano Movement possibly more strongly than my generational counterparts because during its (albeit short) "classic" period (late '60s and early '70s), I was unable to act publicly. But more deeply,

* Chicano queer folk.

I mourn it because its ghost haunts me daily in the blonde hair of my sister's children, the gradual hispanicization of Latino students, the senselessness of barrio violence, and the poisoning of la frontera from Tijuana to Tejas. For me, El Movimiento has never been a thing of the past; it has only retreated into subterranean uncontaminated soils of consciencia, awaiting resurrection in a "queerer," more feminist generation. Or, at least, this is my hope.

What was right about Chicano nationalism was its commitment to preserving the integrity of Chicano people. A generation ago saw the sudden appearance of cultural, economic, and political programs to develop Chicano political consciousness, autonomy, and self-determination. What was wrong about Chicano nationalism was its institutionalized heterosexism, its inbred machismo, and its failure to put into *evolving* praxis a cohesive national political strategy on the page and on the pavement.[4]

Over the last twenty-five years, many progressive nationalisms emerged: Chicano nationalism, Black nationalism, Puerto Rican independence (still viable as evidenced in the recent mass protest on the island against establishing English as an official language), Lesbian Nation and its lesbian separatist movement, and, of course, the most recent Queer Nation. What I have admired about each was its righteous radicalism, its unabashed anti-assimilationism, and its rebeldía. These movements may not have been built to last, but they each, in varying degrees, changed minds and hearts and institutions along the way.

I recognize the dangers of nationalism as a long-term strategy for political change. Its tendency toward separatism and ideological fundamentalism can foster biological determinism, racism, and fascism. This is especially problematic if that "nation" is structurally empowered to enact on those tendencies, which is generally not the case for disenfranchised communities in the US. We are all horrified by the concentration camps and the genocidal rapes in Bosnia, perversely justified by the Serbian call for ethnic cleansing. We are bitterly sobered by the Nazism espoused by Pat Buchanan at the 1992 Republican Convention in which only heterosexual white middle-class US Americans have the right to citizenship and heaven.

We are repeatedly reminded that sex and race do not define a person's politics. Margaret Thatcher is a woman and enforced the policies of the Imperial WhiteMan as the British prime minister and Clarence Thomas is Black and follows suit as US Supreme Court justice. But it is historically evident that the female body, like the Chicano people, has been colonized. And any movement to decolonize our people must address questions of race, gender, class, and sexuality within the context of our internally colonized relationship to the United States.

Chicanos are an occupied nation within a nation, and women and women's sexuality are occupied within Chicano nation. If women's bodies and those of people who transgress their gender roles have been historically regarded as territories to be conquered, they are also territories to be liberated. Feminism has taught us this. The nation I seek is one that decolonizes the brown and female body. It is one in which heterosexism and homophobia are no longer the social order of the day. I hold to the word *nation* because without the specific naming of Chicanos as a pueblo, we—our histories, values, cultural practices—will be lost to United States monoculture. (As when feminism is reduced to humanism, the woman is subsumed.) Let us retain our radical naming but expand it to meet a broader and wiser revolution, recognizing that societal equity and cultural autonomy for historically oppressed ethnic/racialized groups in the US requires relentless and strategic political resistance against cultural amnesia.[5]

Tierra Sagrada: The Roots of a Revolution

Aztlán. I don't remember when I first heard the word, but I remember it took my heart by surprise to learn of that place—that sacred landscape wholly evident en las playas, los llanos, y en las montañas of what is now the North American Southwest. Aztlán gave language to a nameless anhelo inside me. To me, it was never a masculine notion. It had nothing to do with the Aztecs and everything to do with what I can only describe as memory, *a memory of place.* I remember once driving through Anza-Borrego desert, just east of San Diego, the old VW van I had borrowed from a friend whipping around corners and climbing. The tape deck set at full blast, every window open, bandana around my forehead. And I think, *this is México, Raza territory,* as I belt out the refrain . . .

> *Marieta, no seas coqueta*
> *porque los hombres son muy malos*
> *prometen muchos regalos*
> *y lo que dan son puro palos . . .*

That day I claimed that land in the spin of the worn-out cassette tape, the spin of my balding tires, and the spin of my mind. And just as I wrapped around a rubber-burning curve, I saw it: "A-Z-T-L-A-N," in giant-sized letters etched into the granite face of the mountainside. Of course, I hadn't been the first. Some other Chicano came this way, too, saw what I saw, felt what I felt. Enough to put a name to it. *Aztlán. Tierra sagrada.*

A term Náhuatl in root, Aztlán was that historical/mythical land where one set of Indian forebears, Nahua peoples, were said to have resided one thousand years ago. Believed to be located in the US Southwest, Aztlán fueled a cultural nationalist vision twenty years ago, which encompassed much of the pueblo Chicano from Chicago to the borders of Chihuahua. In the late sixties and early seventies, Chicano nationalism meant the right to control our own resources, language, and cultural traditions, rights guaranteed us by the Treaty of Guadalupe Hidalgo signed in 1848 when the Southwest was "annexed" to the United States at the end of the Mexican-American War. At its most radical, Chicano nationalism expressed itself in militant action, with its own share of gunrunners.

In the mid-1960s, Reies López Tijerina entered a campaign against the Department of the Interior to reclaim land grants for New Mexicans, resulting in his eventual imprisonment. In 1968, nearly ten thousand Chicano students walked out of their high schools to protest the lack of quality and Chicano-specific education in Los Angeles barrio schools. The same period also saw the rise of the Brown Berets, a paramilitary style youth organization regularly harassed by law enforcement agencies throughout the Southwest. These are a few highlights of what is best understood as the Chicano Power Movement, running parallel with more mainstream campaigns for civil and labor rights. Certainly violence, especially police violence, was visited upon Chicanos in response to public protests, the murder of journalist Rubén Salazar during the National Chicano Moratorium of 1970 being one of the most notable examples. Like other liberation movements, the Chicano Movement had its share of FBI infiltrators. But students, in the long-term, played a key role in the ideological formation of El Movimiento.

In 1969, El Plan Espiritual de Aztlán was drawn up at the First Chicano Youth Conference in Denver, Colorado, calling for a Chicano program of economic self-determination, self-defense, and land reclamation, including an autonomous taxation and judicial system. By the mid-1970s, the radicalism of El Plan weakened in the face of that formidable opponent—five-hundred years of internal colonization; but, El Movimiento would continue to grow and leave its mark, especially in the one piece of geography Raza could claim: El Barrio. With the flourishing of the movement, Chicano neighborhoods experienced their own "boom" of clínicas, legal aid offices, murals and galerías exhibiting local artists, afterschool programs, bilingual preschools, floricanto poetry festivals and theater, as well as ongoing protests for fair housing and labor practices, immigrant rights, and more. At its best, the *ideas* of Chicano Nation served to support societally sovereign communities in the cultivation and transmission of Raza cultural praxes and knowledges, with the programs and institutions to support them.

Chicanos are not easily organized as a racial/political entity. Is our land the México of today or the México of a century and a half ago, covering thousands of miles of what is now the Southwestern United States? Unlike the island of Puerto Rico whose "homeland" is clearly defined by ocean on all sides, Aztlán has often served as a more metaphysical homeland than a physical territory. As Native/mestizo peoples living in the United States, our relationship to this country has been ambivalent at best. Our birth certificates since the invasion of Aztlán often identified us as white. Our treatment by AngloAmericans branded us brown.

As Latino people of color in the US, we have a distinct history, often misunderstood by the population at large. In the history of African Americans, when the white slaveholder raped a Black woman, the mixed-blood offspring inherited the mother's enslaved status. Over a century later, mixed-raced African Americans overwhelmingly continue to identify as Black, not as mixed blood. Their living memory of slavery and Jim Crow, along with their daily experience of racism, creates little ambivalence about their racial identification.

But the history of Mexicans/Chicanos follows a different historical pattern. The Spanish-American invasions of Indigenous Mexico and its peoples were secured through rape, intermarriage, African and Native slave labor, and the spread of Catholicism and disease. During Spanish colonialism, Spanish America maintained a rigid and elaborate caste system that privileged the pure-blood Spaniard and his children over the mixed-raced peoples. This societal hierarchy remained in place through Mexican independence (1810–1821). But it wasn't until after the Mexican revolution (1910–1920) that the "mestizo" became synonymous with, and institutionalized as, the nation-state Spanish-speaking citizen. A distinct modernist national narrative grew from this mixing, creating a "third mestizo race" that included Indian, African, and European blood, even while the majority of "Mexicans" were more racially Indigenous than not. In short order, "Mexicans" were to simply forget that they were Indians (and for that matter, Black). Mestizaje became conflated with the modern, i.e., with European values and societal structures, while Indian identity was deemed worthless—as a thing of the past.[6]

Chicano Nation recognizes itself as a mestizo nation conceived in a double-rape: first, by the Spanish and then by the Gringo. In the mid-nineteenth century, when AngloAmerica took possession of one-third of México's territory, a new English-speaking oppressor assumed control over the Spanish, mestizo, and Indian peoples inhabiting those lands.

To make alliances with other nationalist struggles taking place throughout the country in the late sixties, there was no room for Chicano ambivalence about being Indians, for it was our Indian inheritance and history of resistance against both Spanish and Anglo invaders that made us rightful residents of Aztlán, alongside other Native peoples of that region, tribal enrollment notwithstanding. Aztlán, whether historical or mythical, provided Chicanos with a land-based struggle, grounded in Raza's living indigenous relationship not only to that particular geographical place that was once México, but also to the larger geography of an original América sin fronteras.[7]

After centuries of discrimination against Native identities, which forced mestizos into denial, many MexicanAmericans found the sudden affirmation of us as Indigenous peoples difficult to accept. And yet the Chicano Indigenous movement was not without historical precedence. Little more than fifty years earlier, México witnessed a campesino and Indian-led agrarian revolution that crossed into the US border states. Oligarchical corruption, of course, would follow.[8]

Radicalization among people of Mexican ancestry in this country most often occurs when the Mexican ceases to identify politically as a Mexican or Mexican-American and becomes a Chicano. I have observed this in my Chicano Studies students (first, second, and third generation); some with acknowledged Native American origins in the Southwest; others from the barrios of San Diego (Barrio Logan), East Los Angeles, Fresno, and all the neighboring California Central Valley towns—Selma, Visalia, Sanger; and in the North—Oakland, Sanjo, and San Panchito. These students are the ones most often in protest, draping their bodies in front of freeway on-ramps and trans-bay bridges, blocking entrances to university administration buildings. They are the ones who, like their Black and Native American counterparts, doubt the "American dream" because even if they got to UC Berkeley, their brother's doing drugs in Boyle Heights, or their little sister is pregnant again, and sorry but they can't finish the last week of the semester cuz Tío Ignacio just got shot in front of a liquor store.

For more recent immigrants the "American dream" may still loom as a possibility on the horizon. Their Mexican pride sustains them through the daily assaults on their intelligence, integrity, and humanity. They maintain a determined individualism within the context of close-knit familias in the effort to support one another on the road to that dream. Still, a new generation of future Chicanos arrives every day with every Mexican immigrant. Some may find their American dream and forget their origins, but most of México's descendants soon comprehend the political meaning of the disparity between their lives and those of the gringo. Certainly, the Mexican women cannery workers of Watsonville who maintained a two-year victorious strike against Green Giant in the mid-eighties and the United Farm Workers union campaigns organized by Cesar Chávez and Dolores Huerta throughout in the 1960s are testimony to the political militancy of the Mexican immigrant worker. More recently, there are the examples of the Mothers of East Los Angeles and the women of Kettleman City who have organized against the toxic contamination proposed for their communities. In the process, la mexicana becomes a Chicana (or at least a Mechicana); that is, she becomes a citizen of this country, not by virtue of a green card, but by virtue of the collective voice she assumes in staking her claim to this land and its resources.

(DES)PLUMADAS:
THE DE-FORMATION OF THE MOVEMENT[9]

With our heart in our hands
and our hands in the soil,
we declare the independence
of our mestizo nation.
                    —Alurista, "El Plan Espiritual de Aztlán"

El Movimiento did not die out in the seventies, as most of its critics claim; it was only deformed by the machismo and homophobia of that era and coopted by the "hispanicization" and the "reaganomics" of the eighties. In reaction against what Chicano men saw as AngloAmerica's emasculation of them through systemic discrimination, the male-dominated Chicano Movement embraced the most patriarchal aspects of its Mexican heritage. For a generation, nationalist leaders used a kind of selective memory, drawing exclusively from those aspects of Mexican and Native cultures that served the interests of male heterosexuals. At times, they took the worst of Spanish machismo and Aztec warrior bravado, combined it with some of the most oppressive male-conceived idealizations of "traditional" Mexican womanhood, and called that cultural integrity. They subscribed to a machista view of women, based on the centuries-old virgin-whore paradigm of la Virgen de Guadalupe and Malintzin Tenepal. Guadalupe represented the Mexican ideal of "la

madre sufrida," the long-suffering desexualized Indian mother, and
Malinche was "la chingada," sexually stigmatized by her transgression of "sleeping with the enemy," Hernán Cortés. Deemed traitor
by Mexican tradition, the figure of Malinche was invoked to keep
Movimiento women silent, sexually passive, and "Indian" in the
colonial sense of the word.*

The preservation of the Chicano familia became the Movimiento's mandate and within this constricted "familia" structure, Chicano politicos ensured that the patriarchal father figure
remained in charge in both their private and political lives. Women
were, at most, allowed to serve as modern-day "Adelitas," performing the "three fs" as one of my Chicana colleagues calls them: "feeding, fighting, and fucking." In the name of this culturally correct
familia, certain topics were censored both in cultural and political
spheres as not socially relevant to Chicanos and typically not sanctioned in the Mexican household. These issues included female
sexuality generally and male homosexuality and lesbianism specifically, as well as incest and violence against women—all of which
are still relevant between the sheets and within the walls of many
Chicano families. In the process, the Chicano Movement forfeited
the participation and vision of some very significant female and
gay leaders and never achieved the kind of harmonious Chicano
"familia" they ostensibly sought.[10]

To this day, although lip service is given to gender issues in
academic and political circles, no serious examination of male
supremacy within the Chicano community has taken place among
heterosexual men. Veteranos of Chicano nationalism are some of
the worst offenders. Twenty years later, they move into elderhood
without having seriously grappled with the fact that their leadership

---

* For more on the impact of "Malinche" on the lives of Chicanas, see "A Long
Line of Vendidas" in this volume.

in El Movimiento was made possible by all those women who kept their "plumas planchadas" (feathers ironed) for every political event.

A Divided Nation: A Chicana Lésbica Critique

We are free and sovereign to determine those tasks which are justly called for by our house, our land, the sweat of our brows, and by our hearts.

Aztlán belongs to those who plant the seeds, water the fields, and gather the crops and not to the foreign Europeans. We do not recognize capricious frontiers on the bronze continent.
— Alurista, "El Plan Espiritual de Aztlán"

A generation ago, when this preamble to "El Plan Espiritual de Aztlán" was conceived and scripted by the poet Alurista, lesbians and gay men were not envisioned as members of the "house"; we were not recognized as the sister planting the seeds, the brother gathering the crops. We were not counted as members of the "bronze continent."

In the last decade, through the efforts of Chicana feministas, Chicanismo has undergone a serious critique. Feminist critics are committed to the preservation of Chicano cultura, but we know that our culture will not survive without organized activism against marital rape, battering, incest, drug and alcohol abuse, AIDS, and the marginalization of lesbian daughters and gay sons. Some of the most outspoken criticism of the Chicano Movement's sexism and some of the most impassioned activism in the area of Chicana liberation (including work on sexual abuse, domestic violence, immigrant rights, Indigenous women's issues, health care, etc.) have been advanced by lesbians.

Since lesbians and gay men have often been forced out of our blood families, and since our love and sexual desire are not housed within the traditional family, we find ourselves in a critical position to address those areas within our cultural family that need to change. Further, to understand and defend our lovers and our same-sex loving, lesbians and gay men must come to terms with how homophobia, gender roles, and sexuality are learned and expressed in Chicano culture. As Ricardo Bracho writes: "To speak of my desire, to find voice in my brown flesh, I needed to confront my male mirror."[11] As a lesbian, I don't presume to understand the intricacies or intimacies of Chicano gay desire, but we do share the fact that our "homosexuality"—our feelings about sex, sexual power and domination, femininity and masculinity, family, loyalty, and morality—have been shaped by heterosexual and heterosexist culture and society. As such, we have plenty to tell heterosexuals about themselves.

When we are moved sexually toward someone, there is a profound opportunity to observe the microcosm of all human relations, to understand power dynamics both obvious and subtle, and to meditate on the core creative impulse of all desire. Desire is seldom politically correct. In sex, gender roles, race relations, and our collective histories of oppression and human connection are enacted. Since the early 1980s, Chicana lesbian feminists have explored these traditionally dangerous topics in both critical and creative writings. Chicana lesbian-identified writers such as Ana Castillo, Gloria Anzaldúa, and Naomi Littlebear Moreno were among the first to articulate a Chicana feminism, which included a radical woman-centered critique of sexism and sexuality from which both lesbian and heterosexual women benefitted.

In the last few years, Chicano gay men have also begun to openly examine Chicano sexuality. I suspect heterosexual Chicanos will have the world to learn from their gay brothers about their shared masculinity, but they will have the most to learn from the "queens," the "maricones." Because they are deemed inferior for not fulfilling the traditional role of men, they are more marginalized from mainstream heterosexual society than other gay men and are especially vulnerable to male violence. Over the years, I have been shocked to discover how many femme gay men have grown up regularly experiencing rape and sexual abuse. The rapist is always heterosexual and usually Chicano like themselves. What has the gay movement done for these brothers/sisters? What has the Chicano Movement done? What do these young and once-young men have to tell us about misogyny and male violence? Like women, they witness the macho's desire to dominate the feminine, but even more intimately, because they both desire men and in varying degrees share manhood with their oppressor (Bracho's "male mirror").*

Until quite recently, Chicano gay men have been silent over the Chicano Movement's male heterosexual hegemony. As much as I see a potential alliance with gay men in our shared experience of homophobia, most gay men still cling to what privileges they can. I have often been severely disappointed and hurt by the misogyny of gay Chicanos. Separation from one's brothers is a painful thing. Being gay does not preclude gay men from harboring the same sexism evident in heterosexual men. It's like white people and racism; sexism goes with the (male) territory.

On some level, our brothers—gay and straight—have got to give up being "men." I don't mean give up their masculinity, I mean, stop their subscription to male superiority. This may be a harder project for men of color, not because they are more sexist than white men, but because they have historically been treated as less than full men in the context of white America.

---

* At the time this essay was written (1992), our understanding of queer identities was largely discussed in terms of sexuality (i.e., lesbian/gay) and binary gender (female-feminine/male-masculine) and not along the spectrum of sexualities, sex, and gender presentations we recognize today. More than thirty years later, the visibility of intersex and trans folk, especially trans women of color, has deepened and progressively complicated queer consciousness and politicization.

I remember during the civil rights movement seeing news-reel footage of the sanitation workers strike in Memphis, Tennessee, where young Black men carried protest signs reading "I AM A MAN." It was a powerful and significant statement, publicly declaring their humanness in a society that historically and violently told them otherwise. But they didn't write "I AM HUMAN," they wrote "MAN." Conceiving of their liberation in male terms, they were demanding the equitable right to be treated as well as any white man and rightfully. This demand would become consciously articulated with the emergence of the male-dominated Black nationalist movement under white capitalist patriarchy. The liberation of Black women per se was not part of the program, except to the extent that better conditions for the race in general might benefit Black women as well.

How differently Sojourner Truth's "Ain't I a Woman?" speech resonates for me. Unable to choose between suffrage and abolition, between her womanhood and her Blackness, Truth's nineteenth-century call for a free Black womanhood in a Black- and woman-hating society required the freedom of all enslaved and disenfranchised peoples. As the Black feminist Combahee River Collective stated in 1977, "If Black women were free, it would mean that everyone else would have to be free since our freedom would necessitate the destruction of all the systems of oppression."[12] No progressive movement can fully succeed while any member of the population remains in submission.

Chicano gay men have been reluctant to recognize and acknowledge that their freedom is intricately connected to the freedom of women. If they insist on remaining "men" in the socially and culturally constructed sexist sense of the word, they will never achieve the liberation they desire. Within people of color communities, violence against women, gay bashing, sterilization abuse, AIDS and AIDS discrimination, gay substance abuse, and gay teen suicide emerge from the same source: a racist and misogynist social and economic system that dominates, punishes, and abuses all that it deems "other." By openly confronting Chicano sexuality and sexism, gay men can do their own part to unravel how both men and women have been formed and deformed by racist America and our misogynist/catholic/colonized mechicanidad. In so doing, we can come that much closer to healing those fissures that have divided us as a people.

The AIDS epidemic has seriously shaken the foundation of the Chicano gay community, and gay men seem more willing than ever to explore those areas of political change that will ensure their survival. In their fight against AIDS, they have been rejected and neglected by both the white gay male establishment and, to some degree, the Latino heterosexual health-care community. They also have witnessed direct support by Latina lesbians.[13]

Unlike the "queens" who have always been open about their sexuality, straight-passing gay men have learned in a visceral way that being in the closet and preserving their masculine front will not protect them, it will only make their dying more secret. I remember my friend Arturo Islas, the novelist. His writing begged to boldly announce his gayness, to dance it beneath a lightning-charged sky just before a thunderstorm. *The Rain God* is a beautiful book that offers a compelling critique of homophobia.[14] Islas died of AIDS-related illness in 1990, having barely begun to examine the complexity of Chicano sexuality in his writing. I also think of essayist Richard Rodriguez, who, with so much death surrounding him, has recently begun to publicly address the subject of homosexuality;[15] and yet, even ten years ago we queer readers all knew "Mr. Secrets" was gay from his assimilationist *Hunger of Memory: The Education of Richard Rodriguez.* Had he come out in 1982, his eloquence as a writer might have told us a different story. For, how many lives are lost each time we cling to privileges that make other people's lives more vulnerable to violence?

At this point in history, lesbians and gay men can make a significant contribution to the creation of a new Chicano Movement, one passionately committed to saving lives. As we are forced to struggle for our right to love free of disease and discrimination, Aztlán as our imagined homeland begins to take on renewed importance. Without the dream of a free world, a free world will never be realized. As queer folk, we do not merely seek inclusion in the Chicano nation; we seek a nation strong enough to embrace a full range of racial diversities, human sexualities, and expressions of gender. We seek a culture that can allow for the natural expression of our femaleness and maleness and our love without prejudice or punishment. In a Queer Aztlán, there would be no freaks, no "others" to point one's finger at.

My Native American friends tell me that in some tribal communities, gay men and lesbians were traditionally regarded as "two-spirit."[16] Displaying both masculine and feminine aspects, they were highly respected members of their community, and were thought to possess a higher spiritual development. Hearing of such traditions gives historical validation for what Chicana lesbians and gay men have always recognized—that we play a significant spiritual, cultural, and political role within the Chicano community. Somos activistas, académicos y artistas, parteras y políticos, curanderas y campesinos. With or without heterosexual acknowledgement, we have continued to actively redefine familia, cultura, y comunidad.

Lo Indígena:
The Re-tribalization of Our People

In recent years, Raza continues to witness the ultimate failure of AngloAmerica to bring justice and true harmony to our lives. We suffer with little notice from the majority population—from a government that has long forgotten those of us whose histories precede them.

Most Chicanos recognize being of Native origin through phenotype alone (I have often heard Raza comment about being the brownest people in a room full of "skins"). This statement does not suggest the illegitimacy of light-skinned Native Americans, it only attests to the ways in which identity construction still remains the literal *business* of the powers that be. We have no right to name/ claim ourselves, not when the government on both sides of the border continues to do so for us.

As de-tribalized peoples, the majority of Chicanos have been historically denied information regarding our Indigenous ancestry, which encompasses a range of nations including Apache, Pueblo, Dineh, Yoeme, Tohono O'odham, Rarámuri, and Kumeyaay—to name only a few from the border regions alone. Despite no verifiable genealogy, many Chicanos are compelled to look to Indigenous philosophies and societal practices to find concrete solutions for the myriad problems confronting us, from the toxic dump sites in our neighborhoods to domestic violence. Many traditional Indigenous socioeconomic tribal or pueblo structures present alternatives that hold considerable appeal for those of us who recognize the weakness in values fixated on the production of capital, buttressed by the privatized patriarchal nuclear family.

In an ideal world—perhaps a "re-tribalized Aztlán"—members are responsive and responsible to one another and the natural environment, collaboration is rewarded over competition, acts of violence against women and children are not allowed to remain secret, and perpetrators are held accountable to the rest of the community. Family is not dependent upon male dominance or heterosexual coupling. Elders are respected and women's leadership is fostered, not feared.

But it is not an ideal world. Any Indian on or off the reservation can tell you about the obstacles to following traditional ways that still hold resonance for their people. The reservation is not indigenous to Native Americans; it is a colonial model invented to disempower Native peoples. The rates of alcoholism, suicide, diabetes, and domestic violence are testimony to the genocidal effectiveness of that system. Chicanos, living in the colony of the US barrio, have the same scars: AIDS, drugs, brown-on-brown murder, poverty, and environmental contamination. Nevertheless, the present-day values and organized struggles of many traditional Native pueblos throughout the Américas represent real hope for halting the quickly accelerating level of destruction affecting all life on this continent.

MADRE TIERRA: THE STRUGGLE FOR LAND

JOURNAL ENTRY

I sit in a hotel room. A fancy hotel room with two walls of pure glass and pure Vancouver night skyline filling them. I sit on top of the bed and eat Japanese takeout. The Canadian TV news takes us east to the province of Quebec, to some desolate area with no plumbing or sewage system, no running water, where a group of Inuit people have been displaced; an uninhabitable place where Inuit children stick their faces into bags and sniff gas fumes for the high, the rush, the trip, for the escape out of this hellhole that is their life. One young boy gives the finger to the TV camera. "They're angry," an Inuit leader states. "I'm angry, too." At thirty, he is already an old man. And I hate this Canada as much as I hate these dis-United States. But I go on eating my Japanese meal that has somehow turned rotten on my tongue and my bloody culpability mixes with the texture of dead fish flesh and no wonder I stand on the very edge of the balcony on the twenty-sixth floor of this hotel looking down on restaurant-row Vancouver and imagine how easy and impossible it would be to leap in protest for the gas-guzzling Inuit children.

The primary struggle for Native peoples across the globe is the struggle for the sovereign protection of their land. In 1992, five hundred years after the arrival of Columbus, on the heels of the Gulf War and the dissolution of the Soviet Union, the entire world is reconstructing itself. No longer frozen into the Soviet/Yanqui paradigm of a Cold and invented War, Indigenous peoples are responding en masse to the threat of a global capitalist monoculture defended by the hired guns of the US military. Five hundred years after Columbus's arrival, they are spearheading an international movement with the goal of sovereignty for all Indigenous nations.

Increasingly, the struggles on this planet are not for nation-states, but for nations of people, bound together by spirit, land, language, history, and blood.[17] The world must pay attention. People do not forget who they are. This is evident from the intifada of the Palestinians residing within Israel's stolen borders and the resistance of the Cree and Inuit Indians in northern Quebec. The Kurds of the Persian Gulf region understand this, as do the Ukrainians of what was once the Soviet Union.* Why is it so radical to accept that Chicanos are also a nation of people, internally colonized within the borders of the nation-state of the USA? How might we find sovereignty over what is rightfully ours? What *is* rightfully ours?

Few Chicanos really believe we can wrest Aztlán away from AngloAmerica. And yet, residing in those Southwestern territories, especially those areas not completely appropriated by Gringolandia, we instinctively remember it as *Mexican* Indian land and can still imagine it as a distinct nation. In our most private moments, we ask ourselves, *"If the Soviet Union could dissolve, why can't the United States?"*[18]

If the material basis of every nationalist movement is land, then the reacquisition, defense, and protection of Native land and its natural resources are the basis for rebuilding Chicano nation—with or without recognition. Without the sovereignty of Native peoples, including Chicanos, and support for our land-based struggles, the world will be lost to North American greed, and our culturas lost with it. The "last frontier" for Northern capitalists lies buried in coal- and uranium-rich reservation lands and in the remaining rainforests of the Amazon. The inhabitants of these territories—the Diñé, the Northern Cheyenne,

---

* And all these embittered struggles continue to this day.

the Kayapó, and others—are the very people who in 1992 offer the world community living models of ways to live in balance with nature and safeguard the earth as we know it. The great historical irony is that five hundred years after the so-called "conquest," the conqueror must now turn to the conquered for salvation.

These are bottom-line considerations. I can't understand when in 1992 with one hundred acres of rainforest disappearing every minute, with global warming, with babies being born without brains in South Tejas, with street kids in Rio sniffing glue to stifle their hunger, with Mohawk women's breast milk being contaminated by the poisoned waters of the Great Lakes Basin, how we as people of color, as people of Native blood, as people with the same last names as our Latin American counterparts, are not alarmed by the destruction of Indigenous and mestizo peoples. How is it Chicanos cannot see ourselves as victims of the same destruction, already in its advanced stages? Why do we not collectively experience the urgency for alternatives based not on what our oppressors advise, but on the advice of elders and ancestors who may now speak to us only in dreams?

What they are telling us is very dear (and clear). The road to the future is the road from our past. Traditional Indigenous communities (our Indian "past" that too many Chicanos have rejected) provide practical answers for our survival. At the Earth Summit in Río de Janeiro in June 1992, representatives from developing countries, and grassroots, Indigenous, and people-of-color organizations, joined together to demand the economic programs necessary to create their own sustainable ecologically sound communities. In a world where eighty-five percent of all the income, largely generated from the natural resources of Indigenous lands and Third World countries, goes to twenty-three percent of the people, Fidel Castro said it best: "Let the ecological debt be paid, not the foreign debt."

And here all the connecting concerns begin to coalesce. Here the Marxist meets the environmentalist. We need look no further than the North American Free Trade Agreement (NAFTA) to understand the connection between global ecological devastation and the United States' relentless drive to expand its markets. NAFTA is no more than a twenty-first-century plot to continue the North's exploitation of the cheap labor, lax environmental policies, and natural resources of the South. The United States has no intention of responding to the environmental crisis. George H. W. Bush's decision to "stand alone on principle" and refuse to sign the Biodiversity Treaty said it all. Profit over people. Profit over protection. No sustainable development is possible in the Americas if the United States continues to demand hamburgers, Chrysler automobiles, and refrigerators from hungry, barefoot, and energy-starved nations. There is simply not enough to go around—no new burial ground for toxic waste that isn't sacred, no untapped energy source that doesn't suck the earth dry. Except for the sun, except for the wind, which are infinite in their generosity and virtually ignored.

The Earth is female. Whether myth, metaphor, or memory, she is called "Mother" by all peoples of all times. Madre Tierra. Like woman, Madre Tierra has been raped, exploited for her resources, rendered inert, passive, and speechless. Her cries manifested in earthquakes, tidal waves, hurricanes, volcanic eruptions are not heeded. But Indian peoples take note and so do the women, the women with the capacity to remember.[19]

Native religions have traditionally honored the female alongside the male. Religions that grow exclusively from the patriarchal capitalist imagination, instead of the requirements of nature, enslave the female body. The only religion we need is one based on the good sense of living in harmony with nature. Religion should serve as a justification against greed, not for it. Bring back the rain gods, corn gods, father sun, and mother-sister moon and keep those gods happy. Whether we recognize it or not, those gods are today, this day, punishing us for our excess. What humankind has destroyed will wreak havoc on the destroyer. Fried skin from holes in the ozone is only one example.

The Earth is female. It is no accident then that the main grass-roots activists defending the Earth, along with Native peoples, are women of all races and cultures. Regardless of the so-called advances of Western civilization, women remain the chief caretakers, nurturers, and providers for our children and our elders. These are the mothers of East Los Angeles, McFarland, and Kettleman City, fighting toxic dumps, local incinerators, and pesticide poisoning, women who experience the Earth's contamination in the deformation and death occurring within their very wombs. We do not have to be mothers to know this. Most women know what it is to be seen as the Earth is seen—a receptacle for male violence and greed. Over half the agricultural workers in the world are women who receive less training and less protection than their male counterparts. We do not control how we produce and reproduce, how we labor and love. And how will our lands be free if our bodies aren't?

Land remains the common ground for all radical action. But land is more than the rocks and trees, the animal and plant life that make up the territory of Aztlán or Navajo Nation or Maya Mesoamerica. For immigrant and Native alike, land is also the factories where we work, the water our children drink, and the housing project where we live. For women and queer folk, land is that physical mass called our bodies. Throughout las Américas, all these "lands" remain under occupation by a Eurocentric, patriarchal, imperialist United States.

LA CAUSA CHICANA: NEARING THE NEXT MILLENNIUM

As a Chicana lesbian, I know that the struggle we share with Indigenous peoples is truly one of sovereignty, the sovereign right to wholly inhabit oneself (cuerpo y alma) and one's territory (pan y tierra). I don't know if we can ever take back Aztlán from AngloAmerica, but in the name of a new Chicano Movement we can work to defend remaining Indian territories. We can work to teach one another that our freedom as a people is mutually dependent and cannot be parceled out hierarchically—class before race before sex before sexuality. A new Chicano Movement calls for the integration of both the traditional and the revolutionary, the ancient and the contemporary. It requires a serious reckoning with the weaknesses in our mestizo culture as it has been handed down to us, and a reaffirmation of what has preserved and sustained us as a people. I am clear about one thing: fear has not sustained us. Fear of action, fear of speaking, fear of women, fear of queers.

As these five hundred years come to a close, I look forward to a new América, where the only discovery to be made is the rediscovery of ourselves as interdependent members of the global community. Nature will be our teacher, for she alone knows no prejudice. Possibly as we ask men to give up being men in its oppressive role, we must ask humans to give up being human in the same way or at least to give up the human capacity for greed. Simply, we must give back to the Earth what we take from it. We must submit to a higher natural authority, as we invent new ways of making culture, making tribe, to survive and flourish as members of the world community in the next millennium.

En Memoriam

For Rodrigo Reyes

January 23, 1992

the death of a brother.
a sudden glimpsed brother
an estranged brother,
a once-touched brother . . .

Last night at the memorial, listening to the tributes made to him, I kept thinking how Rodrigo loved his own kind, his own brown and male kind. It was clear that the hearts he touched the most deeply were his carnalitos. And each one, as lovely as the one preceding him, spoke about Rodrigo, "mi 'mano, mi papito, mi carnal, ese cabrón . . ." con un cariño wholly familial.

For a moment, I wondered if women had ever entered Rodrigo's heart in the same way. Perhaps his mother had when Rodrigo, as a young teenager, told her, "Déjalo," referring to his father. "Leave him, Amá. Yo te cuido. We don't need him." When Rodrigo told me that story from his sickbed, a different Rodrigo came into view—a

---

* Rodrigo Reyes was a community organizer, theater director, actor, poet, and painter who made his life in the Gay Latino Mission District of San Francisco. He died of AIDS-related illness on January 19, 1992.

man who was once a boy with a boy's earnestness to protect and defend his mother—with a boy's desire to conceive of a manhood outside of abuse. We were all inocentes once and we carry that broken innocence into every meeting with every stranger and every potential amante.

Was it in the same visit he asked me, the barriers between us momentarily dissolving?

"Do you see that painting?" He points to a living mass of color on the wall.

"Yes," I answer.

"That painting just passed through me. Rodrigo didn't paint that, it just happened. Rodrigo disappeared. Do you understand?"

And a desire welled up in me to meet this man, to finally speak with a brother about my most private place, that place where the work possesses us and our small egos take flight.

"Yes," I answer. "I understand."

He told me that all he wanted was a little more time, a little more time to repeat that moment, to be the servant of his art, and utterly humbled in the creation of it. There is no greater joy, we agreed. And how I wanted him to live, too, for just that reason.

The gift of the dying is that they allow us, their survivors, to contemplate our own deaths, our own meanings, our own creations. I thank him for this—for this me, with some time still to spare.

I wonder why and how we live in an era when dying is such a visceral part of our daily lives. Possibly, living in San Francisco and not San Salvador, we imagined we would be spared such a relentlessly intimate acquaintance with death, an intimacy seldom experienced except in times of war and natural disaster; but this is the era in which we live. Women dying in droves from cancer;

gay men/folks of color dying of AIDS. I don't know what to make of it. It has barely begun to touch my life. Perhaps I have Rodrigo to thank again for this—initiating me to life with the knowledge of death.

Last night the homage given to Rodrigo convinced me of how rare it is to be colored and queer and live to speak about it. In honoring Rodrigo, one young man said, "Rodrigo devoted his entire life to the community." And I would add, he devoted his entire passion to his own brown brothers. He delighted in their beauty, their desire, and their hope. He wanted them to be free, and righteously. I believe that in Rodrigo's final months and in his final words, he saw a much clearer road toward that freedom, and that it had something to do with the freedom of women, too. I believe he started to understand this, not in his head, but in his gut, when he looked upon so much death and drugs and despair within his own community and saw who remained at his bedside.

The last thing I did for Rodrigo, the last time I saw him, was cut his toenails. I marveled at it, how after all our heated feminist debates, it had come down to this simple act. He was my brother, after all, and he needed his toenails cut. I confess, I did not always feel recognized by Rodrigo as a sister. At times I felt that the sisters simply didn't matter to him. And in each rejection I saw the face of my own blood brother. Let us not kid ourselves, this is what we bring to our meetings as latinos, lesbianas, jotos, políticos—all the wounds of family betrayals and abandonments. But I know—with or without his recognition—that, as artists and queers, we were intimately tied to each other's survival, knowledge, y libertad.

He did make space for them, his brothers.
He did plant seeds.

He did lay ground.

And this is where the young ones pick up . . .
Pa'lante, 'manitos!

Where Beauty Resides

Maya mathematics from the beginning of the Classic Peri-od included the concept of zero, principally as a symbol of completeness.

—Miguel León-Portilla, *Time and Reality
in the Thought of the Maya*

A cup is molded of clay, but its . . . hollow space is the useful part.
—Carolyn Merchant, *Radical Ecology:
The Search for a Livable World*

Your hand, a cup that empties me of myself.
I am reduced to zero.
I meditate on how I will live without
reflection.
The quiet invades.

Thursday morning and minutes ago you were here with me.
I look out onto a city of grey and steel blue structures
I spot you folded into one of them
red brick lining the walls where you work
you are thinking of me
you put pencil to your lip
teeth imbedded into knuckle
you inhale
what was once me or the scent of your own
expectant
desire.

Here, indoors, the city is not grey

the sheets are a steel blue that ignite your eyes
searching me strip searching me,
I have gone no more
your hand has only emptied me of all want.
"Satisfecha," I say
the word hard like sex
whole in meaning.

When you rise I watch you cover your body
your elbows spread like crooked wings
bra snaps behind your back
you step into panties
sliding up thighs
your wound mouth disappears
shirt slipping over head
you emerge, a radiant medusa.

I see you as I was instructed:
"you have a beautiful body"
you smile, snap up the crotch of your jeans
but your beauty resides elsewhere
you know this too,
emptied of ourselves.

I only ask this one thing of you:
beyond woman hidden in woman
resides child hidden in child
resides zero.

There is no loneliness there
but a strangeness, I admit
my eyes scanning the cityscape for your shape

against the fog's haze, I search
strip search these words
emptied of myself.

As a catholic schoolgirl I would have confessed
the sin of you   my body,
the temple of my undoing.

I suspect this feeling is called sadness I suspect
I used to name this loneliness
your back walking out the door
the weight of another being as fragile
as delicate as lonely as mine
heavy upon your shoulders.

I think of others, too, while I kiss you,
pacts we make in the coveted hours of urban life.

I'll promise you anything
for the bowl of your breasts and thighs
to contain me once more
this morning
this bed.

I am speaking of something else here
with no name
it is about the number zero
without loneliness betrayal regret
you emptied me of myself.

When you leave
what I remember as fear

a vague sense of relief
a panicked moment of abandonment
what I remember in myriad
faces of lovers at myriad
numbers of doors in myriad
faceless numberless cities
dissipates from me
I watch you leave emptied of those memories
I watch you leave and enter me
my eyes, liquid prey before her hunter.

Return to me, amor, again
and again with the same animal hunger.
I will not refuse you I have nothing left to lose.
You cannot devour what is infinite you drink
until replenished and drink again
and I am the receiver of your thirst
your tongue, my blessing
your hands, gifts from the gods.

I am emptied of myself
relieved of this burden
my body, a sacrament
a flame
a holy sacrifice.

All else is blasphemy.

    . . . . .

I am writing you to reach you without words
you will not read these words as much as you will see them

this day written in the bay grey sky
you will know me better than you imagined
forgive me everything
and generosity will lay upon us
span the bridge that links and divides us

and I could go on writing like this forever
only guessing
at what lies inside
the shape and size
of these letters.

Codex Xeritzín—El Momento Histórico*

*Amid the fires of the Los Angeles Rebellion, on the eve of a
fading Quinto Sol and a rising new época, I paint in scribe
colors—black ink & fire red—my own Chicana codex. I offer
it as the closing prayer for the last generation.*

Picture this. It is May 1, 1992. Fifty-eight people dead, hundreds
injured, and thousands are arrested across the country. Enflamed
by the Los Angeles uprising, my hometown of San Francisco also
ignites. The mayor calls a state of emergency. Young people—
brown, black, white—are rounded up. Anyone walking the streets
of el barrio after 7 p.m. is arrested: hundreds of protesters spill out
of Dolores Park—two women who happen to be coming home from
a nearby wedding, another risking an emergency trip to the store
(any store she can find open) to buy tampons. Hours later, she's in
the Santa Rita Jail, still bleeding.

---

* This essay was originally written for the Mexican Museum's 1992 "Chicano
Codices Encountering Art of the Américas," curated by Marcos Sánchez-Tranquilino. Representing twenty-five Chicano artists from across the United States,
the exhibit's task was to create a contemporary response to the Mesoamerican
codices, the pictorial record books of Indigenous American thought largely
destroyed by the fires of the Spanish conquest. Much of the visual imagery incor-
porated in this essay was inspired by codices by Amalia Mesa-Bains, Barbara
Carrasco, Emanuel Martinez, Emmanuel Catarino Montoya, Delilah Montoya,
the East Los Streetscapers, Carmen Lomas Garza, Willie Herrón, Kathy Vargas,
Marcos Raya, Marta Sanchez, Larry Yáñez, and Celia Herrera Rodríguez.

After these Roman hieroglyphics have been pressed onto the printed page, history will have advanced well beyond the time of this writing; but as the Maya understood, a date is not a beginning, but the culmination of history in all its totality. What we are witnessing today took five hundred years of invasion to create.

It is 1992 and Los Angeles is on fire. Half a millennium after the arrival of Columbus, the Mesoamerican prophecies are being fulfilled. The once enslaved have taken to the streets, burning down the conqueror's golden cities. A decade-long plague that attacks the very immune system upon which our survival depends assumes pandemic proportions. There is famine and worldwide displacement.

People are living in refrigerator boxes on the streets of Aztlán. Earthquakes jolt the California coastline with increasing regularity. With such violent movement, "El Quinto Sol" will be destroyed. The temple has been toppled and is falling into flames. This is the USAmerican destiny.

> *There are dark patches on the faces of the children.*
> *They are crying.*

It was not always like this.

In the beginning there were no contradictions. God, Ometeotl, the origin of all life, was both woman and man, Omecihuatl and Ometecuhtli. The paradox of our Native existence—that we both govern our fate and are predetermined to live it—was simply a naked truth expressed in a poem, a song, an embroidered mantle, a jaguar god etched into jade-ite. Science was less intelligent than art. And art and its makers were respected. Metaphor depicted what the intellect suffered: la flor de nuestro ser, su belleza, su fragilidad. Her temporal and fleeting essence.

Five hundred years later, our deepest memories are mere color-
less glimpses: paper cutouts of the ancient dalia, maguey, lagartija.
Our reptilian regeneration lies fragmented, hand split from heart.
Decapitated, our speech scrolled tongues float in a wordless sea.

How did we grow so speechless?

> *We know the red path.*
> *Bloody footprints on urban streetscapes.*
> *We assimilated, put on the white mask.*
> *We have been sleepwalking the road of "Davy Crockett"*
> *heroes.*

The Chicano codex is the map back to the original face. Its scribes are
the modern-day tlamatinime. We grab la raza's face and turn it in our
palm. We hold up the obsidian mirror, tell them, "Look, gente, so that
you might know yourselves, find your true face and heart, and see."

The Chicano codex es una peregrinación to an América unwritten.
América: the brown swell of tierra indígena debajo de la Calavera.
Our rapist wears the face of death. In a suit of armor, he rides us—
cross in one hand, sword in the other.

> *This is how they've always taken us*
> *with their gods of war and their men of god.*

The Chicano codex is a demand for retribution—for land and lives
lost. Our records show the sum of Chicano existence engraved on
tombstones: World War I, World War II, Korea, Vietnam, Iraq. Our
records show a five-century-long list of tributes paid to illegal land-
lords. We want it *all* back, Señor!

Keep those "40 pieces of gold the size of communion hosts," and give us
back Colorado, Cabrón. Keep your smallpox infested blankets, syphilis-

infected Spaniards, and give us back los Tainos. Keep your Cortés and give us back Peltier. Return the rainforests and we'll return genocide, alcoholism, drug addiction, and nuclear disaster.

Chicano scribes are deconstructing the gringo history of greed. The real history kept from us, we scratch it on barrio walls, deciphering modern-day hieroglyphs—pachuco slang blending into urban guerrillero tongue, "US out of Aztlán NOW!" "Cada marca escarbando el rostro de nuestra memoria."*

And there at the Mar Vista Gardens, on the stoneface of a housing project, a heart is drawn in the shape of a breast. *Can you see it?*
The soft arc of vulva. There.
The backbone of a woman winding into a Quetzalcóatl mind.

       And the women whisper:

       we are more
       than mujer before metate
       we are more
       than mujer before metate
       we are more.

A Mechicana glyph. Con Safos.

The Chicano codex is a portrait of our daily lives.
How many corn cakes a day do the children of Aztlán need to survive?
Images of spam next to a stack of store-bought tortillas.
Chavalitos working in the family panadería.
We are a codex of lotería and boxing matches.
We pick nopales, graduate from college, are elected County Supervisor.
We low-ride in East Los, bumper to bumper in minitrucks.

---

* From the artist's notes for *Codex Zelia* by Celia Herrera Rodríguez.

We light velas at La Placita.

For whom do we pray?

This time, for Juan.
In the circle of this oración we form a contemporary urban Chicano
glyph. A small group of jotería stand in the shadow de Los Pechos de La
Indígena (San Francisco). Two lush green mounds of female protection.
A radio tower piercing her breast.

We sprinkle his ashes en la comadre's yard, an urban jardín of coffee-can
pots and desert succulents. It's a wonder how the Mexican desert sur-
vives here under the ever-damp serape of bay fog. We fill the mouth of
each can with the white dust of his bones, una cucharita at a time. Sea
birds pass overhead. One woman announces, "Miren, there goes our
brother. See how without flesh, he is free to fly." As in the Mesoamerican
tradition, a small dog bears witness and guides him home.

Our codices are a record of remembering. At times, we can only
sense those memories intuitively like an "internal feather"—always
present, always hidden, yet glowing iridescent under a tejano full
moon. Our memory is the umbilical cord buried beneath the shade
of cottonwoods, where abuelita cuentos pour scroll-like from the
tongue. She is the knowledge of aloe vera for sunburn, nopalitos for
lonche, yerbabuena for just about anything.

Today, I burn the sage Juan brought back from the hills outside Tijuana.
I plant the geraniums that Carmen gave me from her garden. I light a
vela before la Virgen. And on Christmas, Las Comadres will put down
our paintbrushes, turn off our computers, and stick our hands into the
masa como lo han hecho las abuelas por siglos.

In these simple acts, we remember
the forgotten,
the fragmented,
the dismembered.
We re-member the severed serpent.
We feed the dust of our bones pa' las plantas.
And once again fertility is possible.

The Chicana scribe remembers, not out of nostalgia but out of hope. She remembers in order to envision. She looks backward in order to look forward to a world no longer machined by greed, but generated by the sovereign knowledge of nature. And in this, she suffers—to know that fertility is both possible and constantly interrupted.

As it was for the tlamatinime centuries ago, the scribe's task is to interpret the signs of the time, read the writing on barrio walls, decode the hieroglyphs of street violence, unravel the skewed message of brown-on-brown crime and sister-rape. The Chicano codex is our book of revelation. It is the philosopher's stone, serpentine and regenerative. It prescribes our fate and releases us from it. It understands the relationship between darkness and dawn.

> *"Mira que te has de morir. Mira que no sabes cuándo."**

This Fifth Sun is quickly vanishing. Urban Warriors emerge on LA streetscapes. "Every empire falls," says homeboy. "The Romans fell. The Egyptians fell. [The Aztecs fell.] This empire's gonna go, too." He, too, reads the writing on the wall.

Five hundred years ago, our original colonizers came in search of

---

* From "Codex Amalia" by Amalia Mesa-Bains.

Gold. And today, in Los Angeles and San Francisco our babies are being buried under it.

GOLD that's a Whirlpool dryer

GOLD that's a case of Pepsi-Cola

GOLD that's a SONY television/VCR unit

GOLD that's AMERICAN EXPRESS CARD GOLD

And even this will not be sign enough.

Even this will not.

Each uprising es un paso en la jomada, the red path to baptism con la Madre Mescalera. With each action, another feather bursts forth. It splits the chest, the skin bleeds. The planet is Crow Woman in whose mountain-breasts the missiles of destruction have been implanted. We open the wound to make it heal, purify ourselves with the prick of maguey thorns. This Sun will not pass away painlessly!

It is 1992, and we are witnessing a new breed of revolucionario, their speech scrolls are slave tongues let loose. Feathers in full plumage, they burn down the Alamo, Macy's San Francisco, the savings and loan, and every liquor store in South Central Los Angeles! Meanwhile, Tlaliyolo—"corazón de la tierra"—prepares to turn over.

And we, the Codex-Makers, remove the white mask.
We wait and watch the horizon.

Our Olmeca third eye
begins to glisten
in the slowly
rising
light.

COYOLXAUHQUI REMEMBERED*

1995-1999

---

* Writings in this section were originally published in the second edition of *Loving in the War Years*, 2000.

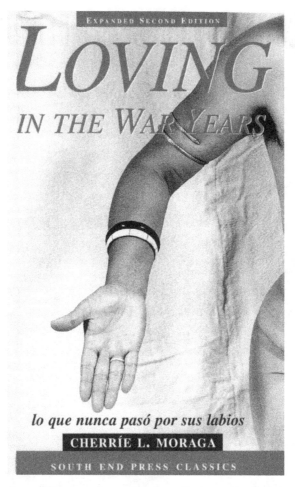

EXPANDED SECOND EDITION

LOVING

IN THE WAR YEARS

lo que nunca pasó por sus labios

CHERRÍE L. MORAGA

SOUTH END PRESS CLASSICS

Cover of the 2000 edition. Photo by Hulleah J. Tsinhnahjinnie; from a performance work by Celia Herrera Rodríguez, *What Part Indian Am I?*, 1994.

Moon in Memoriam

As my Beloved starts the ceremonial fire,
we turn in the moon's direction
to watch its near-fullness crest
over the darkening hills.

Is this not you, Marsha, our warrior-sister—
la Coyolxauhqui returned?
Dismembered by the male gods of war,
are you not that woman of the earth,
broken into pieces?

That moon-diosa rising behind juniper-blue
tejano hills?

For artist-activist Marsha Gómez
(1951–1998)

Coyolxauhqui Re-membered*

ON THE EVE OF THE YEAR TWO THOUSAND

In the late 1970s when I wrote the first poems of what later would become part of *Loving in the War Years*, I had never heard of Coyolxauhqui, severed into pieces in the war against her brother, but I knew her brokenness. I had felt the breast of my lesbian desire amputated from the warrior loins of my cultura.

> *She, an ancient Mexica warrior deported into darkness.*
> *I, a young Xicanadyke, writing in exile.*

What I had imagined would protect me—the armored helmet of my feminism—provided me no shield against the neo-gringo theft of tongue and tierra. Without knowing, I had been looking for Coyolxauhqui in those dark wartime writings of two decades past, the dim reflection of my own pale moon-face lighting my way.

I am not the first, I kept telling myself, *I am not the only one to walk this road.* But I felt it so at the time, the danger of putting the words "lesbian" and "Chicana" together on the same page, within the same line. The danger of walking in the body of she who put them together.

---

* An earlier version of this essay originally appeared as an introduction to the second edition of *Loving in the War Years*. It has been revised and reassigned a chronological place in this collection.

In 1983, in the month that *Loving* was to be released, I had escaped Brooklyn to the anonymity of México, somehow thinking the distance would shield me from a more profound banishment awaiting me. Still, I thought only of return to my Califas, where I could be all my fragmented parts at once: the re-membered Coyolxauhqui taking up permanent residence in Aztlán. Twenty years later, now at the precipice of the millennium, I can say I am returned—neither Aztec goddess nor completely whole, but well-accustomed to the darkness.*

As a child, I had anticipated this "coming of age" moment, regularly counting the years ahead to configure how old I'd be at the turn of the century. Now I barely believe in the calendar of the West—how it counts linearly to invent a history in Christ's birth, and Columbus' arrival into the translucent turquoise waters of a misnomered América.

Still, much has changed between the first and second edition of *Loving*: the USSR was dissolved, the Sandinista Revolution was dismantled, AIDS was discovered and took on pandemic proportions. Cesar Chávez died in his sleep from exhaustion, and Audre Lorde and Toni Cade Bambara passed in ever-warrior resistance to cancer. My abuelita, born in 1888, passed onto the spirit world in 1984 and mis queridos padres grow to fear disability and death in their weakening bodies and advancing years. Affirmative action and bilingual education were outlawed in California, and cancer has clustered throughout the central agricultural valley of California and along the poisoned perimeters of Aztlán.

When I compiled the first edition of *Loving in the War Years*, I did so without the aid of a computer; twenty years later, the computer has invaded the lives of most middle-class citizens of first-world countries. Thanks to a global internet, the computer is the fastest-growing site of US investment of time and money. It is where the US shops,

---

* For earlier references to Coyolxauhqui, see "En busca de la fuerza femenina" in this volume.

dates, reads, writes, makes pornography, and makes profit. It is a new epoch in which middle-class white kids can be college dropouts and become millionaires overnight, and where getting this book to press took about a quarter of the time it would have twenty years ago. It is also where I have found innumerable resources on prison rights, human rights abuse, Xicana Indígena organizing, public protests against Latino-loathing legislation, and more networks of relevant information than one earnest writer can scarcely begin to approach.

Twenty years. A litany of change, political and personal.

Twenty years ago, I was not a mother, only a daughter. Still, I can state, unequivocally, as I did in the first edition of *Loving*, "It is the daughters who are my audience."[1] And any son who will listen. Now, in fact, I have a son of seven years, who I hope is listening. I also have a whole family of queer and blood relations I couldn't have dreamed possible at twenty-seven.

Is this the road to Coyolxauhqui's re-memberment?

Since the first publication of *Loving*, I have also become a playwright, my transition into dramatic writing the direct result of *Loving*'s completion. I had finally told my own story, which (it seems) allowed space for other voices, other stories to enter me. My earliest (late 1980s into the '90s) plays reflect a fictionalized voice made possible through the autobiographical musings of my nonfiction writings. Theater has also become, for me, a new and oftentimes embattled public forum for cultural criticism. In the meantime, I have made a living mostly as a teacher and lecturer, traveling to conferences and colleges around the country, where I have witnessed in just one generation the deradicalization of many ethnic and feminist studies programs. This then, twenty years later, is a bit of the biography of my life, my times.

When they discovered El Templo Mayor beneath the walls of
this city, they had not realized that it was She who discovered

them. Nothing remains buried forever. Not even memory,
especially not memory.

—Giving Up the Ghost[2]

Maybe what I like best about writing is that it always knows better than you where you're going, if you let it. This is what also makes writing so dangerous, that it can reveal to you what you didn't know you knew. I wrote the lines above one year after *Loving in the War Years'* original publication. I was describing how Mexican workers, repairing underground electrical lines in the central Zócalo in Mexico City, had inadvertently unearthed what would later be revealed as the remains of El Templo Mayor, the last of the major Mexica (Aztec) temples. Without thinking, I referred to the temple as "She." I learned later that the first evidence of Templo Mayor under the "walls of (that) city" was the giant, 3.25 meters in diameter, stone disk sculpture of Coyolxauhqui, the dismembered moon goddess. From her, all the rest of El Templo Mayor would be eventually unearthed, where it stands resurrected today.

Had Coyolxauhqui spoken to me? Me, her distant mixed-blood pocha relative, living in the northern land of her descendants? Maybe these are just delusions of my own self-importance. But such self-indulgence is critical to the writing process. Because without indulging our fears, our fantasies, our fury, how then are we to land upon truth? And, from that time forward, I decided maybe I could remember (know) more than what the small biography of my life determined. Maybe I could re-member Coyolxauhqui at least in this writing, this teaching, this praying, this home.

So, this gives me hope.

That as artists we might have something to contribute between and beyond what we are allowed to live here in this americanprison of forgetfulness, durante los años de guerra and its endless Indian Wars.

1999/2000
Oakaztlån, califas

Canto Florido

1
a flor de labios
vivo yo
poeta de la palabra
silenciada

I do not sing
what resides always
on the tip
of the tongue,
la ausencia protegida
en la cuna del cuerpo

it is always
what is not
said
what we remember
fleetingly
as the flower.

a petal drops between my teeth

(the Spanish Poets did not know
this, the Spanish Poets tasted
only dust
on their stingy
tongues.)

2
la flor fugaz

En la boca del río
that is our bed
we return a la tierra salada,
a los huesos molidos.
a los mitos antiguos
we return
fertilizer pa' las flores
born of sea.

You are not so much sea
as desierto, the hot
animal-glove que me cubre
por la noche
     Cihuacoatl

membrane molten onto fist,
the sieve of my pored-skin left
wanting
nothing.

Cells reorganize
we prepare to die.

tú
tú, mi flor
en la flor de la edad
ya
     a petal drops between my teeth

mi querida
muerte.

Looking for the Insatiable Woman[1]

One day a story will arrive in your town. There will always be disagreement over direction—whether the story came from the southwest or the southeast. The story may arrive with a stranger; a traveler thrown out of his home country months ago. Or the story may he brought by an old friend, perhaps the parrot trader. But after you hear the story, you and the others prepare by the new moon to rise up against the slave masters.
    —Leslie Marmon Silko, *Almanac of the Dead*[2]

Most of us can name the story that came into the town of our hearts which changed our lives forever. For me, they were the earliest stories I can remember of my mother's childhood as a farmworker, so little the family used to drag her along between the rows of crops like the sack of potatoes they were picking. Thirty years later, those stories would become the farmworker familias of my plays. The place the same: the Central Valley of Califas; the people—composites of stories told, remembered, witnessed, and invented.

Ironically, the story of La Llorona, the Mexican Weeping Woman, was never told to me by my mother or any family member; and yet, it has had a more profound impact upon my writer's psyche than any story they recounted. One traditional Mexican version of La Llorona tells the tale of a woman who is sexually betrayed by her man, and, in what was either a fit of jealous rage or pure retaliation, she kills their children by drowning them in a river. Upon her own death, she is unable to enter heaven because of her crime. Instead, she is destined to spend all eternity searching for her dead children. Her lament, "Mis hijos!," becomes the blood-chilling cry heard along irrigation ditches and country creeks, warning children that any misbehavior (straying too far from camp, for example) might lead to abduction by this female phantom.

The story of La Llorona first arrived in the town of *my* heart quite by accident through the mouth of an almost-stranger. She was a "traveler," as Leslie Marmon Silko writes, "thrown out of (her) home country" of bible-belt California years before. At the time, the mid-1970s, I was working as a waitress in a vegetarian restaurant on the borderline between San Francisco's gay Castro district and el barrio de la misión. The "traveler" was a white woman who'd come in, an hour before closing, every other weeknight for a bowl of brown rice and stir-fry vegetables and a cup of tea. I liked the look of the woman from the start: thirty-something-ish, bleached-blonde permed hair, broken-toothed and full-chested. She had a wide smiling face. I spied the button she wore on her too-tight tee shirt, which read "Commie Dyke," and I instantly knew the girl was family. Amber (I'll call her by her real name because she'd like being the protagonist of her own story) came in most nights after she closed up shop at the collectively owned leftist Modern Times Bookstore just down the road. She'd walk in, throw a load of new titles onto the decoupage tabletop, and crack open one of those revolutionary texts.

The books drew me to her. I remember one title in particular, the blue and red letters against the silver background, *The Romance of American Communism*.[3] There in the post-rush-hour lull, over a cup of Darjeeling and within earshot of a few scraggly looking hippies, I got my first real introduction to Mr. Karl Marx as told to me by Ms. Amber Hollibaugh,[4] an honest-to-god member of the working class. She informed me that I, too, had been holding membership without ever fully understanding it until it poured from this girl's lips like salve for the wounded and ignorant. *But that's another story.*

The story I want to tell is how this whitegirl from the "asshole of nowhere," as another working-class friend's momma used to call anywhere not Los Angeles or New York, opened my heart to the story of La Llorona. Not that this girl from some truck stop in the Central Valley *consciously* knew anything about the Mexican myth, but what she told me shook loose that memory bone in me that had stored the cuento for at least one generation.

At the time, Amber was doing prison support work for a thirty-nine-year-old very butch lesbian, who had been locked up in an Oregon prison for half her life. Jay Freeman was a child-killer. A contemporary La Llorona. And the required betrayal involved not a man, but what looked more like a kind of self-betrayal, as feminist philosopher Maria Lugones understands internalized homophobia between two female lovers. Twenty years earlier, the dyke and her lover got into some mess of a conflict. It seems the two kids were the "problem." It seems the couple drove the kids to a cliff and, taking that innocence into their hands, each threw a child off the cliff. They were drunk, no doubt. Crazed, no doubt. And they both, no doubt, were guilty of the crime. But it's redneck Oregon. And the biological mother takes the stand and testifies that "the dyke made me do it"; that under the spell of the pervert, she was forced to commit the gravest female crime against nature: infanticide. The biological mother walks. The lesbian lover, twenty years later, is still in jail. Twenty years a model prisoner and each time she is up for parole the word gets out, "lesbian child-killer to go free," and public pressure keeps her behind bars.

Today, another twenty years later, and I don't know if Jay's still in prison.[5] Amber's in New York now and still working with prisoners and queer folk. And I am left here, still unraveling this story. In

1976, I wrote a poem about it called "The Voices of the Fallers."* I just couldn't get the kid or the killer out of my head, that child falling. "I'm falling," he cries, "can't you see? I'm falling?" The child's plea echoes the voice of my high school classmate, another very masculine young woman, crying as she tossed herself off a cliff in Baja California. (But *that's another story as well.*) I couldn't get those voices out of my head because I know what it's like to be a lesbian mom, biological and not. I have witnessed when the kid and the homophobia and the fear and shame of ourselves can lead to blows against the walls, against each other, against a child's heart. It's not so far away from me. But the poem didn't satisfy my hunger to know the story, the real story, the story of why a woman kills her child. The story of La Llorona.

Why did I need to know the story? I am a sub-urban Chicana. Kids drowned in the local plunge, not the nearby river. I never heard anyone say "La Llorona's gonna get you." It was the "Boogie Man" in our neighborhood, or that simple inarticulate terror inspired by some *Twilight Zone* episode (the original ones), where the short trip down the hall to the bathroom became a long, labyrinth-like journey into the unknown.

"C'mon, JoAnn, walk down the hall with me. I gotta go."

"Okay, but you go first."

"No, you first."

"No, you."

"You."

"Then hold my hand."

But as the daughter of a thoroughly Mexican mother, I did know about women being punished for the rest of their lives for some sin that happened somewhere in our collective history. "Eres mujer." That's all we need to know. That's the crime we feministas are still

---

* "The Voices of the Fallers" appears in this volume.

solving. I echo here Helena Maria Viramontes's story, "Growing," wherein she writes of a father reprimanding his daughter: "*Tú eres mujer,* he thundered, and that was the end of any argument, any question, and the matter was closed because he said those three words as if they were a condemnation from the heavens and so she couldn't be trusted."[6]

When I first learned the Mexican story of La Llorona, I immediately recognized that the weeping woman, that aberration, that criminal against nature, was a sister. Maybe by being a lesbian my identification was more easily won, fully knowing my crime was tantamount to hers. Any way you slice it, we were both a far and mournful cry from obedient daughters. But I am convinced that La Llorona is every Mexican woman's story, regardless of sexuality. She is sister to us all.

I began to investigate the myth. From the first paragraph I ever read on the subject in *Literatura chicana: texto y contexto,* to José Limón's[7] analysis and Rudolfo Anaya's fictionalization,[8] to interviews with farmworkers in Oregon, to finally sitting for days in the San Francisco Public Library scanning roll upon roll of that neon blue microfilm for every account of infanticide ever printed in the daily news—no version ever told me enough.

The official version was a lie. I knew that from the same bone that first held the memory of the cuento. *Who would kill their kid over some man dumping them?* It wasn't a strong enough reason. And yet everyone from Anaya to Euripides was telling us so. Well, if traición was the reason, could infanticide then be retaliation against misogyny, an act of vengeance not against one man, but man in general for a betrayal much graver than sexual infidelity: the enslavement and deformation of our sex?

A partera friend posed another possibility to me. A Yaqui woman who had worked en la frontera as a nurse-midwife for many years, Angelita Borbón was intimately knowledgeable about a full range of maternal instincts, both sanctioned and taboo. "Infanticide is not a homicide," she told me, "but a suicide. A mother never completely separates from her child. She always remains a part of her children." *But what is it then we are killing in ourselves and why?*

The answer to these questions resides, of course, in allowing La Llorona to speak for herself, to cry out something other than "Mis hijos!" for all eternity. When this dawned on me, so did the beginnings of a play I began four years ago and still has me working and wondering. I called it a "Mexican Medea" in reference to both the Greek Euripides tragedy and the Llorona story. As Euripides's dramatization of the story of Medea turned to the Greek gods as judge and consul, I turned to the pre-Columbian Aztec deities. In my research, I discovered another story, the Aztec creation myth of "The Hungry Woman," and this story became pivotal for me, an aperture in my search to unlock la fuerza de La Llorona in our mechicana lives.

In the place where the spirits live, there was once a woman who cried constantly for food. She had mouths in her wrists, mouths in her elbows, and mouths in her ankles and knees. . . .

Then to comfort the poor woman [the spirits] flew down and began to make grass and flowers out of her skin. From her hair they made forests, from her eyes, pools and springs, from her shoulders, mountains and from her nose, valleys.

At last she will be satisfied, they thought. But just as before, her mouths were everywhere, biting and moaning . . . opening and snapping shut, but they [were] never filled. Sometimes at night, when the wind blows, you can hear her crying for food.[9]

Who else other than La Llorona could this be? It is always La Llorona's cries we mistake for the wind, but maybe she's not crying for her children. Maybe she's crying for food, sustenance.

Maybe que tiene hambre la mujer. And at last, upon encountering this myth—this precapitalist, precolonial, pre-catholic mito—my jornada began to make sense. This is the original Llorona y tiene mucha hambre. I realized that she has been the subject of my work all along, from my earliest writings, my earliest feminism. She is the story that has never been told truly, the story of that hungry Mexican woman who is called puta/bruja/jota/loca because she refuses to forget that her half-life is not a natural-born fact.

I am looking for the insatiable woman. The statement resonates with the Mexican artist Guadalupe Garcia's cry in her performance piece *Coatlicue's Call*.[10] She announces, "I am looking for a woman called Guadalupe." Maybe we're all looking for the same woman, in ourselves. When La Llorona kills her children, she is killing a male-defined motherhood that robs us of a self-determined womanhood. I first discussed this desire to interrupt patriarchal motherhood through a re-vision of the Mexica story of Huitzilopochtli's birth.* The myth recounts Coyolxauhqui's efforts to halt the birth of the War God by murdering her mother, Coatlicue. She is convinced that Huitzilopochtli's birth will also mean the birth of slavery, human sacrifice, and imperialism (in short, patriarchy). She fails in her attempt and is murdered and dismembered by her brother and banished into the darkness to become the moon.

This ancient myth reminds Mexican women that, culturally speaking, there is no mother-woman to inhabit who is defined by us outside of patriarchy. We have never had the power to do the defining.[11] We wander not in search of our dead children, but our lost selves, our lost sexuality, our lost spirituality, our lost sabiduría. No wonder La Llorona is so irrefutably punished, destined to walk the earth en busca de sus niños. To find and manifest our true selves—that "woman before the fall"—what might we have to change in the

---

* See "La fuerza femenina" in this volume.

world as we know it? "¡Mis hijos!" Llorona cries. But, I hear her saying something else. "¡Mis hijas perdidas!" And I answer. "Te busco a tí también, madre/hermana/hija." I am looking for the hungry woman.

"La Llorona," "The Hungry Woman," "The Dismemberment of Coyolxauhqui"—these are the stories that have shaped us. We, Chicanas, remember them in spite of ourselves, in spite of our families' and society's efforts to have us forget. We remember these stories even where mothers worked in factories, not fields, and children played in city plunges, not country creeks. The body remembers.

Each of my plays, each poem, each piece of fiction has been shaped by a story. Most writers will tell you the same. My play *Shadow of a Man*[12] grew out of an extended image, a story my mother told me of her dead father appearing to her at the foot of her bed. He was silhouetted against the soft intruding urban light, hat dipped over one eye, a shadow across his face. "I knew it was a sign of death," she said. "But I didn't know whose." Her eldest brother, Esteban, would die soon after.[13]

In another play, *Heroes and Saints,*[14] the protagonist, a seventeen-year-old Chicana without a body, was inspired by Luis Valdez's *The Shrunken Head of Pancho Villa.*[15] In it, Valdez is looking for Villa's missing body. In *Heroes,* I am looking for la Chicana's missing body. In both plays, we both are looking for a revolution.

What does it take to uncover those stories with the power
to inspire insurrection?

How do we breed a revolutionary generation of Chicana art?

Stories inspire stories, and the best and most revolutionary of stories are recuperated from the deepest places of our unconscious, which is the reservoir for our collective memory. The best writers may employ an "I" in their work, but it is generated by the "we" of our shared knowing. So that when we truly succeed at our storytelling, we cannot wholly take the credit. I grow impatient with any

tendency toward "tourist" literature in Latino works, writings that
seem directed toward audiences that are strangers to the cultural
and political geography of our symbols, images, and history. When
we write in translation, we never move beyond our colonized status.
When we write for ourselves, our deepest selves, the work travels
into the core complexity of our experience with a quality of veracity
that illuminates a total humanity. I have glimpsed our promise—
sometimes in the first few forbidden chapters of an unfinished novel
by the published poet; sometimes in the roughly scripted mono-
logue of a sixteen-year-old Xicana-Navajo dyke thinking she's a vato
loco; sometimes in the bleeding trails of watercolor taking the shape
of a severed vulva-heart on a piece of amate paper.

Sometimes.

I believe in the power of story to change our lives, whether it's
a story you stumble across spilling out of the mouth of a commie
dyke at a vegetarian restaurant or one your bisabuela told your
abuelita and your abuelita told your mami, but your mami forgot to
mention to you, but somehow you knew it all along. There is revolutionary potential in the story. True stories empower, the way lies
disempower.

At the time of this writing, I am still working on my Llorona
story. Of course, I want to believe it is revolutionary, but at some
point, I may have to accept that my Mexican Medea may only succeed in capturing a splinter of what I know in my bones about Llorona. I confess, it's a harder story to write now, being a mother, with
all the beauty and burden of those lessons of Mexican motherhood.
Pero sigo pa' lante.[16]

And if this play doesn't satisfy my hunger for La Llorona's story,
maybe another later work will. Maybe it's a story I'll work on for
the rest of my life in many shapes and voices and styles. Maybe, as
James Baldwin once said, we each have just one story to tell and
every writing effort is just an attempt to say it better *this time*. Maybe

somewhere in me I believe that if I could get to the heart of Llorona, I could get to the heart of the meXicana prison and in the naming I could free us, if only just a little.

Maybe the effort is a life well spent.

Entre nos

I am not

the indian she is
but bear witness
to the story
of the dirt
and the trees
and the land
before the road
they built
through the mountain.

Thistle

thistle
she tells me
with thistle they awaken
the mind back
into the living body

I see it bloom purple
like flowering bruises

here

and here.

Out of Our Revolutionary Minds—
Toward a Pedagogy of Revolt[1]

HISTORY

In the beginning was the letter: a conversation between Nat Turner and an enslaved African American from the play *Insurrection: Holding History.*

> NAT: [Hammet] you been studin' 'em letters?
> HAMMET: I been studin' em.
> NAT: let me see one 'em A's then.
>
> *(HAMMET moves to NAT's Back.
> With his finger he begins drawing the letter "A".)*
>
> HAMMET *(Slowly):* . . . arrow.
> . . . stick.
> NAT: nah do me one 'em B's.
> HAMMET *(Concentrates):* . . . stick.
> . . . rock. rock.
> NAT: do that one again and don't speak it this time. . . .
> okay nah befo' we split i'm gon' teach you a new one.
>
> *(NAT begins drawing the letter "C" on HAMMET's back.)*
>
> moon
> this letter "C."

(He points to sky.)

think "see" "moon."
"C"²

And the letter was made flesh. And became the word. And the word was "insurrection" because literacy was forbidden. "If you teach [the enslaved] how to read, [it] would forever unfit him to be a slave."³ The slaveholder knows and fears: to take up the master's tools threatens the foundation of the master's house. However, a century and half later, poet Audre Lorde admonishes: "The master's tools will never dismantle the master's house."⁴ Maybe it is more complicated than we ever imagined: this practice of the word and pen.

For playwright Robert O'Hara, the bent back of Nat Turner is the metaphor for revolution, where the lash is repulsed and replaced by the letter. More than a hundred years later, literacy is still popularly viewed as the best escape from economic enslavement for people of color while this country continues to handpick which bodies can "darken (which) doorways" to educational advantage.

Education was the single-word mantra I heard growing up via my mother's counsel: "If I'd only had the education, hija . . . nothing could've stopped me." This is the rare gift the undereducated (my mother got no further than the third grade) can offer to the next generation: "ganas"⁵—the desire for that which was not their class-secured right, and so all the more coveted. I, too, learned to covet education, not for the job out of the factory, but for a world wider than the confines of my hometown working-class rituals of work and worry.

In my innocence, as a first-generation college student, I imagined books as that stolen inner-world sanctum where one was allowed to contemplar one's existence, the meaning of one's life, and the source of one's suffering. In the 1970s, I read imaginative literature because it was more complex than psychology, truer than history, and tended toward dissent (at least what I read did). As such, literature and its makers became my teachers. I fell in love with literature, looked to literature for personal insights into political contradictions, as I also sought to extract from poems, novels, and essays the political meaning of my most intimate inquiries.

Twenty-five years ago, however, there was little *me* to read. Chicana and lesbian literature as a genre had not been invented. So, I rifled through whatever queer turn of the page I could get my hands on, beginning with a 1928 edition of Radclyffe Hall's *The Well of Loneliness*, which portrayed lesbian desire through the vantage point of a ruling-class English woman-wannabe-man. Closer to home, I found my own otherness reflected in the hunchbacked and queer figures of Carson McCullers novels. I did not know at that time that she, too, was a lesbian. And for "colored" womanhood, I finally encountered Black women's fiction.

In 1975, with so little *me* to read, I wrote to fill in the blanks. Hélène Cixous reminds us: "Writing and reading are not separate, reading is a part of writing. A real reader is a writer. A real reader is already on the way to writing."[6] For many of us, that ability to read and write was not passed down como herencia familiar. As Chicana poet Lorna Dee Cervantes puts it, "[We] come from a long line of eloquent illiterates / whose history reveals what words don't say."[7] My generation, coming of age in the 1960s and early 1970s, the period of affirmative action and bilingual education, may be the first to have paradoxically suffered en masse the promise of union with, and threat of separation from, our origins proffered by our collective literacy. But the proximity of our literacy to that eloquently illiterate generation that preceded us served as a continual reminder of our questionable and questioning relationship to the gringo world of arts and letters. It kept us humble before the work-worn faces and fingers of our parents and grandparents, but more importantly, critical of the unilateral authority of academic knowledge and aesthetics of letters. Our crianza had proven there were other ways of knowing and expressing knowledge.

Significantly, in those early years of Chicano cultural production, that one-generation-working-class proximity served as a kind of barometer to gauge the significance of our work in relation to the people we supposedly represented. If our letters, i.e., our art and thought praxis, continued to emerge from our actual lives—our history, memory, instincts, and intuitions—it promised to more directly impact our *body* politic. As O'Hara's play suggests, ideas inscribed upon the body can inspire insurrection.

BODY

I know that most of the students of color I teach at the university turned to books for the same reasons I did. Most of them have a love for language and ideas and an innate sense of social responsibility that was, in part, inspired by books that responded in radical ways to the contradictions and inequities in their lives. Kafka writes:

> I think we ought to only read the kind of books that wound and stab us. If the book we are reading doesn't wake us up with a blow on the head, what are we reading it for? . . . We need books that affect us like a disaster, that grieve us deeply, like the death of someone we loved more than ourselves, like being banished into the forest far from everyone, like a suicide. A book must be the axe for the frozen sea inside us.[8]

A book must be the axe for the frozen sea inside us.

When the Chicana writer sits down to table with tinta and text in hand, she brings the history of "eloquent illiteracy" with her. The body of her literature is not only decoded from those imported black glyphs pressed upon the dead leaves of América's trees, it is also experienced spontaneously from the home-grown language of cuento and canto. As we bend toward the turn into the twenty-first century, the lament of many poets and public thinkers is that there is little place for such origin(al) thinking in the US academy. In fact, academia requires separation from some of our most regenerative ethnically specific resources, unless translated ideologically into a Western point of reference. Imaginative literature and the arts as expressions of the body Latino have become, as my friend Alberto Sandoval-Sánchez suspects, merely "a pretext for do[ing] theoretical work."

At the Crossing Borders conference at the City University of New York,[9] that same Alberto—poet, politico, and scholar—referenced his ten-year battle with AIDS, stating, "Alberto had become a body." He spoke of the disease, ironically, as a kind of ally in his relentless attempt to reckon with his physical self and the life of the mind. AIDS was the rude awakener that put his entire academic life into question. He openly admitted a kind of contempt toward the academy, which is, by some definition, "theoretical . . . without practical purpose or intention," and as such, remains incompatible to the body and its needs. So, AIDS gave Alberto a body and as such, practical purpose. He states: "I am dying to write. I am not dying to be published. It is a popular misconception that to be published is to achieve immortality. For me, immortality is in the moment of writing, an act that confirms I am alive." In Alberto's daily confrontation with death and in his survival of the assaults the academy has visited upon his erased Latino queer body, Alberto has uncovered an enormous amount to teach us.

If the academy, in its very mission, denies the body, except as the object of theoretical discourse, one wonders how the radical-thinking "othered" body (the queer, the colored, the female) can find full expression there. The presence of Ethnic Studies on the college campus has not ensured the cultural survival of US people of color. As Audre Lorde reminds us, "Survival is not an academic skill."[10] In his book *Chicano Poetics*, poet Alfred Arteaga suggests that Ethnic Studies may have done no more than unwittingly "define [our] world for the benefit of the colonizer."[11] Of course, it is more contradictory and complicated than this; for, while the academy assimilates the Richard Rodriguez "scholarship boy,"[12] it also instructs disloyal faculty of color, along a roadmap toward liberation, situated well beyond the gates of the neo-colony. The question remains: Can we, collectively, take the whole of our body politic to that place?

LANGUAGE

I am a writer. Language matters to me. I am acutely aware of those moments when language illuminates, gives shape to something which was before vaguely known to me, like a dream that stays, haunting, indecipherable. I am grateful when words teach me something I forgot I knew. I am equally aware of the times when language kills, diminishes, truncates the creative impulse and the dream of change. I know when someone uses language to do violence against me/us. In response, language becomes a form of self-defense, a mechanism of survival.

I am reminded of N. Scott Momaday's story, *The Man Made of Words*, about the Arrowmaker whose survival is utterly dependent upon language.[13]

It is late at night. The Arrowmaker sleeps in his tepee with his woman when he is suddenly awakened by a human shadow on the other side of the tepee wall. If the shadow understands the Arrowmaker's language, there is nothing to fear. If the shadow doesn't respond when the Arrowmaker addresses him in his own tongue, the shadow will receive an arrow into his heart.

Language and survival. Momaday's story serves as an allegory to our own survival, seeking out those whose language we can trust.

I put my faith in the stories, the language of the body where the word is made flesh by the storyteller. "Words are intrinsically powerful," Momaday writes. "They are magical. By means of words one can bring about physical change in the universe.... To be careless in the presence of words ... is to violate a fundamental morality."[14]

I think often of the immoral waste of words in academic life; the labyrinth of postmodern methods of inquiry, the intention of which may be to liberate one's thinking from the ideological limitations and impositions of Western thought, while all along maintaining a conversation—in voice, form, and content—with it. After over two decades of teaching creative/critical writing at the university, I can attest to the loss of profound original sites of knowing by young scholars of color, due to the prescriptive approaches of research required by academia; the foreign Eurocentric sources that must be cited to substantiate one's own unauthorized (what may be intuitively known) ideas; and, the ubiquity of once powerful, even sacred, words, appropriated to the point of impotence.

In academic life, theoretical language is, as a rule, profane. It tends to obfuscate rather than illuminate. Moral words, as Momaday tells us, "can bring about physical change in the universe." In an unjust society, moral words would bring about justice. Some of the finest young thinkers of color in this country are being held captive within the university system. Moral words would free them from their enslavement to Western thought. Free words would bring about revolutionary change. Free words are sacred.

"Go home to your Maya grandmother," I tell my Guatemalan-born-US-raised Stanford undergrad. "She'll teach you what you want to know. You don't have to suffer their words here any longer." Still, we tell ourselves (queers, feminists, people of color) that we are here at Stanford, at Yale, at Dartmouth, at Duke, at Cal, to engage in radical re-visions of history in the effort to construct a radical agenda for the future, *once we get their theory down.*

From *Insurrection: Holding History,* a dialogue between a graduate student, Ron, and his 189-year-old formerly enslaved great-great-grandfather (Mutha Wit speaks on his behalf):

RON: I just gotta finish my thesis.

MUTHA WIT: What's a thesis?

RON: It's a long paper I gotta write.

MUTHA WIT: Then what you do after you don' wrote it?

RON: Then I gotta show it to a bunch of white folks.

MUTHA WIT: Then what?

RON: Hopefully I can get paid like one of them white folks.

MUTHA WIT: Then what?

RON: ... Gramps ...

MUTHA WIT: Then what?

RON: Then nuthin. What you mean then what? Then I'm
done. I git a job. I live, become fabulously rich and
mildly famous.

MUTHA WIT: Then what?

RON: Then I drop dead I guess I don't know.[15]

REVOLT

I came of age with images of brave. Brave in the face of scared. Student sit-down strikes, civil rights activists bludgeoned by police; Chicanos picketing grape vineyards and lettuce fields; Vietnam protests—young faces streaked with blood, burning flags at their dancing feet; Black Panthers holstered against sharpshooters peering off of inner-city rooftops.

Martin Luther King Jr. was moving from an integrationist nonviolence to a critique of imperialism when he was violently murdered. Martin Luther King Jr. would not be content with Black people eating from a poisoned pie. A piece of the American Dream was not The Dream.

Real political struggle always poses the threat of violence, real and imagined. The Chicano Moratorium of 1970 (which I witnessed ten miles away on television news reports) was real and highly imagined. Real heads were beaten in, real girls my age were dragged away by helmeted, baton-swinging police. I imagined myself so near and far from them.

There are less dramatic dangers, visible and invisible, and many fronts of struggle. But always hard sacrifices are made for change:

Undocumented workers challenge the eviction of a fellow worker and block the entrance to the factory. They stand face-to-face with police. Danger.

A woman hangs off a redwood in a protest of protection. Chain saws buzz in the background. Danger.

It's 1968, and he burns a draft card.

It's 1998, and she won't scab in the strawberry fields. She needs a job. Bad.

I think the only real dangerous moves I've ever made in my life were out of necessity, so they felt not very dangerous at all. When you have time to think about it, you think better of it, you think yourself out of danger. You don't move. So sometimes it's better not to think at all. At times, I ask myself, have I ever really been brave? Words have hurt me. The worst. Words by lovers, brothers, intimates. Words that were hurled at me because I spoke up. First. At all.

Getting arrested in protest against an unconscionable war was not brave. It was performance. A rehearsed act of resistance, as Luis Valdez has written.[16] What wasn't rehearsed was my claustrophobia. I didn't know how jammed we'd be in the police van. I hadn't thought about being restrained, how the plastic of the makeshift handcuffs behind my back would turn my hands swollen and blue and make me want to crawl out of my skin, being confined so. But all that was an *accident* of courage. And basically not dangerous.

It was brave of me the first time to sit down in a circle of women of color and say "we" without apology. Brave each time. Brave to do so without titles of books in my hand. Like proof. Of what? Authenticity? Belonging?

Brave risking the enemy's ammunition to hurt me, my child. I am a lesbian mother and practice both out loud.

Brave to leave my lover of eight years.

Brave to tell my mom I was a lesbian. Brave at twenty-two.

Brave to refuse to give up my wages to my boss who decided, when *his* business was failing, he wanted to collectivize all *our* earnings. Brave at twenty-seven to be the only one.

Brave to eat sacred medicines when I was afraid and didn't know a thing.

Brave to speak Spanish like a fool in front of people who knew plenty.

These are seemingly mundane, unimportant examples, but each one had consequence, perhaps unrecognizable to anyone but myself.

None of us can judge what is courage in another.

"Go toward the fear," I tell my students. "Feel its pulse. Let it speak to you." I'm bravest in my writing. But that's not the same as action; only that writing *can* sometimes require action in yourself and others. Sometimes. Sometimes you read or write words you got to live up to. Never know what it's going to dig up. Dig up the dirt of memory, the dirt of land. Make you want some back for us. Make you fight to have it.

THE PEDAGOGY

Revolt: verb. "To rise in rebellion; to refuse to acknowledge someone or something as having authority."

I have taught professionally for over twenty years. I have taught high school, poets-in-the-schools, the Marxist school, myriad youth programs, gang-prevention and high-risk programs, theater for queer youth and immigrant women, writing groups for Indígenas and other women of color, and playwrights' groups. I've served as an adjunct instructor (mostly) in Women's Studies, Ethnic Studies, Creative Writing, Drama, and in Spanish and English Departments from the country club of Stanford University to the inner-city campuses of community colleges and state universities on both coasts.

I love teaching and remain in conflict with it. Fundamentally, it takes me away from my primary vocation, which is to write. To make art. I teach well, I believe, and chose teaching over political activism in the fourth decade of my life, because I couldn't do both *and* write . . . *and* raise my son . . . *and* support an extended family. One could make an impact, I believed, through teaching, while making some semblance of a living.

Now, I wonder.

Over the successive years of university teaching, I have found that the profession, in its increasing corporatization, has moved further and further away from a radical agenda. Since I have been situated primarily in Ethnic Studies or Women's/Gender Studies, I have witnessed academic programs that once emerged out of political struggle separate themselves from that struggle.[17]

A movement doesn't happen in a book, but it doesn't happen without books either.[18]

Through the writing of this essay, I am aware of the possibility that my ideas may be misconstrued as anti-intellectual. If so, I have no one to blame but my poet's passion to expose the Academic Emperor in all his nakedness, even at the risk of the generalization that belies the exception and the exceptional. There *are* exceptional students and exceptional faculty. There are remarkable moments where critical consciousness, as described in Paulo Freire's *Pedagogy of the Oppressed*, is awakened; where the most visionary and dangerous of teachers inspire thoughts that directly impact the bodies sitting in front of them. The bodies think. They stand up. They act.

In recent years, students of color can't help but be aware of the increase in the state-sanctioned violation of their right to an education and a future. Last winter, with the introduction of yet another assault on the rights of youth of color (California Proposition 21), students took to the streets and filled campus plazas in protest. Most impressive was students' willingness to connect their struggle against carceral racism with opposition to the anti–gay marriage legislation of Proposition 22. I attribute this to the coalition activism initiated by queer students of color. It was their bodies, after all, that provided the living connection between the issues.[19]

The revolutionary body.
The revolutionary body that reads and writes.

I saw it happen. In April 1999, in recognition of the thirtieth anniversary of the Third World Liberation Front strike at UC Berkeley, students occupied Barrows Hall to protest the "state of regression" of Ethnic Studies at the Berkeley campus. Stating that "the systematic decline of [Ethnic Studies] programs [was] causing a slow and steady death" of the department. Protesters demanded a substantial increase in funding and faculty for Ethnic Studies to be implemented immediately and to continue over a five-year period. To press their demands, students held daily protests and nightly vigils, suffered mass arrests for civil disobedience, and maintained a ten-day hunger strike until the administration was forced to concede.

The rescue of Ethnic Studies is not, in and of itself, revolutionary. It does not alter the racist *system* of higher education in this country. It is, however, an impressive act of revolt, requiring radical consciousness. It challenges the unilateral authority of the university to determine *what* and *how* we learn and from whom.[20]

In the 1960s, from the high school walkouts in East Los Angeles to the Third World strike, education remained the fundamental concern of young Raza because education is about the future of a people. And we saw ourselves as such, as a *people, un pueblo,* distinct from mainstream America, requiring culturally specific methods and materials of intellectual inquiry. Questions were raised then that remain unanswered because we have not, as the Marxists mandate, continued to question the question. These acts of revolt in the last few years by students of color and their allies have given me renewed hope that possibly the questions have not been buried forever beneath the ethereal cover of the postmodern.

What is worth knowing?

How does one acquire knowledge?

How do we best learn within our communities?

Who are our true teachers? And how do we find and support them?

And of course, for what purpose, what result, do we educate ourselves and our children?

The system of education in this country from the public elementary school to the private university will not, by definition, permit a culturally autonomous approach to these inquiries. As Freire points out, "It would be a contradiction in terms if the oppressors not only defended but actually implemented a liberating education."[21]

When I think of my own Chicano/a people and the state of California's betrayal of its soon-to-be-majority Latino population, I lose patience with liberal attempts at remedy. I've come to believe that the less we see ourselves as a distinct and distinctive pueblo, the less we will be able to define and realize the intellectual, cultural, and educational needs and profound promise of our community.

EDUCATING A NATION

Today I am writing Nation. It is not a dirty word.

A North American Indian woman is kidnapped and murdered crossing the borders of nation-states. And the nations of people within those borders—Menominee and U'wa, Chicana and Hawai'ian—cry out in outrage. "The body of [Ingrid] Wash-inawatok, 41, and two others—Hawaiian activist Lahc'ena'e Gay and environmental activist Terence Freitas—were found bound and blindfolded Thursday in a field just across the Arauca River in Venezuela. . . . All the victims were shot multiple times with 9mm weapons."[22]

My friend Ingrid Flying Eagle Woman Washinawatok El-Issa had "ignored the State Department's warnings to stay away from rural Colombia."[23] She went anyway because the U'wa people asked her, in the traditional way, to come. She could not refuse. According to a family spokesperson, she had gone to Colombia to develop an Indigenous-based school curriculum for the tribe. Ingrid, in her many roles as an activist, had instituted models of pedagogy where the cultural integrity of Indigenous people is preserved and honored.

You have a belief. You dedicate your life to the realization of that belief. That's brave.

Ingrid believed in sovereignty, complete sovereignty of mind, body, spirit, nation. Sovereignty was *her* most dangerous word. Months before her death, she wrote: "Europeans relegate sovereignty to only one realm of life and existence: authority, supremacy and dominion. In the Indigenous realm, sovereignty encompasses responsibility, reciprocity, the land, life and much more."[24]

Ingrid left her family, a son and a husband, to make good on her beliefs, to assist other Indigenous peoples in creating models of education in accord with their own traditions. It was a dangerous time to make the trip. For several years, the Indigenous U'wa have been in protest against oil exploration by Occidental Petroleum Corporation on their ancestral lands in northeast Colombia and, as a consequence, have encountered US-sanctioned violence from the Colombian government.[25] Ingrid could've stayed home, like the "officials" had advised; she could've minded her own business. She didn't. That's brave.

Nationhood. I stay up nights and wonder. If sovereignty could be realized, just the way Ingrid wrote about it, well, just maybe there'd be an actual Chicano/a body to name and some land to claim to share. Ingrid returned home to her Menominee Nation in a black body bag. No American flag draped over it. At least that much was true. The United States of America was not her nation.[26]

"Perhaps the greatest stories," Scott Momaday writes, "are those which disturb us, which shake us from our complacency, which threaten our well-being."[27] This is Ingrid's story—the greatest story ever told. The story about a woman who was murdered for practicing what she preached. She was someone who put into practice the art of teaching people how to teach themselves through their own cultural symbols, languages, values.

The U'wa are not a people unconscious of their oppression. The invitation to Ingrid and her acceptance was a reciprocal gesture between Native peoples who viewed their survival as integrally interdependent and who viewed education from an Indigenous perspective as critical to that survival. To teach is to empower. And to teach the oppressed in their own language with their own tools is to create (or in the case of the U'wa, sustain) a sovereign people. This, the most valorous job I can envision.

Do we have to die to be teachers of revolt?

I want to think not. I want to believe that our teaching and artists' acts of resistance can do some damage to the cultural hegemony of EuroAmerica—and, in the process, do some good for the political consciousness of the many oppressed peoples of this nation-state.

For that reason alone, I continue to teach Chicano Nation in my own queer tongue.

I am trying to find the right words.

I am learning to spell

revolution.

La danzante

1
I dream red
since our return
from cactus-stone and full white
moon light
I awaken to red
wet between your dusted thighs.

Was it a birthing
or a death
you danced
days ago—
the measured step, toe
to pebbled earth, knee
rising to heaven
down again
this time
back to ground
again

we walk
together

then part   the boy by my side.

2
We spy the whitebardyke
of native seed,
Its memory planted

in Indian
ink across the broken-edged
blades of her back
down to buttbone.

There is all manner of medicine
prescribed there
on loose pale skin
eagle/coyote/wolf/and bear—
and the boy wonders
   a living cartoon?

We walk on, sobered
by the naked revelation:
chain-smokin-mid-fifties-12-steppin
queer girl/once Indian
is too much regret
for any of us
to carry.

How does she bear the weight of all that medicine?

She broke her bone
she said
she dragged a broken bone
that met the low end of her thigh
on that high desert road
she called red.

3
Not
us

Mexicans. Our road
less rose, mas amarillo
in its southern descent
hacía el sol
the sculpted sudden
slope
de tus nalgas
more "forever" than any tattoo.

4
Behind eyes sheltered
from the sky's relentless azure
I too step toe to earth
mouth words whose meaning
becomes evident in the repetition
I wait to know
you in the light
of the darkness of sleep
death, I mean to say

and it is the simplest of knowing.

When I open my eyes
you are already walking
away from me
fifty years from now
now
it makes no difference

your face, the face of every ancestor
in every stone
we stumble over with clumsy worldly feet.

At some point you'll have no need to cry over it
the mistakes.

Of course it is not a matter of words
it is not of matter
when the molecules of your body
mix with the earth and the sky
in a prayer I do not enter.

But
I won't forget your *red*
woven-crowned head
amid arizona
blue
the bleached *white*
sheet of cloud
rumpling snail to viejita
red
white
blue
the colors of a nation
only dreamed.

5
Nationless
I take you into my arms
in the ordinary bed of a california
valley roadside motel
unwind the crimson cotton
wrapped 'round your hips

and I enter you as deep and as hard as we want

because you were there too dying
in the midday sun singing
to the same god
and we want to touch it
somehow
because our bodies are remembering
we want to gather all the touch
we can
before we go

back.

The Dying Road to a Nation—
A Prayer para un Pueblo[1]

For CHR

We, you and I, must remember everything.
We must especially remember those things we never knew.
                    —Jimmie Durham, *A Certain Lack of Coherence*

DYING LESSONS[2]

My comadre, Marsha, comes to me in dreams. I stand in a circle of
women on Indígena land in Tejas. Marsha is impatient with the group,
their shocked inaction upon the news of her violent death. She tells me,
"Build me a dome," a roundhouse she means. Her work must continue.
There is no time to waste.

In September 1998, Marsha Gómez, artista-activista-lesbiana-madre
-hermana, was murdered by the hand of her only son. Marsha was an
Indigenous-identified mestiza. Off-season, she could be mistaken for
Jewish or something else not quite white, but not necessarily always
Choctaw, not siempre the darker side of Mexican. "Cajun and Hispanic" is what her blood relations called themselves. But unlike those
relations, Marsha was one hundred percent "colored girl," "red-skin,"
and "kickin' butt." Thoroughly. And her thorough-courage compelled
me because I knew Marsha was afraid, always a little; some place in

her not quite convinced she belonged in either world—Mexican or
Indian. No Native enrollment card. Few Spanish-language skills.
Queer in both worlds. But my god, that other world, a dead world: the
woman-hating white world from which she fled, from which she could
not protect her white-skinned son.

He used the instruments of her work to murder her.

This is not a metaphor.

He bludgeoned his mother to death with the tools of her trade.

She was a sculptor.

Marsha's son, that once soft golden-haired boy, saw in his own illness a female vulnerability he learned to despise.[3] There are those
who look away from this killing as an aberration, but it is not an
aberration. It is its own impossible truth—that speaks to the real
incarcerated state of the Xicano/Native/queer familia and the
wounded heart of our nations—

because we cannot imagine it;

because our minds cannot conjure it;

because she was so so unworthy of it;

because we recognize ourselves in it and are forced to rethink
everything about our lives; why we are standing on this road, at
this hour, brokenhearted as we are. With desperate fingers we try to
unknot the noose of this tragedy, how to change that fate, steer our
pueblo's children away from hopelessness. *We give birth to sons, who
become men. And we are unable to defend ourselves against this most
intimate, most beloved of oppressors.*

I still want to believe that at some point Marsha made a decision
toward life, that she offered up her body to save her son from himself;
to save other women from the violence de su corazón inquieto. (She
was *not* the first woman he had harmed.) But I know those responsible for Marsha Gomez's death have faces and do not have faces;
that in my speechless shocked heart only one truth resounds—*that*

her death was not an accident, but the result of a murderous misogynist political history still in the making.

None of us is immune to that history. I recognize myself in Marsha's middle-aging body, in her son's rage she used as a weapon against herself. I've seen my own son's anger at only five years old.

"Mom, the tears won't stop." He tells me con ojos lagrimosos. He slaps each of his own cheeks. "They just keep coming down. Make them stop, please." I bring a tissue, the end of my shirttail, or maybe a sleeve to his moist puppy-nose, soaked lashes. He stops crying. For now.

Did Marsha's son ask for anything more complicated than that? "Relieve me of myself, Mom, make the tears stop coming down." But what a mother may cure at five, twenty years later is not enough. It is never enough. It is not ours to cure our sons of the "manhood" imposed on them.

A few days following Marsha's death, I learned from friends that hours after the murder, her son was seen on a nearby country road looking for the man who killed his mother. The bitter irony is that maybe this is la búsqueda that all sons and brothers and fathers should undertake along with us—that search for our murdered mestiza/Indigenous mothers, sisters, daughters, lovers.[4]

I awaken every morning remembering that there was a life before greed. Before family as private property. Before competition, linear plotlines, and Western Romance and Reason. I know there was a time when "two-spirit"[5] people like Marsha held a place in tribal circles without compromise to their/our being. I am fighting for my young son's life and the values that might shape that life. I want to walk with him through my own opening heart to a different country, one that we may still only inhabit within the walls of our home or inside the circle of those with whom we sit and eat and maybe even pray.

THE RETURN

"¿Qué vale la vida if we can't take each other back?"

That's all my new love, so long in the knowing, had to say to finally bring me to her. But, how far back is Return? What radical action does Return require?

You want to change your life, I tell myself, you light a candle. You pray on it. Daily. All day long. Then you do the hard work of living the prayer.

Years ago, I made a prayer. Same prayer. Every day. Bring me family. And I knew in the praying, I was inviting the sons of lovers and brothers of many nations and the children of every shade to return to me. It took them a long time to arrive, but now that the time has come, I know that the hardest work is in front of me.

I am learning in hard ways. Daily. That we live in a violent and unforgiving world and all our acts of heartlessness return to us. I have also learned there is a time for heartlessness, for an unmoving warrior-stance. I have learned this most palpably for my son. Our leaving the family of our first home together was one of the hardest moves I ever made. But Return is harder yet.

This naked step I take toward a clouded mirror
that is this woman, myself.

JOURNAL ENTRY

I feel very young, unremarkable, an ordinary student nada más.

Daily, I have to ask my Beloved many things. I have to ask her what the pain in this desert means, why the women cry so awkwardly. I have to ask her how to enter the arbor, how to tie a prayer tie, wrap a sage stick, roll a cigarette of prayer tobacco. And I wonder how can she want me, baby that I am.

"Teach me how to pray," I say.

She takes me by the hand, presses the copal between my finger-tips, then releases the pebbles into the burning embers. And in the act, I am sent home to what I already learned at my mother's breast: faith.

I turned to her for god. I break some taboo in writing this; that god is found in bed, in the open-face of consummated desire; that death is found there, too, limpio y sencillo; that fear of death has a way of subsiding in love. All I prayed for was to find a woman with whom I could make familia, with whom I could wake up each morning with a shared purpose, a shared prayer, a shared praxis. Sin mentiras, no illusions that death did not await us at every turn.

How do we love on the dying road? What does that kind of spiritual practice look like?

Maybe my spiritual practice is nothing more than this writing. Maybe one wakes up every morning and just really wakes up. Maybe that is the daily prayer. The "Give Us This Day Our Daily Breath." And the bread, something as simple as bread, the matter of a revolution. Still, "the revolution begins at home." A cliché born of truth.

HOME TRUTHS

On the Day of the Dead, we put out food for our ancestors. Tequilita for my Tía Tencha, white roses for Marsha (her favorite), tamales, chocolate, water, black coffee with a tablespoon of sugar for Doña Domitila. Cigarettes for my Tío Bobby who died of lung cancer. Frijoles and pan. We pray.

I wonder if they come to visit, my relatives. Or if, upon death, they are relieved of us. Finally. I wonder if this offering is really for them or for us. I pray for the dead; that when they come to visit us in our sleeping and waking dreams, they are large enough to hold a place that remembers us, but where their hearts no longer ache, want, as we do now. I pray that our spirits are something much grander than this pitiful longing and all the beauteous attachment we have to it. I am una llorona, my tears, at times, my most faithful companions. I cry Marsha away from this earth. I pray that with the release (the relief) of the body, her spirit is not encumbered by the ego through which she thrived and suffered. I also pray for her son.

These prayers are my preguntas. I write this as if I were without faith, but when la curandera María Cristina carries Marsha's spirit back into our home through the few small worldly tokens of Marsha's life (a piece of hair, an earring), I am altered by the spirit's presence. I believe in the dead and the dying; the lessons they leave with their descendants.

LESSON 1

On the way across the Bay Bridge my son asks me, "Can God count to infinity?" I answer yes, since Rafaelito, newly acquainted with letters and numbers and long fascinated with superheroes, wants to understand the limits of power and numerical comprehension.

He goes on. "Is God more powerful than Batman?"

Again, I answer yes, adding an explanation about the nature of the power to which I refer. Power of the heart, of the spirit, etcetera, etcetera, knowing on some level he just wants to know if God can kick Batman's butt. Now, that *would* be a comfort, someone infinitely strong in charge of it all.

Since I know my son is thinking hero equals male, my feminism kicks in to remind him that God is both male and female—well, really neither male nor female but all energies simultaneously. And my Indigenous perspective and Buddhism prompt me to remind my son of the presence of God in all things living, even things that can't punch back.

Yes, even rocks breathe. I've seen them.

My answers are pitiful as I try to separate in my mind truth from lie from myth and cuento. I teach myth's truth. I teach my son about a God personified in his mind as a superhero because that's what he understands about power. It's the best I can get for now but only because I want him to know humility. I am a mother in search of a language that finds awe in the face of beauty, art, the ongoing creativity of nature and its insistent survival, its flourishing in the face of death. Because whatever my religion is, it counters the solipsism of American greed and the egotism of the "rugged individual." Because I want him to know he is not the center of the universe, but that the universe resides within him as in the flower. I want to relieve him of the burden, but reinforce the responsibility, of knowing his interdependent place upon this planet and its consummate heavens.

He is one among many, as am I.

LESSON 2

Superheroes and his male-identification firmly intact, my son is attracted for some of the same reasons to the image of Christ on the cross. But it is not Christ the Hero that draws my son in, but the Naked Christ. Christ the Unjustly Scorned. Christ the Martyr. At five years old, Rafael Angel is also fascinated with child-imagined bondage and can often be found tied up with all manner of shoestring, curtain cord, or discarded packing twine. My compadre and I joke that he may have inherited this need for self-imposed restraint from his mother's residual Catholicism, or, I suggest, he is responding to a vague memory of his earliest months of premature life spent within the confines of a doll-sized hospital isolette, his body tied to IV lines.[6] Who knows? But undeniably this image of the bound Christ moves my son.

I don't have crucifixes in my house as a rule. As a rule Christ never answered a prayer I can remember. But my son discovers the one crucifix I've packed away, given to him by his grandmother when he was about two years old. I am sure my mother fully expected that I would nail the dying figure above my son's sleeping head the night that I received it. Well, I could neither display the Crucified Christ (a dream catcher hangs in its stead) nor toss it away, imbued as it was with my mother's faith. Upon spying the half-naked and bleeding figure, Rafael immediately begins hammering me with questions about him.

"Who hurt him like that?"

"Why doesn't he have more clothes on?"

"Did his mama know?"

And in spite of my rejection of Catholicism at the age of eighteen, the Life, Death, and Resurrection of Christ is probably the best religious story I know. So, I tell him what I remember and can live with. I refer to Jesus as a holy man and explain that people were jealous of him, that they wanted to stay cruel and greedy and he wanted change and peace in the world. I'm fumbling badly, I think, when he asks why they hung him on the cross to die. I don't remember my answer; but later, when he retells the story to a friend, I overhear him say—

"They killed Jesus because he knew God."

And I think, *maybe my answers aren't so pitiful after all.*

La ve p'atrás—She Who Looks Back

Months later, I attend a Latino academic conference in New York City. I am speaking with The Critic about Nation. We are on stage and I am trying to make a point. I turn my whole body away from the audience, a full one hundred and eighty degrees. I look behind me. I am trying to illustrate the point with my body. I am trying to teach the teachers something about ourselves, about looking backward toward our Indian and Black mothers to find a future.

An image stays in my mind: an eighteenth-century New Spain casta painting by Miguel Cabrera. It is a portrait of miscegenation. In the painting, the mixed-blood child sits on the lap of his Spanish father. The child's facial features and coloring are a delicate blend of Gachupín and Indio. His Indigenous mother stands just behind and to the side of them, but the child is looking back, back at her, to his Indian antecedents, to his past and to the future he will choose.

And in his face, I see my own face looking back. Not all of us are compelled to return, but I am. And I want to take the others with me. I tell them so.

"¿Qué vale la vida si we can't take each other back?"

A young man in the audience is outraged. He stands in the second row from the rear and accuses me of feigning shamanhood, playing "some kind of curandera" role. He is angry that he is white enough to move forward effortlessly into americanmanhood and I am his mama reeling him back in and backwards. Into darkness.

We were not always like this, stupid and forgetful.

There *is* nothing new. No theory, no computer program, no virtual nada that has anything more profound to teach us than what is found in the dark quietude of this ancestral knowing. This is "infinity," I want to tell my son. And as close to god as we can get.

> *We, you and I, must remember everything.*
> *We must especially remember those things we never knew.*
> —Jimmie Durham

My family is dying. My blood and heart relations are vanishing with each passing of seasons. I am next. I know. Always next. I pray only for the courage to remember what I may never have the chance to live. And in the remembering may I know and, in the knowing, may I teach.

It's the little bit we have to offer the exiled and forgotten I call my nation.

Afterword

If we were only
to write poetry
there would be no need
of the foreword   before
nor the afterword
afterwards

only inexplicable poetic truths
as the poet knows them

something closer to the bone
of knowledge.

She once wrote:
"words are a war to me."
And so they remain
a near half-century
later.

Since that first writing,
the weaponry of words continues.

May 2023

Agradecimientos

I hope this book speaks for itself, of my profound gratitude to those I have loved. Those here and gone—familia, camaradas y compas—who've continued to hold me as I hold them, at least through these pages. I am grateful for the return of *Loving* and *The Last Generation* and that Haymarket Books took on the task. It seems especially fitting, since its original publisher was the leftist South End Press, now closed. Over the years, Haymarket has picked up that calling; and I am especially taken by the poetics of its politic. I thank Anthony Arnove's leadership in this regard and Rachel Cohen for the ease and attentiveness with which she navigated this production process. I also thank Jim Plank, Publicity Director at Haymarket. As always, I honor my agent, Stuart Bernstein, perhaps because our relationship feels genuinely reciprocal in what we bring to the shared table of our work together; and the ways in which we seem to make the other laugh when it is most needed. Sobretodo agradezco a mi amor Celia y a mi hijo Rafael Angel because they live their lives closest to my writer-self. I know it's not always easy (and neither are they). And that's why I am grateful.

Notes

Loving in the War Years 1978–83

Passage

1. The historical site, in the greater area of present-day northern New Mexico, from where the Aztecs were to have migrated before settling in what is now Mexico City. It is the mythic homeland of present-day Chicano peoples.

La Güera

1. "La Güera" was originally conceived for *This Bridge Called My Back: Writings by Radical Women of Color,* coedited by Gloria Anzaldúa and me, published by Persephone Press in 1981. The first *published* version of the essay (pre-*Bridge*) was selected by poet Adrienne Rich for inclusion in the 1980 lesbian writers anthology, *The Coming Out Stories,* from the same publisher and edited by Julia Penelope Stanley and Susan J. Wolfe. Adrienne Rich wrote the foreword to the collection and had personally requested "La Güera" for inclusion, noting that the women of color perspective in the book was noticeably limited.
2. Emma Goldman, *Red Emma Speaks: An Emma Goldman Reader,* ed. Alix Kates Shulman (New York: Random House, 1972), 388.
3. Maxine Hong Kingston, *Woman Warrior: Memoirs of a Girlhood Among Ghosts* (New York: Knopf, 1976).
4. From "The Brown Menace or Poem to the Survival of Roaches," in *The New York Head Shop and Museum* (Detroit: Broadside Press, 1974), 48.

It Got Her Over

1. Michelle Cliff, *Claiming an Identity They Taught Me to Despise* (Watertown, MA: Persephone Press, 1981).

A Long Line of Vendidas

1. Sometime in the mid-1990s, I happened upon Vivian (not her real name) at Sunday Mass at the New Mission Church in San Gabriel. We each were accompanying our mother and, exiting the church, we spied one another. The mutual recognition was palpable. We spoke briefly, warmly, then went on about our lives, our mothers each hooked into the elbow of her daughter's arm, akin to lovers.

2. Norma Alarcón examines this theme in her essay "Chicana's Feminist Literature: A Re-Vision Through Malintzin / or Malintzin: Putting Flesh Back on the Object," in *This Bridge Called My Back: Writings by Radical Women of Color* (Watertown, MA: Persephone Press, 1981).

3. The Smithsonian's recent discussion on the subject: https://www.smithsonianmag.com/smart-news/was-la-malinche-indigenous-interpreter-conquistador-hernan-cortes-traitor-survivor-or-icon-180978321/.

4. Octavio Paz, *The Labyrinth of Solitude: Life and Thought in Mexico*, trans. Lysander Kemp (New York: Grove Press, 1961), 77.

5. See Aleida R. Del Castillo, "Malintzin Tenepal: A Preliminary Look into a New Perspective," in *Essays on La Mujer*, ed. Rosaura Sánchez and Rosa Martínez Cruz (Los Angeles: UCLA Chicano Studies Research Center, 1977), 133.

6. Del Castillo, "Malintzin Tenepal," 131.

7. Del Castillo, "Malintzin Tenepal," 141.

8. Bernal Díaz del Castillo, *Historia verdadera de la conquista de la Nueva España*, vol.1, chap. 37 (México, Distrito Federal: Oficina Tipográfica de la Secretaría de Fomento, 1904, 1905).

9. Gloria Anzaldúa, unpublished writings.

10. For more on this subject, see my essay "Coyote's Daughter," in *Native Country of the Heart: A Memoir* (New York: Farrar, Straus and Giroux, 2019), 9–20.

11. Until the 1980s, "heterosexism," like the word "homophobia," had seldom appeared in Chicano publications. Heterosexim is the view that heterosexuality is the "norm" for all sexual relationships and as such the heterosexist imposes this model on all individuals through homophobia (fear of homosexuality) and institutionalized discrimination, such as laws defining marriage as between "a man and a woman." In 2015 same-sex marriage was legalized by the Supreme Court.

12. Sylvia S. Lizarraga, "From a Woman to a Woman," in *Essays on La Mujer*, 91.

13. Alfredo Mirandé and Evangelina Enríquez, *La Chicana: The Mexican-American Woman* (Chicago: University of Chicago Press, 1979), 225.

14. In acknowledging these women, I think of so many other Chicanas and other Latina feminists who were the first to politicize the particular oppression suffered by brown women. Speaking up in isolation, without a woman of color movement to support them, these women had little opportunity to record their own history of struggle. And yet, it is they who make this writing and the writing of my contemporaries possible.

　　The 1981 publication of *This Bridge Called My Back* unexpectedly bore witness to a sudden "boom" of Chicana writing in the 1980s, including Lorna Dee Cervantes's *Emplumada* (Pittsburgh: University of Pittsburgh Press, 1981); my own *Loving in the War Years* (Boston: South End Press, 1983); and four works published by Arte Público Press of the University of Houston, including Sandra Cisneros's *The House on Mango Street* (1983), Helena María Viramontes's *The Moths and Other Stories* (1985), Ana Castillo's *Women Are Not Roses* (poetry, 1984), and Denise Chávez's *The Last of the Menu Girls*. (1986). Also in 1986, Ana Castillo's *Mixquiahuala Letters* was published by Bilingual Press of New Mexico, and, one year later, Gloria Anzaldúa would publish her seminal *Borderlands / La Frontera: The New Mestiza* (San Francisco: Spinsters/Aunt Lute, 1987).

　　The paths that opened for us via these first works could not have been imagined, each of us growing up at a time when there was so little of ourselves to read. A full generation of writings followed, emerging from all corners of the country and quarters of thought. Still, we ask: *how is it that the complexity of Chicana lives remains so invisible in the public eye? How has our writing impacted the social conditions of Raza here and across borders?* I can think of no better project than our continuing to write toward that imperative.

15. Toni Cade Bambara, *The Salt Eaters* (New York: Random House, 1980), 3, 10.

16. See Adrienne Rich's "Compulsory Heterosexuality and Lesbian Existence," in *Blood, Bread, and Poetry: Selected Prose 1979–1985* (New York: Norton, 1986).

17. Since 2016, this no longer holds true for China. Due to rapidly decreasing birth rates, China raised the limit to two and then three children. Now, there is increasing political pressure to abolish all such restrictions. See, for example, Yaqiu Wang, "It's Time to Abolish China's Three-Child Policy," Human Rights Watch, February 22, 2023, https://

www.hrw.org/news/2023/02/22/its-time-abolish-chinas-three-child-policy.

18. In the 1973 *Roe v. Wade* Supreme Court decision, abortion was legalized in the United States. Since that time, the movement to pass a Human Life Amendment, which consists of multiple proposals to secure the rights of the fetus over that of the mother, has remained very much alive (some proponents of which insist that human life begins with conception or fertilization). With Republican control of the Senate headed by Mitch McConnell and four years of a Donald Trump presidency, along with the untimely death of Justice Ruth Bader Ginsburg in September 2020, three antiabortion judges—Neil Gorsuch, Brett Kavanaugh, and Amy Coney Barrett—were appointed to the Supreme Court. Along with Justices Alito and Thomas, they created an antiabortion majority. As a result, on June 24, 2022, *Roe v. Wade* was completely overturned, eliminating the federal constitutional right to abortion. See https://www.plannedparenthoodaction.org/issues/abortion/roe-v-wade.

19. Sonia A. López, "The Role of the Chicana Within the Student Movement," in *Essays on La Mujer,* 26.

20. Alarcón, "Chicana's Feminist Literature," 184.

21. I use "mestizo" here to address the mestizaje (mixture)—Indigenous and Spanish—of Mexican Catholicism. In the years ahead, I would come to understand and identify more clearly that the suffering I experienced in relation to my sexuality, dictated first by the Catholic Church and later by El Movimiento Chicano, was rooted in a profoundly patriarchal Spanish colonialism.

22. Paz, *Labyrinth of Solitude,* 77.

23. As discussed in the introduction to this collection, the distinction between gender, sex, and sexuality was not the vernacular of the early 1980s, but I employ it here for the clarity it offers.

24. "Played Between White Hands," in *Off Our Backs* 12, no. 7 (July 1982).

25. Mirtha Quintanales with Barbara Kerr, "The Complexity of Desire: Conversations on Sexuality and Difference," in *Conditions: Eight* (1982), 60.

26. In this regard, see Audre Lorde's 1981 critique of white feminist ethnocentrism in "An Open Letter to Mary Daly," in *This Bridge Called My Back,* 5th ed. (Albany, NY: SUNY Press, 2021), 90–93.

27. Bernice Reagon, "Turning the Century Around," in *Home Girls: A Black Feminist Anthology,* ed. Barbara Smith (New York: Kitchen Table: Women of Color Press, 1983), 361.

28. Audre Lorde, "The Uses of the Erotic/ The Erotic as Power" in *Sister*

Outsider: Essays and Speeches (Trumansburg, NY: The Crossing Press, 1984), 53.

29. Combahee River Collective, "A Black Feminist Statement" (1977) in *This Bridge Called My Back*, 5th ed., 210.

30. Barbara Smith, unpublished paper.

31. Combahee, "Black Feminist Statement," 215.

32. From an unpublished letter.

THE LAST GENERATION 1985–1992

PROPHECY OF A PEOPLE

1. "Poetry Is Not a Luxury" in *Sister Outsider: Essays and Speeches* (Trumansburg, NY: The Crossing Press, 1984), 136–39. Originally published in *Chrysalis: A Magazine of Female Culture* no. 3 (1977).

ART IN AMÉRICA CON ACENTO

1. An earlier version of this essay first appeared in *Frontiers: A Journal of Women Studies*, 12, no. 3 (1992). It was originally presented as a talk given through the Mexican American Studies Department at the California State University of Long Beach on March 7, 1990.

2. In the 1990 the National Opposition Union (UNO), a coalition of opposition parties in Nicaragua, formed to support the presidential candidacy of Violeta Chamorro. She succeeded in securing the election over incumbent president Daniel Ortega of the Sandinista National Liberation Front (FSLN).

3. At the time of this writing the civil war in El Salvador continued between the government's US-backed military and the leftist FMLN (Farabundo Martí National Liberation Front). It would not officially end until the signing of the Chapultepec Peace Accords in Mexico City. In the twelve-year war (1979–1992) over 75,000 people were killed. The most horrific and genocidal slaughters by government forces took place among Indigenous and campesino communities.

4. Gloria Anzaldúa, *Borderlands/La Frontera: The New Mestiza* (San Francisco: Spinsters/Aunt Lute Press), 24.

5. Lorna Dee Cervantes, "Oaxaca, 1974," in *Emplumada* (Pittsburgh: University of Pittsburgh Press, 1981), 44.

En busca de la fuerza feminina

1. This essay was originally written for the Symposium on "Current Debates in Chicano Culture" on July 20, 1991. The symposium was organized by the Mexican Museum in conjunction with the exhibition "Chicano Art: Resistance and Affirmation, 1965–1985" at the San Francisco Museum of Modern Art.

2. One notable exception was Celia Rodríguez's "La Llorona." The watercolor figure appears with a bundle, which the artist calls "her constant companion, symbolizing loss and psychic suffering." La Llorona's burden is identified as specifically female and mestiza.

3. My gratitude to Mexican performance artist Guadalupe Garcia, who first introduced this myth to me.

The Breakdown of the Bicultural Mind

1. Although this essay concerns my personal experience of mixed parentage—one white and one of color—the "twenty-first century mestizo" is increasingly born of two parents of color of different races and/or ethnicities. As such, their particular histories of migration and economic class may greatly impact the ways in which mixed-raced folks perceive their role as people of color in the US and internationally. Also, often one's experience is largely impacted by how one "presents" racially.

2. *Chicana Lesbians: The Girls Our Mothers Warned Us About*, ed. Carla Trujillo (Berkeley, CA: Third Woman Press, 1991),

3. Alice Walker, "The Divided Life of Jean Toomer," from *In Search of Our Mothers' Gardens* (New York: Harcourt Brace Jovanovich, 1983),

Queer Aztlán

1. An earlier version of this essay was first presented at the First National LLEGO (National Latino/a Lesbian and Gay Organization) Conference in Houston, Texas, on May 22, 1992. A later version was presented at a Quincentenary Conference at the University of Texas in Austin on October 31, 1992.

2. It's important to add that "Queer Nation" certainly served its purpose in bringing radical in-your-face awareness about the AIDS pandemic to a national level.

3. Earl Shorris, *Latinos: A Biography of the People* (New York: Norton, 1992), 100.

4. Perhaps this became an impossible task, given the FBI's Counterin-

telligence Program (COINTELPRO) infiltration of some of the more
radical organizations of the Chicano Movement at the time. See Pedro
Caban, "Cointelpro," *Latin American, Caribbean, and U.S. Latino Studies
Faculty Scholarship* 18 (2005), https://scholarsarchive.library.albany.
edu/lacs_fac_scholar/18.

5.   From a 2022 perspective, I am certainly less wedded to the word
"nation," given the reactionary damage that has been done in its name,
both in terms of its conflation with the neoliberal lie of the "democratic"
nation-state, as well as with racist separatist movements. I retain its usage here, however, as I understood it in the original writing: as a viable
strategy toward economic and social equity and cultural sovereignty
generated by peoples who have been historically oppressed by the
monolith that is WhiteAmerica.

I continue to believe in the strategic implementation and progressive activism possible in viewing Raza as a pueblo, a people, i.e., a
"nation" culturally distinct from the colonizer nation-state of the US.

6.   In *México Profundo: Reclaiming a Civilization*, trans. Philip A. Dennis
(Austin: University of Texas Press, 1996), Guillermo Bonfil Batalla
refers to this phenomenon as "the de-Indianization" of México. On page
17, he writes, "De-Indianization is not the result of biological mixture,
but of the pressure of an ethnocide that ultimately blocks the historical
continuity of a people as a culturally differentiated group." Chicanos as
Mexican Americans inherited this process of "de-Indianization."

7.   In recent years, the notion that United States Mexicans (Chicanos) are
settler colonizers has gained considerable intellectual traction among
many Northern Native Americans, Latinx, and white academics alike.
In some sectors, the Chicano Movement's reclamation of Aztlán is
interpreted as settler colonial appropriation. Certainly, this *was* the
case in Reies Tijerina's campaign in which he used Spanish land grants
to justify the Chicano right to land ownership. Given that from an Indigenous perspective, ownership (land as property) *is* the problem, the
critique is not without foundation. But El Movimiento was the farthest
thing from appropriation. These were de-tribalized Chicanos in search
of return to their homeland—a site of origin—in collaboration with
northern Native activists. In fact, Chicanos played a considerable role in
the American Indian Movement, not as "allies" but as Native-identified
peoples, the affinity of which is still evident to this day.

8.   The 1993 North American Free Trade Agreement with Mexico, the
United States, and Canada (NAFTA) marked another traitorous blow

to any remaining remnants of the Mexican revolution. In signing NAFTA, the government of Mexico capitulates to First World profiteering, furthering the surrender of the Mexican people's sovereign right to land and livelihood. Mass migration and abandoned milpas and maquiladoras would follow, as well as the consequent horrifying rise in femicide along Mexico's border.

9. "Pluma" in Spanish refers both to the "pen" and "feather," the double meaning of which was often applied to Chicano nationalist poets the likes of Alurista, who might appear wearing Aztec-style plumage at poetry readings. "Desplumada," on the other hand, means "plucked."

10. This was certainly the case with the Chicano Teatro movement from the mid-1960s into the 1980s. Initiated by the Chicano visionary Luis Valdez and his Teatro Campesino in 1965 to support the United Farm Workers (UFW) movement, a network of Chicano teatros emerged nationally. For nearly two decades, with some exceptions, el teatro chicano tended to reflect the male dominance of El Movimiento, even within its often-self-proclaimed collective structure.

Today, there are fewer and fewer recognizable Chicano teatros, given that there is less and less public money to support them. But a case might also be made that their entrenched patriarchal perspective about what is, indeed, "Chicano" has not broadened nor deepened sufficiently with the times. Once the site of radical transformation in form and content, Chicano Theater has remained fairly conventional in its cultural ideologies and theater praxes.

11. From an unpublished work.

12. Combahee River Collective, "A Black Feminist Statement," in *This Bridge Called My Back*, 5th ed. (Albany, NY: SUNY Press, 2021), 215.

13. In contrast to the overwhelming response by lesbians to the AIDS crisis, breast cancer, which had disproportionately affected the lesbian community, received little attention from the gay men's community, as well as the public at large. And yet, the statistics at the time were devastating and remain so. In 2022, one in eight women will be diagnosed with breast cancer, and one in three of those cases will become metastatic. Although breast cancer rates remain high and have even increased, survival rates have been improving, due to early detection and better screening and treatment options. See https://www.nationalbreastcancer.org/breast-cancer-facts.

14. Arturo Islas, *The Rain God: A Desert Tale* (Palo Alto, CA: Alexandrian Press, 1984).

15. See Rodriguez's essay "Late Victorians" in his collection, *Days of Obli-*

gation: An Argument with My Mexican Father (New York: Viking Press, 1992).

16. This was not the case among all tribes nor is homosexuality generally condoned in contemporary Indian societies. For more on the usage, see Ramón A. Gutiérrez, "Must We Deracinate Indians to Find Gay Roots?" *Outlook: National Lesbian & Gay Quarterly* 1, no. 4 (Winter 1989); also, note 4 in "The Dying Road to a Nation—A Prayer para un Pueblo" in this volume; and my essay "Still Loving in the (Still) War Years/2009: On Keeping Queer Queer" in *A Xicana Codex of Changing Consciousness: Writings 2000–2010* (Durham, NC: Duke University Press, 2011), 187–88.

17. The dissolution of what was heretofore the nation-state of Yugoslavia, composed of Serbs, Slovenes, Croats, Albanians, and Macedonians, including Muslim and Orthodox practitioners, resulted in the rise of bitter nationalist sentiments gone awry. It is a horror story of ethnic and cultural nationalism twisted into covetous militarism, patriarchal madness, mass rapes, and ethnic cleansing. It serves as a painful warning—a bloody cautionary tale—of the risk of fascist extremism poisoning what may be the rightful liberatory campaigns of oppressed peoples.

18. This is a line spoken by the character Medea in my play *The Hungry Woman: A Mexican Medea*. It takes place "in an imagined future of a history that never happened," after of the United States has been "balkanized." It is, in part, a dystopian portrait of a postrevolutionary Aztlán from which queer people of color have been exiled. "Nationhood," thus, is not without this writer's critique. Originally conceived in 1995, *The Hungry Woman: A Mexican Medea* was published in a preproduction version through West End Press of Albuquerque, New Mexico, in 2001.

19. In 1993, this note read: "I wish to thank Marsha Gómez, the Indigenous Women's Network (IWN), and the Alma de Mujer Center for Social Change in Austin, Texas, for providing me with statistical and other current information about Indigenous peoples' struggles for environmental safety and sovereignty, as well as published materials on the '92 Earth Summit in Brazil."

Today, I add the following: Although much of the leadership of the Indigenous Women's Network has now passed on, including Marsha Gómez and Ingrid Flying Eagle Woman Washinawatok (see multiple references to them in the final section of this volume), I remain indebted to them, to IWN, and to that piece of land called "Alma de Mujer" outside Austin, Tejas, which Marsha stewarded for many years. For a time, the place realized a feminist vision of Xicana, Indigenous, and other women of color residing in reciprocity with one another and with the Earth. I was privileged to have spent some considerable time there in the eighties and nineties. See http://www.almademujer.org/about.html.

Coyolxauhqui Remembered 1995–1999

Coyolxauhqui Re-membered

1. For reflections on those earlier years of pregnancy and mothering see *Waiting in the Wings: Portrait of a Queer Motherhood*, published in 1997 (and reprinted in 2022 by Haymarket).

2. In *Giving Up the Ghost*, originally published in 1986. Also in *Heroes and Saints & Other Plays* (Albuquerque, NM: West End Press, 1994), 25.

Looking for the Insatiable Woman

1. This essay was originally presented as an address at El Frente Latina Writers' Conference at Cornell University on October 14, 1995, organized by Helena Maria Viramontes, among others. Feminist philosopher Maria Lugones, whom I reference later in this essay, was also present at the conference. On February 22, 1996, the lecture was again delivered at the University of California, Los Angeles, sponsored by the César Chávez Center and the English Department.

2. Leslie Marmon Silko, *Almanac of the Dead* (New York: Simon & Shuster, 1991), 135–36.

3. Vivian Gornick, *The Romance of American Communism* (New York: Basic Books, 1977).

4. Amber Hollibaugh, from commie dyke organizer to published writer, is the author of *My Dangerous Desires: A Queer Girl Dreaming Her Way Home* (Durham, NC: Duke University Press, 2000).

5. More than two decades after writing this essay, it troubles me to state that the actual murder of the two children, by Jay (Jeannace June) Freeman and her femme lover collaborator, was far more brutal than I understood at the time. Having access to internet sources now, I believe that the specific conditions of the murder are so heinous as to be unforgivable. The children were not simply shoved off a cliff in Oregon but were brutally beaten and abused at the site in order to affect the appearance of a male rapist-murderer. What holds true is my shared perception,

with Amber Hollibaugh, as Freeman's advocate, that the murders were fundamentally generated by Jay's deeply internalized homophobia and her unbridled rage perhaps ignited by the sexual abuse she endured as a child by her stepfather. If not equally disturbing, but definitely unsettling, were the public depictions of Freeman drawn from a decidedly homophobic and misogynous lens, common in the 1960s, especially toward butch lesbians (folks whom today we would understand as transgender). The murdered children are clearly the victims, but without a feminist and queer comprehension of the structural heteropatriarchy that gave rise to the crime, Jay Freeman is simply rendered a monster.

6. *Cuentos: Stories by Latinas*, ed. Cherríe Moraga, Alma Gómez, and Mariana Romo-Carmona (New York: Kitchen Table: Women of Color Press, 1983), 66.

7. *Literatura chicana: texto y contexto*, ed. Antonia Castañeda Shular, Tomás Ybarra-Frausto, and Joseph Sommers (Englewood Cliffs, NJ: Prentice-Hall, 1972). And José E. Limón, "La Llorona, the Third Legend of Greater Mexico: Cultural Symbols, Women, and the Political Unconscious," in *Between Borders: Essays on Mexicana/Chicana History*, ed. Adelaida R. Del Castillo (Encino, CA: Floricanto Press, 1990), 399–432.

8. Rudolfo A. Anaya, *The Legend of La Llorona* (Berkeley, CA: Tonatiuh-Quinto Sol International, 1984).

9. From *The Hungry Woman: Myths and Legends of the Aztecs*, ed. John Bierhorst (New York: William Morrow and Company, 1984), 23, 25.

10. *Coatlicue's Call/El llamado de Coatlicue* (conceived and performed by Guadalupe Garcia; written and directed by Cherríe Moraga) premiered at Theater Artaud in San Francisco on October 25, 1990. It was produced by Brava! for Women in the Arts.

11. After decades of activism to secure women's reproductive rights, *Roe v. Wade* was overturned in 2022. Abortion is outlawed by the Supreme Court. Is there any doubt about the patriarchal control of women's bodies?

12. *Shadow of a Man* is published in my *Heroes and Saints & Other Plays* (Albuquerque, NM: West End Press, 1994).

13. My tío Esteban Moraga died of an infection due to wounds received in an altercation that took place in a restaurant in LA in the mid-1930s.

14. Moraga, *Heroes and Saints*.

15. See *West Coast Plays* 11/12 (Berkeley, CA: California Theater Council, 1982).

16. A full production of *The Hungry Woman: A Mexican Medea* premiered by Stanford University, Piggott Theater, May 11–22, 2005. It was

codirected by the playwright and Adelina Anthony; conceptual design by Celia Herrera Rodríguez. The play has been presented at universities throughout the country, along with an adaptation that took place in Málaga, España, in 2002. Still, the presence of Llorona in our MeXicanx lives continues to haunt us as artists.

On September 15 and 16, 2018, Celia Herrera Rodríguez and I collaborated on a protest-performance work entitled *Un Llanto Colectivo*. Some forty Chicanas/Latinas participated in the ceremonial protest in response to the separation of familias at the border. In the spirit of La Llorona, our protest centered on a collective outcry against the loss of our children. Organized by Las Maestras Center for Xicana[x] Indigenous Thought, Art and Social Praxis in collaboration with Otay Mesa Detention Resistance and Centro Cultural de la Raza, the two-day protest took place at the ICE headquarters and the Otay Mesa Detention Center, along the San Diego/Tijuana border. See https://www.detentionresistance.org/ and https://www.lasmaestrascenter.ucsb.edu/causa-caravana.

Out of Our Revolutionary Minds

1. First presented as the keynote address for the conference entitled Chicano Cultural Production: The Third Wave at the University of California, Irvine, on April 15, 1999.

2. Robert O'Hara, *Insurrection: Holding History* (New York: Theater Communications Group, 1999), 38–39.

3. In response to his "master's" admonition, Frederick Douglass writes: "From that moment, I understood the pathway from slavery to freedom.... I set out with high hope, and a fixed purpose, at whatever cost of trouble, to learn how to read." *Narrative of the Life of Frederick Douglass, An American Slave* (New York: Penguin Books, 1982), 78–79. First published in 1845 by the Anti-Slavery Office in Boston, Massachusetts.

4. Audre Lorde, "The Master's Tools Will Never Dismantle the Master's House," in *This Bridge Called My Back*, 5th ed. (Albany, NY: SUNY Press, 2021), 95.

5. The truest thing said by Mr. Escalante, through the mouth of Edward James Olmos, in the film *Stand and Deliver*, dir. Ramón Menéndez (Burbank, CA: Warner Bros. Pictures, 1988).

6. Hélène Cixous, "The School of the Dead," in *Three Steps on the Ladder of Writing* (New York: Columbia University Press, 1993), 21.

7. Lorna Dee Cervantes, "Visions of Mexico While at a Writing Sympo-

sium in Port Townsend, Washington," *Emplumada* (Pittsburgh: University of Pittsburgh Press, 1981), 45–47.

8. Franz Kafka, *Letters to Friends, Family and Editors*, trans. Richard and Clara Winston (New York: Schocken, 1978), 16.

9. The conference was sponsored by the Center for Lesbian and Gay Studies of the Graduate School and University Center of the City University of New York in Winter 1999.

10. Lorde, "Master's Tools," 95.

11. Alfred Arteaga, *Chicano Poetics: Heterotexts and Hybridities* (Cambridge: Cambridge University Press, 1997), 75.

12. Richard Rodriguez, *Hunger of Memory: The Education of Richard Rodriguez: An Autobiography* (Boston: D. R. Godine, 1982).

13. N. Scott Momaday, "The Arrowmaker," in *The Man Made of Words: Essays, Stories, Passages* (New York: St. Martin's, 1997), 9–12.

14. Momaday, "The Native Voice in American Literature," in *The Man Made of Words: Essays, Stories, Passages* (New York: St. Martin's, 1997), 15–16.

15. O'Hara, *Insurrection*, 14.

16. See *Actos* by Luis Valdez y El Teatro Campesino (San Juan Bautista: Cucaracha Publications, 1971). In his introductory essay, "Notes on Chicano Theater" (p. 2), Valdez describes the performance of resistance: "A demonstration with a thousand Chicanos, all carrying flags and picket signs, shouting Chicano Power!! is not the revolution. It is theater about the revolution . . . The Raza gets excited, simón, but unless the demonstration evolves into a street battle . . . it is basically a lot of emotion with very little political power, as Chicanos have discovered by demonstrating, picketing, and shouting before school boards, police departments, and stores to no avail . . . [The 1966 Huelga march's] emotional impact was irrefutable. Its actual political power was somewhat less." See also *Luis Valdez Early Works* (Houston: Arte Publico Press, 1990).

17. In the 1970s, feminist activists initiated a movement of critical engagement regarding the female body, especially in the areas of domestic abuse, sexuality and sexual assault, reproductive rights, and lesbian rights. This same activism catalyzed the formation of Women's and Feminist Studies programs across the country. Over the years, as many of these programs began to be replaced with "Gender Studies," the complexity of our theoretical understanding of gender and sexuality broadened and evolved, allowing greater space for discussions of genderqueer and trans identities; however, the focus on the condition of women (and transwomen) as living bodies became more theoretical and less geared toward direct activism.

18. In the foreword to the 1983 edition of *This Bridge Called My Back: Writings by Radical Women of Color*, I wrote: "The *idea* of Third World feminism proved to be much easier in a book than between real live women (of color)." I lamented what was, at the time, a lack of multicultural organizing among women of color across racial and ethnic differences. Still, *Bridge*, eighty-five thousand copies and twenty years later thanks to the vision of its multiple contributors, did serve to raise consciousness and provide an ideological base for political activists working on women of color issues.

    (Another twenty years after writing the statement above, I am gratified to state that *Bridge* celebrated its fortieth anniversary with a fifth edition, published by SUNY Press. It continues to stay in print and resonate for succeeding generations.)

19. Proposition 21, the "Gang Violence and Juvenile Crime Prevention Act of 1998," was passed in March 2000. The California initiative statute created to "deter" juvenile crime significantly changed the legal treatment of youths arrested for crimes, and specifically targeted youth of color and the poor. The statute increased the punishment for all gang-related felonies. Youth offenders fourteen years of age or older charged with murder or certain sex offenses would automatically receive adult trials without judicial review. Informal probation was eliminated for youths committing felonies. Youths were subjected to longer sentences for serious felonies (85 percent of the sentence given versus the usual 50 percent as stipulated by the California "Three Strikes" law).

    Any youths sixteen years of age or older convicted in adult court were to be sentenced to the California Detention Center (California Department of Corrections), instead of the California Youth Authority (now called the Division of Juvenile Justice), without protected separation from the larger adult population.

    Proposition 22 also passed in March of 2000. The "California Defense of Marriage Act," otherwise known as the "Knight Initiative," added a new provision to the California Family Code: "Only marriage between a man and a woman is valid or recognized in California." At the time of the initiative's introduction, the state of California had already only recognized marriages between a man and woman as a legal union; however, the inclusion of this clause would in effect cancel out the recognition of same-sex legal unions obtained in other states. In 2008, however, the California Supreme Court decision guaranteeing the right to same-sex marriage nationwide, invalidated Prop. 22.

20. In 1995, another example of successful student of color organizing

occurred. Nine students and one professor conducted a heavily pub-
licized fourteen-day hunger strike to protest the underfunded state
of Chicano Studies at UCLA. The outcome, although a compromise
(students had demanded a fully funded Chicano Studies Department),
was the establishment of the César E. Chávez Chicano Studies Center.
Over the succeeding decades, UCLA Chicana/o Studies continued to
grow. In 2005 it was established as a department; and, in 2019 "an overwhelming majority" of its faculty voted to change its name to the César
E. Chávez Department of Chicana/o and Central American Studies.
See https://chavez.ucla.edu/about/history/.

21. Paulo Freire, *Pedagogy of the Oppressed* (New York: Continuum, 1993),
39. Written in Portuguese, *Pedagogía del oprimido* was first published
in Spanish in 1968, translated by Mayra Bergman Ramos. The English
translation was published in 1970; the Portuguese original, in 1972.

22. "Washinawatok, Freitas and Gay were believed to have been abduct-
ed and murdered by members of the leftist rebel organization, FARC
(Revolutionary Armed Forces of Colombia). The motive for the murders remains unclear; but, at the time of the murders, family members
suspected a connection between the deaths and a U.S. grant of $230
million to Colombia to fight the drug war and to crackdown on FARC."
Amy Weaver, *Shawano Leader*, 118:56 (Sunday, March 7, 1999).

23. Associated Press, *Green Bay Press-Gazette*, Sunday, March 7, 1999.

24. "Sovereignty Is More Than Just Power," *Indigenous Woman* 2, no. 6
(January 1999).

25. Damien Whitworth, *Washington Times*, March 13, 2000: "The U'wa
have threatened to commit mass suicide by hurling themselves of a cliff,
should the 'the blood of Mother Earth' be removed. Mass suicide as an
act of resistance against colonization was employed by U'wa ancestors
as early as the 17th century in opposition to Spanish rule."

26. For more info on Ingrid Washinawatok-El-Issa's life and legacy: https://
en.wikipedia.org/wiki/Ingrid_Washinawatok

27. N. Scott Momaday, "The Storyteller and His Art—Introduction," in *The
Man Made of Words: Essays, Stories, Passages* (New York: St. Martin's
Griffin, 1998), 169.

The Dying Road to a Nation

1. First presented at the American Academy of Religion conference in Or-
lando, Florida, in November 1998; subsequently presented in a revised

version at the National Association for Chicana/Chicano Studies Conference in San Antonio, Texas, on April 30, 1999. (This current version has been considerably updated.)

2. Parts of this writing on the passing of Marsha Gómez became the eulogy I offered at her memorial at Alma de Mujer Center for Social Change, just days after her death. It was later published in the chapter "And It Is All These Things that Are Our Grief," in *A Xicana Codex* (2011).

3. Mekaya Gomez, a talented visual artist, had been diagnosed with schizophrenia in his early twenties; his suffering was also complicated by drug-induced mental problems. A Travis County jury convicted him of the murder of his mother, whereupon he received a fifty-six-year sentence. In 2002, two years after the conviction, he was found dead in his prison cell under questionable circumstances. All of us in Marsha's community locally in Austin and around the country were shocked by the news—a tragic ending to the tragic loss of Marsha. Mekaya was in desperate need of psychiatric care while incarcerated. We all knew Marsha would have wanted that for him.

4. Of course, it is impossible to read this line more than twenty years later without it resonating, almost prophetically, with the horror of the femicide taking place in México and Central América.

5. The term "two-spirit" is used to refer to contemporary Native American/ First Nation gay men, lesbians, and transgender individuals, as well as to traditions of multiple gender categories and sexualities in tribal cultures. Some Xicanas who recognize themselves as Native have also employed the term. For a diverse discussion on the subject, see *Two-Spirit People: Native American Gender Identity, Sexuality, and Spirituality*, ed. Sue-Ellen Jacobs, Wesley Thomas, and Sabine Lang (Urbana and Chicago: University of Illinois Press, 1997). Current 2022 writings, websites, and social media outlets on queer identities from an Indigenous American perspective are more readily accessed today. See, as one example, https://www. wernative.org/my-relationships/sexual-health/lgbt-two-spirit.

6. The premature birth and fight for his life are in my 1997 memoir, *Waiting in the Wings: Portrait of a Queer Motherhood*.

References/Selected Works*

IN CONVERSATION WITH THEIR TIMES

Alarcón, Norma, et al, eds. *The Sexuality of Latinas*. Berkeley: Third Woman Press, 1993.

———, ed. *Third Woman: SouthwestMidwest* 2, no. 1 (1984).

Alexander, M. Jacqui and Chandra Talpade Mohanty, eds. *Feminist Genealogies, Colonial Legacies, Democratic Futures*. New York: Routledge, 1996.

Allen, Paula Gunn. *Off the Reservation: Reflections on Boundary-Busting, Border-Crossing Loose Cannons*. Boston, Beacon Press, 1999.

Allison, Dorothy. *The Women Who Hate Me*: Poetry 1980–1990. Ithaca, NY: Firebrand Press, 1991.

Anaya, Rudolfo, Francisco A. Lomelí, and Enrique R. Lamadrid, eds. *Aztlán: Essays on the Chicano Homeland*. Albuquerque: University of New Mexico Press, 2017. First published 1989, by el Norte Publications/Academia.

Anzaldúa, Gloria. *Borderlands / La Frontera: The New Mestiza*. San Francisco: Spinsters/Aunt Lute Press, 1987.

Arteaga, Alfred. *Chicano Poetics: Heterotexts and Hybridities*. Cambridge: Cambridge University Press, 1997.

Baldwin, James. *James Baldwin: Collected Essays*. Edited by Toni Morrison. New York: Library of America, 1998.

Bambara, Toni Cade. *The Salt Eaters*. New York: Random House, 1980.

———. *Those Bones Are Not My Child: A Novel*. New York: Pantheon, 1999.

Berg, Stepthen. *Nothing in the Word: Versions of Aztec Poetry*. New York: Grossman Publishers, 1972,

Bethel, Lorraine and Barbara Smith, eds. *Conditions: Five: The Black Women's Issue*. Brooklyn, NY: Conditions, 1979.

---

* "Selected works" reflect critical writings that especially impacted my own Chicana thinking at that time. It is by no means exhaustive.

Bonfil Batalla, Guillermo. *México Profundo: Reclaiming a Civilization*. Translated by Philip A. Dennis. Austin: University of Texas Press, 1996.

Bracho, Ricardo. "Sexual Sovereignty: Towards an Erotic of Chicano Liberation," "Refracting Voices: Race, Gender, Desire," and "The Alphabet Isn't Sopa." Unpublished manuscript.

Broyles-González, Yolanda. *El Teatro Campesino: Theater in the Chicano Movement*. Austin: University of Texas Press, 1994.

Castellanos, Rosario. *Balún Canán*. Mexico: Fondo de Cultura Económica, Colección Popular 92, 1986.

Castillo, Ana. *The Mixquihuala Letters*. Tempe, Arizona: Bilingual Review Press/Editorial bilingüe, 1986.

Cervantes, Lorna Dee. *Emplumada*. Pittsburgh: University of Pittsburgh Press, 1981.

Cixous, Hélène. *Three Steps on the Ladder of Writing*. New York: Columbia University Press, 1993.

Codex Mendoza: Aztec Manuscript. Commentary by Kurt Ross. London: Regent Books/High Text Ltd., 1984.

Churchill, Ward. *From a Native Son: Selected Essays on Indigenism, 1985–1995*. Boston: South End Press, 1999.

The Combahee River Collective. "A Black Feminist Statement." In *This Bridge Called My Back: Writings by Radical Women of Color*, edited by Cherríe Moraga and Gloria Anzaldúa, 210–18. New York: Kitchen Table Press, 1983. (Original publication, 1977.)

Díaz del Castillo, Bernal. *Historia verdadera de la conquista de la Nueva España*, Vol.1, Chap. 37. México, Distrito Federal: Oficina Tipográfica de la Secretaría de Fomento, 1904, 1905.

Douglass, Frederick. *Narrative of the Life of Frederick Douglass, An American Slave*. New York: Penguin Books, 1982.

Durham, Jimmie. *A Certain Lack of Coherence: Writings on Art and Cultural Politics*. London: Kala Press, 1993.

Eisenstein, Zillah R., ed. *Capitalist Patriarchy and the Case for Socialist Feminism*. New York: Monthly Review Press, 1979.

Feinberg, Leslie. *Stone Butch Blues: A Novel*. Ithaca, NY: Firebrand Books, 1993. https://www.lesliefeinberg.net/

Fernández, Adela. *Dioses prehispánicos de México: Mitos y deidades del panteón náhuatl*. Mexico City: Panorama Editorial, 1989.

Freire, Paulo. *Pedagogy of the Oppressed*. New York: Continuum, 1993.

Galeano, Eduardo. *Open Veins of Latin America: Five Centuries of the Pillage of a Continent*. New York: Monthly Review Press, 1973.

———. *The Memory of Fire Trilogy: Genesis, Faces and Masks, and Century of the Wind*. New York: Pantheon, 1982–86.

Goldman, Emma. *Red Emma Speaks: An Emma Goldman Reader*. Edited by Alix Kates Shulman. New York: Random House, 1972.

Gómez-Peña, Guillermo. *The New World Border: Prophecies, Poems, and Loqueras for the End of the Century*. San Francisco: City Lights, 1996.

Gutiérrez, Ramón A. "Must We Deracinate Indians to Find Gay Roots?" *Outlook: National Lesbian & Gay Quarterly* 1, issue 4 (Winter 1989).

Instituto Nacional de Antropología e Historia Secretaria de Educación Pública. *Los Códices de México*. Mexico City, INAH, 1979.

Islas, Arturo. *Migrant Souls: A Novel*. New York: William Morrow, 1990.

———. *The Rain God: A Desert Tale*. Palo Alto, CA: Alexandrian Press, 1984.

Keane, Dolores. "Solid Ground." By Dougie MacLean. 1993. Shanachie, compact disc.

León-Portilla, Miguel. *Aztec Thought and Culture*. Norman, OK: University of Oklahoma Press, 1963.

Lorde, Audre. *The Black Unicorn*. New York: W. W. Norton, 1978.

———. "The Brown Menace or Poem to the Survival of Roaches." In *The New York Head Shop and Museum*. Detroit: Broadside Press, 1974.

———. *Sister Outsider: Essays and Speeches*. Trumansburg, NY: The Crossing Press, 1984.

Martínez, Rubén. *The Other Side: Fault Lines, Guerrilla Saints, and the True Heart of Rock 'n' Roll*. London: Verso, 1992.

Merchant, Carolyn. *Radical Ecology: The Search for a Livable World*. New York: Routledge, 1992.

Midnight Sun. "Sex/Gender Systems in Native North America." In *Living the Spirit: A Gay American Indian Anthology*, edited by Will Roscoe with Gay American Indians, 32–57. New York: St. Martin's Press, 1988.

Mirandé, Alfredo, and Evangelina Enríquez. *La Chicana: The Mexican-American Woman*. Chicago: University of Chicago Press, 1979.

Mohanty, Chandra Talpade. "Under Western Eyes: Feminist Scholarship and Colonial Discourses." *Feminist Review*, no. 30 (Autumn 1988): 61–88.

———. "'Under Western Eyes' Revisited: Feminist Solidarity through Anti-capitalist Struggles." *Signs* 28, no. 2 (Winter 2003): 499–535.

Momaday, N. Scott. *The Man Made of Words: Essays, Stories, Passages*. New York: St. Martin's, 1997.

Moraga, Cherríe. *Heroes and Saints & Other Plays*. Albuquerque, NM: West End Press, 1994.

————. *The Hungry Woman: A Mexican Medea*. Albuquerque, NM: West End Press, 2001.

————. *Native Country of the Heart: A Memoir*. New York: Farrar, Straus and Giroux, 2019.

————. *A Xicana Codex of Changing Consciousness: Writings, 2000–2010*. Durham, NC: Duke University Press, 2011.

Moraga, Cherríe, and Gloria Anzaldúa. *This Bridge Called My Back: Writings by Radical Women of Color*. Watertown, MA: Persephone Press, 1981. Subsequent editions: New York: Kitchen Table: Women of Color Press, 1983; Berkeley, CA: Third Woman Press, 2002; Albany, NY: SUNY Press, 2015, 2021.

Morrison, Toni. *Sula*. New York: Knopf, 1974.

Muñoz, José Esteban. *Disidentifications: Queers of Color and the Performance of Politics*. Berkeley: University of California Press, 1999.

Nuttall, Zelia, ed. *The Codex Nuttall: A Picture Manuscript from Ancient Mexico*. New York: Dover Publications, 1975.

Ortiz, Simon J., ed. *Speaking for the Generations: Native Writers on Writing*. Tucson: University of Arizona Press, 1997.

Pauli, Hertha. *Her Name Was Sojourner Truth*. Pasadena: Appleton, 1962.

Paz, Octavio. *The Labyrinth of Solitude: Life and Thought in Mexico*. Translated by Lysander Kemp. New York: Grove Press, 1961.

Pérez, Emma. *The Decolonial Imaginary: Writing Chicanas into History*. Bloomington: Indiana University Press, 1999.

————. "Sexuality and Discourse: Notes from a Chicana Survivor." In *Chicana Lesbians: The Girls Our Mothers Warned Us About*, edited by Carla Trujillo. Berkeley, CA: Third Woman Press, 1991.

Pina, Michael. "The Archaic, Historical, and Mythicized Dimension of Aztlán." In *Aztlán: Essays on the Chicano Homeland*, edited by Rudolfo A. Anaya and Francisco A. Lomelí, 43–74. Albuquerque: Academia/El Norte Publications, 1989.

Rich, Adrienne. "Compulsory Heterosexuality and Lesbian Existence." In *Blood, Bread, and Poetry: Selected Prose 1979–1985*, 23–75. New York: Norton, 1986.

————. *Of Woman Born: Motherhood as Experience and Institution*. New York: W. W. Norton, 1976.

————. *On Lies, Secrets, and Silence: Selected Prose 1966–1978*. New York: W. W. Norton, 1979.

Rodriguez, Richard. *Days of Obligation: An Argument with My Mexican Father*. New York: Viking Press, 1992.

———. *Hunger of Memory: The Education of Richard Rodriguez: An Autobiography*. Boston: D. R. Godine, 1982.

Said, Edward W. *Out of Place: A Memoir*. New York: Vintage, 2000.

Sánchez, Martha Ester. *Contemporary Chicana Poetry: A Critical Approach to an Emerging Literature*. Berkeley/Los Angeles: University of California Press, 1985.

Sánchez, Rosaura, and Rosa Martínez Cruz, eds. *Essays on La Mujer*. Los Angeles: UCLA Chicano Studies Research Center, 1977.

Sandoval, Chela. *Methodology of the Oppressed*. Minneapolis: University of Minnesota Press, 2000.

Segrest, Mab. *Memoir of a Race Traitor: Fighting Racism in the American South*. New York: The New Press, 1994.

Shorris, Earl. *Latinos: A Biography of the People*. New York: Norton, 1992.

Silko, Leslie Marmon. *Almanac of the Dead*. New York: Simon & Shuster, 1991.

———. *Ceremony*. New York: Viking Press, 1977.

Smith, Barbara, ed. *Home Girls: A Black Feminist Anthology*. New York: Kitchen Table: Women of Color Press, 1983.

Steiner, Stan, and Luis Valdez, eds. "El Plan Espiritual de Aztlán." In *Aztlán: An Anthology of Mexican American Literature*. New York: Vintage Books, 1972.

Taylor, Diana and Juan Villegas. *Negotiating Performance: Gender, Sexuality, and Theatricality in Latin/o America*. Durham, NC: Duke University Press, 1994.

Thompson, William Irwin. *Blue Jade from the Morning Star: An Essay and a Cycle of Poems on Quetzalcoatl*. Hudson, NY: Lindisfarne Press, 1983.

Trujillo, Carla, ed. *Chicana Lesbians: The Girls Our Mothers Warned Us About*. Berkeley, CA: Third Woman Press, 1991.

Vasconcelos, José. Translated by Didier T. Jaén. *The Cosmic Race/ La raza cósmica*. Baltimore: Johns Hopkins University Press, 1997. First published in Spanish 1925.

Walker, Alice. "The Divided Life of Jean Toomer." In *In Search of Our Mothers' Gardens*. New York: Harcourt Brace Jovanovich, 1983.

Wolf, Christa. *Medea: A Modern Retelling*. New York: Doubleday, 1998.

Index

abortion, 6, 119, 369, 376. *See also*
    reproductive rights
Afghanistan, 3
African American. *See* Black identity
African identity, 200, 279
AIDS, 6, 157, 202, 283, 290, 296,
    298, 317, 339, 371, 373
Alamo, 311
Alarcón, Norma, 117, 122
Alma de Mujer Center for Social
    Change, 374, 381
Almanac of the Dead (Silko), 323
Alurista, 281, 283, 373
Amazon, 291
América, 4, 8, 197, 200, 203–5, 215,
    279, 290, 294–95, 305, 307,
    317, 338
American Indian Movement, 6, 372
Anaya, Rudolfo, 327
AngloAmerica, 4, 19–20, 62–65, 67,
    107–8, 135, 199–204, 211, 281,
    288, 372
    Aztlán and, 278–79, 291, 294
    institutional violence and, 120
Anglo identity, 100, 107–8, 198, 213,
    257, 271
Anti-Apartheid, 6
Anti (Vietnam) War Movement, 6
Anzaldúa, Gloria, 5, 19, 98, 111, 117,

125, 204, 368
Apache nation, 289
Arizona, 261
Arteaga, Alfred, 340
Asian American Political Alliance, 6
Austin, Texas, 374
Aztec Empire, 54, 108–111, 156,
    213, 215, 276, 281, 310, 317,
    319, 328, 366, 373
Aztlán, 137, 157, 212–13, 216,
    275–79, 283, 288–89, 306, 308,
    317, 366
    AngloAmerica and, 278, 291, 294
    as colonial settler concept, 372
    dystopian, 374
Azuela, Rocky, 104–5

Baja California, 326
Balam, Chilam, 226
Baldwin, James, 331
Bambara, Toni Cade, 118, 317
Barrio Logan, 280
Bay Area, 158
Berg, Stephen, 54
Berkeley, 15, 253, 280, 346
Biodiversity Treaty, 293
Black feminism, 67–68, 139–40, 286
"Black Feminist Statement" (Com-
    bahee River Collective), 139

Black identity, 65, 106, 246, 248–51, 275, 278–80, 335, 342, 362
   class and, 66
   Los Angeles Rebellion and, 305
   womanhood and, 117, 136, 139–40, 286, 337
Black nationalism, 274
Black Panthers, 6, 342
Black Power, 6
Borbón, Angelita, 327–28
Bosnia, 274
Boston, 15, 106, 136, 249
Boyle Heights, 280
Bracho, Ricardo, 211, 271–72
Brazil, 157, 292, 374
Brooklyn, 15, 249, 317
Brown Berets, 6, 277
Buchanan, Pat, 275
Bush, George H. W., 197–98, 200–201, 293

Cabrera, Miguel, 362
Califas/California, 3, 15, 71, 123, 136, 157, 163, 199, 201, 251, 280, 306, 317, 319, 323–24, 347. *See also specific cities and towns*
   Central Valley, 62, 280, 323, 325
   Proposition 21, 346, 379
   Proposition 22, 379
Cambodia, 199
Canada, 290, 372
Cane (Toomer), 259
capitalism, 3, 66, 111, 115, 119–20, 140, 199, 259, 289, 291, 293
CARA Exhibit, 211
Caribbean, 8, 199, 253
Carrasco, Barbara, 305
Castañeda, Carlos, 252
Castellanos, Rosario, 155

Del Castillo, Aleida, 110, 117
Castillo, Ana, 171, 368
Castro, Fidel, 292
Catarino Montoya, Emmanuel, 305
Catholic Church, 128, 212, 369
Catholicism, 15, 105, 110, 114, 128–30, 133, 216, 218, 278, 361–62, 369
Central America, 6, 8, 381
Central Valley, 62, 280, 323, 325
Centro Campesino Cultural, 176
Centro Cultural de la Raza, 377
A Certain Lack of Coherence (Durham), 355
Cervantes, Lorna Dee, 204, 337, 368
Cervántez, Yreina, 211
Chapultepec Peace Accords, 370
Chávez, César, 155, 280, 317
Chávez, Denise, 368
Chicago, 136, 276
Chicana feminism, 5, 18, 103, 108, 110, 111, 115–17, 135–36, 142–43, 272, 275, 283–84, 326–27, 329, 368, 377
Chicana identity, 3, 8, 121–22, 126, 133–36, 139, 200, 251–54, 294–95, 305
   ancestors and, 5, 310
   betrayal and, 106–8, 113–14, 121–23, 125–16, 142
   Chicano Movement and, 122, 271–72, 282–84
   Coyolxauhqui and, 214, 216, 330
   family and, 66–67, 98–103, 110–19, 212, 249, 330, 337–38
   Heroes and Saints and, 330
   heterosexism and, 115–23, 125, 143, 213, 282
   Llorona and, 326, 330

love and, 103, 143, 252–53,
283–84

Malinche and, 110–13, 258, 282

Mexican identity and, 200, 202,
253–54, 281–22

migration and, 347

oppression of, 64, 107–21, 120,
127, 129, 212

outsider to, 16, 20, 103

privilege and, 106

Virgen de Guadalupe and, 108,
281–282

visibility and, 4, 19, 139, 251, 272,
337, 368

women's movement and, 116–17,
122, 139

La Chicana (Mirandé and Enriquez),
117

Chicana lesbian identity, 64–65,
103, 121–23, 126–27, 133–37,
139, 142–43, 212, 215, 247,
252, 257, 271, 283, 284, 288,
294, 316

AIDS and, 287

Black feminism and, 139

Chicano Movement and, 115,
122, 273, 283–84, 287

family and, 103, 143, 282–84, 355

Chicano codex, 307–10

"Chicano Codices Encountering Art
of the Américas," 305

Chicano culture, 117, 127–28, 158,
201–05, 211, 277, 283, 305,
337, 373

Aztlán and, 137, 273, 275–77, 279,
283, 366

Catholicism and, 128, 309

family and, 66–67, 98–103, 111–
19, 212, 282–84, 308, 338

heterosexism and, 115, 122, 143,
282–87, 367

sexism and, 115, 121–22, 127–28,
275, 282–83, 373

Chicano gay identity, 106, 121, 143,
201, 211, 212, 272–73, 282–88,
296

Chicano identity, 8–9, 17, 106–7,
202, 204–5, 257, 273, 275–83,
291, 347

ancestors and, 203–5, 276, 295,
307–11

colonialism and, 156–57,
199–201, 275–76, 278–79,
282, 291–92, 331, 372

heterosexism and, 115, 122, 274,
284–87

Indigenous identity and, 9, 199,
200, 203, 278–79, 281,
288–92, 318, 372

male identity and, 8, 114–16, 120,
281–84, 296

Malinche and, 111

Mexican identity and, 9, 111, 113,
121–22, 204, 271, 278–82,
372

oppression, 116–17, 120, 289–90,
292

privilege and, 63, 107, 257

Spanish language and, 273

Chicano Movement, 6, 121, 143,
201–3, 271–74, 277, 281–83,
295, 342–43, 346, 369, 372, 373

Chicano nationalism, 122, 273–74,
276–79, 282, 288, 349, 372, 373

Chicano Poetics (Arteaga), 340

Chicano Power Movement, 277, 378

Chicano Studies, 280, 380. *See also*
Ethnic Studies

Chicanx identity, 5, 8
Chihuahua, 276
China, 119, 368
Cisneros, Sandra, 368
City University of New York, 339
civil rights movement, 4, 6, 138, 342
Cixous, Hélène, 337
*Claiming an Identity They Taught Me
    to Despise* (Cliff), 79
Cliff, Michelle, 79
Coatepec, 213
Coatlicue, 5, 213–15, 329
Coatlicue's Call (Garcia), 329
Cochiti (K'úutìim'é) people, 193
"Codex Amalia" (Mesa-Bains), 310
Codex Zelia (Herrera Rodríguez),
    308
Cold War, 290
Colombia, 348, 380
Colón, Cristóbal, 156
colonialism, 4–5, 126, 163, 247, 275,
    289, 305–6, 308, 310, 340, 380
    Chicano identity and, 156,
        199–201, 275–76, 278–79,
        282, 291–92, 331, 372
    patriarchy and, 108–110, 119–20,
        275, 369
Columbus, 290–91, 306, 317
Combahee River Collective, 139,
    286
Contra War, 197
Cortés, Hernán, 108–110, 126, 282,
    308
Cotera, Martha, 117
Coyolxauhqui, 5, 213–16, 252,
    316–19, 329–30
Cree Indians, 291
Cuba, 200

Denver, 277
Depression, 256
Díaz del Castillo, Bernal, 110
Diñé people, 260, 289, 291
Doña Marína, 108
Douglass, Frederick, 377
Durham, Jimmie, 355, 363

Earth, 293–95, 311, 375, 380
Earth Summit, 157, 292, 374
East Los Angeles, 271, 272, 280–81,
    294, 308, 346
East Los Streetscapers, 305
education, 16, 62–63, 67, 104–5,
    128, 141, 203, 251, 277, 308,
    317–18, 336, 337, 341–49
El Salvador, 140, 157, 198, 370
Engels, Frederick, 116
English language, 68, 71, 106, 137,
    257, 274
Enriquez, Evangelina, 117
ethnic cleansing, 275, 374
ethnicity, 8–9, 115, 134, 136, 138,
    275, 372, 374, 379
Ethnic Studies, 280, 318, 339–40,
    345, 346, 380
Euripides, 327–28
Europe, 123, 128, 294, 341, 349
European identity, 9, 156, 200,
    202–3, 254, 279, 283

FBI, 277, 371
femicide, 373, 381
femininity, 70, 117, 215–16, 250,
    284, 285, 288, 375
feminism, 8, 140, 201–2, 275, 298,
    325, 360, 375, 378
    anti-feminism, 121–22
    Black, 67–68, 139–40, 286

bourgeoise, 115, 134

Chicana, 5, 18, 103, 108, 110, 111, 115–17, 135–36, 142–43, 272, 275, 283–84, 326–27, 329, 368, 377

criminalization and, 376

Latina, 368

lesbian, 70, 103, 115–16, 118, 134–37, 272, 274, 378

Third World, 134–36, 138–40, 379

white, 70–71, 116, 134–36, 369

women of color, 4, 6, 68, 71–72, 115–16, 118, 140, 379

First Chicano Youth Conference, 277

FMLN (Farabundo Martí National Liberation Front), 6, 370

Foreign Club, 113

Four Hundred Stars, 213

Freeman, Jay, 33, 325–26, 375–76

Freire, Paulo, 345, 347

Freitas, Terence, 348, 380

Fresno, 280

"From Woman to Woman" (Lizarraga), 115

FSLN. *See* Sandinista National Liberation Front

García, Cathy, 124

Garcia, Guadalupe, 329, 371

Garcia, Rupert, 212

Gay and Lesbian Movement, 6, 118, 201–2, 272

gay identity, 65–66, 69–70, 272–73, 282–88, 324. *See also* Chicano gay identity

AIDS and, 157, 298, 373

homophobic violence and, 140

marriage rights, 346, 367, 379

two-spirit identity, 381

Gay, Lahe'ena'e, 348, 380

genderqueer identity, 134, 378. *See aslo* nonbinary gender; transgender identity

genocide, 119–20, 274, 289, 308, 370

Giving Up the Ghost (Moraga), 253, 319

Goldman, Emma, 62, 64

Gómez, Marsha, 258–59, 261, 315, 355–57, 359–60, 374, 381

Great Lakes Basin, 292

Green Giant, 280

Grenada, 199

Guatemala, 157, 192, 199

Gulf War, 157, 290

Hall, Radclyffe, 337

Harlem, 250

Hernández, María, 116–17

Herrón, Willie, 305

heterosexism, 65, 70, 114–15, 125, 212, 274, 275, 284, 367, 376

heterosexuality, 64, 114, 115, 119, 130, 134–35, 137–39, 141, 143, 212–13, 275, 281–89

Historia verdadera de la conquista de la Nueva España (Díaz del Castillo), 110

Hollibaugh, Amber, 94, 324–25, 375, 376

Hollywood, 67

homophobia, 70, 121, 141, 272, 275, 281, 284, 325–26, 367, 376

homosexuality, 121, 122, 158, 255, 282, 284, 287, 367, 374

Huerta, Dolores, 280

Huitzilopochtli, 109, 213–15, 329

Hungry Woman, 328–30
*The Hungry Woman: A Mexican
Medea* (Moraga), 374
Huntington Beach, 123

I-Hotel, 6
Indian Wars, 319
Indigenous cultures, 211, 252, 292,
293, 360, 381
capitalism and, 111, 289, 290–91
education and, 345, 348–49
family and, 356
gender and, 278, 357, 381
sexuality and, 374, 381
Indigenous identity, 5, 136, 156,
162–63, 249, 252, 254, 260–62,
356
Chicano identity and, 9, 199, 200,
203, 278–79, 281, 288–92,
318, 372
colonial connotations of, 281–82
erasure of, 212
mestizo identity and, 8–9,
108–10, 126, 200, 278–79,
292, 355–56, 369
re-indigenization, 7, 288–90
Indigenous people, 156–58, 216,
252, 260–61, 279, 283, 305,
362–363. *See also* Native Americans; *specific peoples*
Catholicism and, 15, 192
in El Salvador, 370
enslavement and, 278
international campaigns of, 157,
272, 291
land and, 199, 247, 276, 291–95,
355, 372, 374
Malinche and, 108, 110, 126, 282
reservations and, 140, 289

sovereignty and, 291, 294, 348,
374
Indigenous Women's Network, 374
Insurrection: Holding History (O'Ha-
ra), 335–36, 342
Inuit people, 290–91
Iraq War, 307
Israel, 291

Jim Crow, 278
JoAnn (Lawrence), 16, 20–21,
98–101, 123, 126, 131–32, 161,
255, 258, 326

Kafka, Franz, 338
Kahlo, Frida, 213
Kayapó people, 292
Keane, Dolores, 263
Kenwood Hotel, 123
Kettleman City, 281, 294
King, Martin Luther, Jr., 342
Kingston, Maxine Hong, 69
Kitchen Table: Women of Color
Press, 251
Korea War, 307
Kumeyaay nation, 289
Kurdish people, 291

El laberinto de la soledad (Paz), 109
The Last Generation, 2, 154, 156–57
Latina feminism, 368
Latina identity, 136, 248, 250, 252
Latin America, 8–9, 199, 215, 272,
292
Latino identity, 197–200, 249, 272,
274, 298, 331, 339
Latinos (Shorris), 273
Latinx identity, 8, 372
León-Portilla, Miguel, 300

lesbian feminism, 70, 103, 115–16, 118, 134–37, 272, 274, 378

lesbian identity, 2, 64–65, 70, 115–16, 125, 127, 248, 251–52, 285, 298, 331. *See also* Chicana lesbian identity; Gay and Lesbian Movement

  AIDS and, 373

  Catholicism and, 130

  class and, 337

  community of, 133, 373

  criminalization and, 33, 325, 327, 376

  family and, 103, 121, 143, 282, 283, 344

  homophobic violence and, 140

  motherhood and, 258, 325–26, 344–45

  two-spirit identity and, 288, 381

  visibility and, 123–24, 139, 142, 202, 324, 337, 366

  white identity and, 122–24, 137, 273

  women of color feminism and, 284

Lesbian Nation, 274

Limón, José, 327

Literatura chicana: texto y contexto (Shular), 327

Un Llanto Colectivo (Moraga and Rodríguez), 377

La Llorona, 5, 323–32, 371, 377

Lomas Garza, Carmen, 305

López, Sonia A., 122

Lorde, Audre, 69, 72, 138, 155, 158, 250, 251, 317, 336, 340

Los Angeles, 15, 67, 135, 163, 277, 311. *See also* East Los Angeles

Los Angeles Rebellion, 157, 305–6

Loving in the War Years

  1977 edition, 2, 316–17, 319

  1983 edition, 12, 316–17, 368

  2000 edition, 2, 313–14

Lugones, Maria, 325, 375

Luna, Carmen, 104–5

machismo, 212, 214, 274, 281

Las Maestras Center for Xicana[x] Indigenous Thought, Art and Social Praxis, 377

Maidu ancestral lands, 7

Malcolm X, 245

male supremacy, 117, 282, 289

Malinche, 5, 108–111, 122, 126, 213, 249, 259, 282

The Man Made of Words (Momaday), 340

manhood, 257, 285, 297, 357

Martinez, Emanuel, 305

Marxism, 292, 344, 347

Marx, Karl, 3, 116, 324

masculinity, 8, 99, 109, 256, 276, 284–85, 287–88, 326

Maya people, 294, 300, 306, 341

McCullers, Carson, 337

McFarland, 294

Medea, 328, 331, 374

Menominee people, 347, 349

Merchant, Carolyn, 300

Mesa-Bains, Amalia, 305, 310

Mesoamerica, 5, 109–10, 156, 158, 294, 305–6, 309

mestizo identity, 5, 8–9, 108, 126, 128, 144, 157, 198, 200, 246, 258, 278–79, 355, 357, 369, 371

Me-Wuk ancestral lands, 7

Mexican-American War, 276

Mexican culture, 108, 127–28, 133,

272, 323–29
Catholicism and, 369
Day of the Dead, 359
Mexican identity, 8, 108–13, 124–26, 134, 157, 205, 246, 253–54, 256, 326, 355–56
Chicano identity and, 9, 111, 113, 121–22, 204, 271, 278–82, 372
motherhood and, 331
white identity and, 105, 108, 198, 248–49, 258
Mexican Museum, 305
Mexican revolution, 278–79, 373
Mexico, 15, 135, 211, 215, 249, 252–54, 276, 278, 317
colonialism and, 108–11, 113, 216
El Templo Mayor, 318–19
femicide in, 373, 381
US and, 198–99, 203–4, 279, 291, 373
Mexico City, 15, 215, 252, 319, 366, 370
migration, 2–5, 199–200, 247, 251–59, 262, 280, 283, 294, 343, 345, 347, 371
family separation, 377
immigrant rights movement, 6
NAFTA and, 373
Mirandé, Alfredo, 117
misogyny, 107, 109, 110, 119, 202, 212, 327, 356–57, 376. See also patriarchy; sexism
Mission District, 296
Mission Dolores, 247
Miwok ancestral lands, 7
The Mixquiahuala Letters (Castillo), 171
Modern Times Bookstore, 324

Mohawk people, 292
Molina, Vivian, 104, 107
Momaday, N. Scott, 340–41, 349
Monte Albán, 253
Montoya, Delilah, 305
Montoya, José, 211
Moraga, Elvira, 1, 15–18, 20–21, 123–24, 126, 130–31, 143, 160–61, 246, 250, 255–56, 330, 344
Catholicism and, 128, 216, 361
class and, 62–64, 323
education and, 105–6, 336
gender roles and, 99–103, 112–14
Moraga, Rafael, 344–45, 358, 360–63, 381
Mothers of East Los Angeles, 281

Na Bolom Center Library, 198
NAFTA. See North American Free Trade Agreement
Nahua people, 276
National Chicano Moratorium, 277, 343
Native Americans, 140, 157, 205, 249, 280, 288, 372, 381. See also Indigenous people; specific peoples
Navajo Nation, 260, 294, 331
Nazism, 275
New Mexicans, 277
New Right, 119
New York, 15, 20, 199, 203, 251, 325
New York City, 140, 201, 362
Nicaragua, 197–198, 200, 370
Nisenan ancestral lands, 7
nonbinary identity, 8, 306. See aslo genderqueer identity; transgender identity

North America, 199–200, 276, 291, 347

North American Free Trade Agreement, 293, 372–73

Northern Cheyenne people, 291

Nothing in the Word (Berg), 54

Oakaztlán, 319

Oakland, 68, 280

Oaxaca, 211, 252

Occidental Petroleum Corporation, 348

O'Hara, Robert, 335–36, 338, 342

Omecihuatl, 306

Ometecuhtli, 306

Ometeotl, 306

Oregon, 325, 327, 375

Ortega, Daniel, 370

Otay Mesa Detention Resistance, 377

Palenque, 253

Palestine, 3, 6, 291

Panamá, 198–99

patriarchy, 70, 111, 138, 140, 214, 259, 281–82, 289, 293–94, 329, 373. *See also* misogyny; sexism

colonialism and, 108–10, 119–21, 275, 369

ethnic cleansing and, 374

reproductive rights and, 376

Paz, Octavio, 109, 133

Pedagogy of the Oppressed (Freire), 345

Peltier, Leonard, 308

Pérez, Emma, 257

Philippines, 199

Phoenix, 260

"El Plan Espiritual de Aztlán" (Al-urista), 277, 281, 283

privilege, 20, 65–67, 70–71, 104–6, 111, 257, 278

Pueblo nation, 289

Puerto Rican identity, 136–37, 249, 251, 253

Puerto Rico, 136, 199, 274, 278

Queer Aztlán, 272–73, 288

Queer Nation, 272, 274, 371

queer people, 6, 255, 294, 309, 318, 337, 349, 356, 374. *See also* Gay and Lesbian Movement; heterosexism; homosexuality; homophobia; *specific identities*

academy and, 339, 341, 346

alliances among, 65–66, 260, 285, 286, 298, 318, 346, 373

Catholicism and, 15, 98, 128

Chicano literature and, 201–2, 287

desire and, 3, 17–18, 118, 123–24, 127–28, 130, 134, 135, 141, 143, 272

incarceration of, 325, 376

liberation, 2, 118, 138

representation of, 337

transgender identity and, 285

Quetzalcóatl, 109–10, 245, 308

Quintanales, Mirtha, 98, 135, 142

racism, 9, 65–71, 86, 106–8, 116–118, 138–42, 199–200, 205, 212, 272–74, 278, 285–88, 346, 372, 379

rape, 65, 109, 116, 126, 140, 203, 259, 278–79, 307, 310, 375

Bosnia, 274

Chicano gay identity and, 285

Madre Tierra, 293
  Malinche and, 122
  Quetzalcóatl and, 245, 247
  slavery and, 278
  Yugoslavia, 374
Rarámuri nation, 289
Raya, Marcos, 305
La raza cósmica (Vasconcelos), 9
Raza, 4–5, 8, 17, 107–8, 121, 134,
  143, 156, 202, 205, 258, 273,
  276–79, 288, 347, 368, 372, 378
Reagan, Ronald, 201
Reagon, Bernice Johnson, 136
reproductive rights, 6, 116, 119–20,
  140, 294, 369, 376
Republican Party, 197, 200, 275, 369
revolution, 72, 119, 139–40, 197,
  200, 204, 245, 251, 271, 275,
  295, 341, 346, 349, 378
  literature of, 324, 330, 336, 374
  Mexican, 278–79, 373
  Sandinista, 317
Reyes, Rodrigo, 296–99
Rich, Adrienne, 366
Richard, Rodriguez, 340
Río de Janeiro, 292
Rodríguez, Celia Herrera, 305, 308,
  314, 371, 377
Roe v. Wade, 369, 376
Roosevelt, Franklin Delano, 256
Russia, 3. *See also* Soviet Union

Salazar, Rubén, 277
The Salt Eaters (Bambara), 118
same-sex marriage, 346, 367, 379
Sanchez, Marta, 305
Sánchez-Tranquilino, Marcos, 305
San Cristóbal, Chiapas, 198, 211
San Diego, 276, 280, 377

Sandinista National Liberation
  Front, 157, 317, 370
Sandoval-Sánchez, Alberto, 339
San Francisco, 15, 197, 216, 246,
  247, 297, 305, 309, 311
  Bay Bridge, 158, 360
  Castro District, 324
  Filmore, 248
  Mission District, 296, 324
  Public Library, 327
San Gabriel, 124–25, 162, 271–72,
  367
Sanger, California, 280
Sanjo, California, 280
San Panchito, 212, 280
San Salvador, 297
El Santuario de Chimayó, 192
Santa Paula, California, 62
Santa Rita Jail, 305
Selma, California, 280
Senate, 369
sex (biological), 8, 19, 101, 107–8,
  113, 116, 119–20, 122, 134,
  139, 295
sexism, 115, 118, 284, 285, 287. *See
  also* misogyny; patriarchy
  Chicano Movement and, 121–22,
  272, 283, 285
  heterosexism and, 115, 117, 272
  internalized, 107
  in literature, 68–69
sexual abuse, 114, 283, 285, 376
sexual assault, 109, 378
sexuality, 8, 107–9, 126–28, 130–43,
  204, 212–13, 275, 282, 284. *See
  also* specific identities
  freedom and, 18, 118–21, 288,
  295
  Indigenous cultures and, 381

Llorona and, 327, 329
privilege and, 66, 107
representation and, 19
spectrum of, 285
women's movement and, 66
"Sexuality and Discourse:
Notes from a Chicana Survi-
vor" (Pérez), 257
sexual politics, 113–15, 118–21, 126,
136
Shadow of a Man (Moraga), 330
Shange, Ntozake, 67–68
Shorris, Earl, 273
The Shrunken Head of Pancho Villa
(Valdez), 330
Silko, Leslie Marmon, 323–24
slavery, 108, 111, 140, 163, 278,
286, 293, 306, 311, 323, 329,
335–36, 342, 377
Smith, Barbara, 67–68, 139, 251
Sonoma, 67
Sonora, 135, 260
South Africa, 6
South Central Los Angeles, 311
South Tejas, 135, 292
Soviet Union, 157, 290–91, 317
Spain, 9, 108–10, 156, 163, 199–200,
278–79, 305, 308, 369, 380
Spanish language, 8, 20, 63–64, 71,
137, 157, 254, 260, 273, 278,
344–45, 356
State Department, 348
sterilization abuse, 6, 116, 119–20,
140. *See also* reproductive rights
Supreme Court, 275, 367, 369, 376

Taino people, 308
Teatro Campesino, 373
Tenepal, Malintin, 108, 281

Tepotzlán, 215
Texas, 120, 135–36, 274, 292, 355
Thatcher, Margaret, 275
Third World Liberation Front, 6,
346
Third World Women's Alliance, 6
This Bridge Called My Back (Moraga
and Anzaldúa), 4, 19, 368, 379
Thomas, Clarence, 275
Thompson, William Irwin, 245, 247
Tijerina, Reies López, 277
Tijuana, 63, 113, 135, 274, 309, 377
Tlaliyolo, 311
Tohono O'odham nation, 289
Tongva people, 163
Toomer, Jean, 259
transgender identity, 6, 8, 119, 285,
376, 378, 381
Treaty of Guadalupe Hidalgo, 276
Trump, Donald, 369
Truth, Sojourner, 286
Tsinhnahjinnie, Hulleah J., 314
Turner, Nat, 335–336
two-spirit identity, 288, 357, 381

UC Berkeley, 280, 346
UCLA, 380
United Kingdom, 275
Ukraine, 3, 291
United Farm Workers, 6, 280, 373
United States, 157, 246, 248–49,
274–75, 290, 306, 317, 349, 361
academy in, 339, 362
Afghanistan and, 3
Chicanx identity in, 5–6, 212,
275, 278, 279, 289, 305, 341,
347–349
Department of the Interior, 277
enslavement in, 278

imperialism of, 120, 140, 157, 197–98, 200, 275, 279, 291, 294, 308, 342, 348, 370, 380

Latinx identity in, 8, 136, 197–200, 252, 272, 278, 362

liberatory movements in, 6

Mexico and, 198–99, 203–4, 279, 291, 373

NAFTA and, 293

reproductive rights in, 119–20

Southwest, 201, 203, 276–78, 280, 291

State Department, 348

US Third World women, 116–17, 134–137, 253

U'wa people, 347–348, 380

Valdez, Luis, 330, 343, 373, 378

Vargas, Kathy, 305

Vasconcelos, José, 9

Venezuela, 348

Vera Cruz, Mexico, 109

Vietnam, 161, 199, 307, 342

Villanueva, Alma, 117

Villareal, Rita, 106–107

Viramontes, Helena Maria, 327, 375

la Virgen de Guadalupe, 15, 108, 213, 267, 281

Visalia, California, 280

Waiting in the Wings (Moraga), 381

Walker, Alice, 259

War of Flowers, 213

Washinawatok El-Issa, Ingrid Flying Eagle Woman, 348–49, 374, 380

Watsonville, California, 267, 280

The Well of Loneliness (Hall), 337

What Part Indian Am I? (Herrera Rodriguez), 314

white supremacy, 117, 259

Whitman, Walt, 183

Wilson, Pete, 197

womanhood, 103, 124, 129, 167, 214, 251, 257, 272, 281, 286, 329, 337

Woman Warrior (Kingston), 69

Women's (and Gender) Studies, 318, 345, 378

women's movement, 6, 66, 70–72, 115–17, 134–36, 272

Woolf, Virginia, 93

Works Progress Administration, 256

World War I, 307

World War II, 307

Xicana/x identity, 5, 8, 316, 318, 331, 356, 375, 381

Yáñez, Larry, 305

Yoeme nation, 289

Young Lords, 6

Yugoslavia, 374

Zamora, Bernice, 117

Zapotec people, 211

Also Available from Haymarket Books

All the Blood Involved in Love
Maya Marshall

The Anti-Racist Writing Workshop
How To Decolonize the Creative Classroom
Felicia Rose Chavez

The Billboard
Natalie Y. Moore, foreword by Imani Perry

Black Women Writers at Work
Edited by Claudia Tate, foreword by Tillie Olsen

Community as Rebellion
A Syllabus for Surviving Academia as a Woman of Color
Lorgia García Peña

LatiNext: The Breakbeat Poets Vol. 4
Edited by Felicia Chavez, José Olivarez, and Willie Perdomo

So We Can Know
Writers of Color on Pregnancy, Loss, Abortion, and Birth
Edited by Aracelis Girmay

There Are Trans People Here
H. Melt

Waiting in the Wings
Portrait of a Queer Motherhood
Cherríe Moraga

About the Author

Cherríe Moraga is an internationally recognized poet, essayist, and playwright whose professional life began in 1981 with her coeditorship of the avant-garde feminist anthology *This Bridge Called My Back: Writings by Radical Women of Color.* She is the author of *A Xicana Codex of Changing Consciousness: Writings 2000–2010* and the memoirs— *Waiting in the Wings: Portrait of a Queer Motherhood* and *Native Country of the Heart.* Moraga is the recipient of the United States Artists Rockefeller Fellowship for Literature, a Lambda Literary Foundation award and the American Studies Association Lifetime Achievement Award among many other honors. As a dramatist, her awards include an NEA, two Fund for New American Plays Awards, and the PEN/ West Award. Moraga is a Distinguished Professor in the department of English at the University of California, Santa Barbara, where, with her partner Celia Herrera Rodríguez, she co-founded Las Maestras Center for Xicana/x Indigenous Thought, Art and Social Praxis.

About Haymarket Books

Haymarket Books is a radical, independent, nonprofit book publisher based in Chicago. Our mission is to publish books that contribute to struggles for social and economic justice. We strive to make our books a vibrant and organic part of social movements and the education and development of a critical, engaged, and internationalist Left.

We take inspiration and courage from our namesakes, the Haymarket Martyrs, who gave their lives fighting for a better world. Their 1886 struggle for the eight-hour day—which gave us May Day, the international workers' holiday—reminds workers around the world that ordinary people can organize and struggle for their own liberation. These struggles—against oppression, exploitation, environmental devastation, and war—continue today across the globe.

Since our founding in 2001, Haymarket has published more than nine hundred titles. Radically independent, we seek to drive a wedge into the risk-averse world of corporate book publishing. Our authors include Angela Y. Davis, Arundhati Roy, Keeanga-Yamahtta Taylor, Eve L. Ewing, Aja Monet, Mariame Kaba, Naomi Klein, Rebecca Solnit, Olúfẹ́mi O. Táíwò, Mohammed El-Kurd, José Olivarez, Noam Chomsky, Winona LaDuke, Robyn Maynard, Leanne Betasamosake Simpson, Howard Zinn, Mike Davis, Marc Lamont Hill, Dave Zirin, Astra Taylor, and Amy Goodman, among many other leading writers of our time. We are also the trade publishers of the acclaimed Historical Materialism Book Series.

Haymarket also manages a vibrant community organizing and event space in Chicago, Haymarket House, the popular Haymarket Books Live event series and podcast, and the annual Socialism Conference.